George Frederick Beaumont

A History of Coggeshall, in Essex

With an account of its church, abbey, manors, ancient houses and biographical

sketches of its most distinguished men and ancient families, including the family of

Coggeshall from 1149

George Frederick Beaumont

A History of Coggeshall, in Essex
*With an account of its church, abbey, manors, ancient houses and biographical sketches of its
most distinguished men and ancient families, including the family of Coggeshall from 1149*

ISBN/EAN: 9783337012076

Printed in Europe, USA, Canada, Australia, Japan

Cover: Foto ©ninafisch / pixelio.de

More available books at **www.hansebooks.com**

A History of Coggeshall.

Printed by Edwin Potter,
The Coggeshall Press, Essex.

A HISTORY

OF

COGGESHALL, IN ESSEX

WITH AN ACCOUNT OF ITS

Church, Abbey, Manors, Ancient Houses, &c.

AND

Biographical Sketches

OF ITS MOST DISTINGUISHED MEN AND ANCIENT FAMILIES

INCLUDING

THE FAMILY OF COGGESHALL

From 1149, to the re-union at Rhode Island, U.S.A., in 1884

BY

GEO. FRED. BEAUMONT

, One of the Local Secretaries of the Essex Archæological Society.

London :
MARSHALL BROTHERS,
PATERNOSTER ROW.

Coggeshall :
EDWIN POTTER,
MARKET END.

MDCCCXC.

To the beloved Memory of

JOSEPH BEAUMONT

Who died at Coggeshall, July 18th, 1889

Preface.

HE following pages contain the embodiment of notes collected during some few years of research, with the intention in the first instance of simply allowing them to remain in manuscript, and providing as far as possible for their preservation for the historian of some future day. As these notes increased in bulk, and were not arranged in any particular order, and as I conceived that there were many of my contemporaries both at home and abroad, who would be glad to know something of the Church, the Abbey, the Manors, the Charities, the Chapels, the families, and the ancient houses of this interesting town, I determined to mould the collected materials into a "History of Coggeshall."

To the end that the work might be as complete as possible, the Court Rolls of the Manors of Great and Little Coggeshall, the Registers of Baptisms, Marriages, and Burials, from their commencement to the present time, the other parish papers—unfortunately but few and of modern date,—very many ancient deeds and other muniments have been subjected to personal examination, and such time as could be spared has been spent in the Public

Record Office and in the Library of the British Museum, resulting fortunately in the unearthing of some few items of interest.

The valuable early 18th century MS.S. of Holman (now in the Colchester Museum), so far as they relate to this town and the family which bears its name, have been transcribed, and I have not hesitated to draw freely from this antiquarian store. "Dugdale's Monasticon," "Weaver's Funeral Monuments, "Newcourt's Repertorium," "Morant's Essex," "Dale's Annals of Coggeshall," the various papers contributed by the Rev. Dr. E. L. Cutts, and Mr. H. W. King to the Journal of the Essex Archæological Society, and other well known and reliable authorities have been frequently consulted and have furnished many interesting details.

To the non-antiquarian reader it will seem that there has been an unnecessary introduction of personal names and genealogical notes, but this will be understood when it is stated that the work has been prepared in the interest not only of the general reader, but also of those who may desire to connect the families of to-day with those of past ages ; a desire which is now singularly pregnant in New England, Australia, and the other Colonies. In order that the task of the genealogist may be rendered as easy as practicable I have supplied an Index of all the personal names occurring throughout the volume.

As the importance of place names in connection with the history of a parish is now fully recognised by antiquaries, I have felt it incumbent upon me to put on record the field and other names occurring here, and to add a few notes with reference to the localities and their appellations, in the hope that, with the assistance of the map which is supplied, they will be found interesting as well to the local antiquary and general reader as to the onamatologist.

For much valuable aid in the production of the illustrations,

I am indebted to Mr. J. D. Webster, whose excellent photographs of local views have been of great service. The Ancient Gateway, the Interior Elevation of St. Nicholas Chapel, and the Norman Capital are from drawings kindly lent to me by Mr. Robert Williams, A.R.I.B.A. Most of the other illustrations have been sketched by my wife, whose willing help in this and many ways in preparing the work for the press I gratefully here acknowledge.

Every endeavour has been made to render the work as accurate as possible, but as it has been prepared during the short hours of leisure which follow the professional labours of the day I dare not entertain the hope that it will be found faultless.

The communication of notes bearing upon the history of this place, and the notification of errors occurring in the following pages will be much appreciated.

GEO. FRED. BEAUMONT.

THE LAWN,
  COGGESHALL,
    January, 1890.

Contents.

List of Illustrations.

CORRIGENDA.

Page 11, line 24, *for Ansum, read Ansam.*

,, 26 ,, 13, *for* Malchus with Judas, *read* St. Peter with Malchus.

,, ,, ,, 14, *for* Repentance, *read* Denial.

,, ,, ,, 24, *for* busts of Angels, *read* emblems of St. Peter.

,, 44 ,, 31, *for Quoadam, read Quondam.*

,, 45 ,, 34, *for* Grimes, read Grime.

,, 66 ,, 16, *for* The Rev. E. W. Mathew, read Col. W. Mathew.

INTRODUCTION.

OGGESHALL comprises two parishes, intersected by the ancient course of the river Blackwater, the greater part of which now bears the name of "The Back Ditch." To the north of this channel lies the parish of Great Coggeshall, and to the south, Little Coggeshall. The larger parish covers an area of 2,632 a. 1 r. 10 p., exclusive of the detached portion* comprising 5 a. 1 r. 15 p. adjoining the bridge at Blackwater, making a total of 2,637 a. 2 r. 25 p., of which about 47 acres are roads and 12 acres water. The smaller parish contains 1,107 a. 2 r. 17 p., exclusive of the detached portion † near Rye Mill, Feering, containing 6 a. 2 r. 7 p., making a total of 1,014 a. 0 r. 24 p., of which about 20 acres are roads and 11 acres water. The former parish is in Lexden Hundred and the latter in Witham Hundred.

. The highest point is by Nunty's Farm, near Monk Wood; here an elevation is reached of upwards of 228 feet above the mean level of the sea, gradually descending to about 88 feet, O.D. in the pastures by the river. The whole area is drained by the river Blackwater and its contributory streams, the chief of which is Robin's Bridge Brook.

The principal street traverses, approximately, the old Roman Road from *Verulamium* to *Camulodunum*, and at its western extremity is known as Stock Street; from Highfield's Farm to Market End it is called West Street; proceeding towards Colchester the name is changed to East Street or Gallows Street, and beyond the Mount it is degraded to Rotten Row. From Market End, Stoneham Street runs at right angles to the Roman Road, and in

---

* Amalgamated with Pattiswick Parish on 25th March, 1889.
† Now part of Feering Parish.

B

a northerly direction towards Halstead, bifurcating at the 'Yorkshire Grey' and changing name to Robin's Bridge Road and
Tilkey Road, the former leading to Halstead and the latter to
Mark's Hall. From Market Hill, Church Street takes a north-
easterly direction and leads to the Church and thence to Earls Colne
and Great Tey. Beyond the Church, on the one hand, and the
Mount on the other, Church Street is connected with East Street
by Dead Lane. Bridge Street, the upper part of which was
formerly called Cellar Lane, leads from the Market Place past the
two bridges, when its name is changed to Grange Hill and Pointell Street [Tedric Pointell had property at Coggeshall at the time
of the Domesday Survey]; at the Hamlet is a road running to
the mill and called Pointell Mill Lane. Bridge Street is connected with West Street by the Gravel. Church Lane, Back
Lane, or Queen Street runs to the north of and almost parallel with
Church Street. There are also minor ways known as Wayne or
Vain Lane, Horn Lane, Crouches Alley, Curd Hall Lane, and
Cuthedge or Coleman's Lane.

From 4,198 inhabitants, in the united parishes, in the year
1861, the population has gradually decreased, the last census
(1881) giving the number of inhabitants at 3,361, of whom 2,998
resided in Great Coggeshall and 363 in Little Coggeshall; since
1881 these figures have been further considerably reduced. The
number of houses in 1881 was in Great Coggeshall, 683, inhabited
by 704 families or separate occupiers, and in Little Coggeshall 82
houses occupied by 85 families or separate occupiers.

Great Coggeshall was from very early times in the Diocese of
London, and so remained until the year 1845 when it was trans-
ferred to Rochester. It is now in the See of the Bishop of St.
Albans, which was founded about 1877.

Little Coggeshall, until 1846, was a peculiar of Canterbury,
and the Vicars of Coggeshall up to that date attended the Visitation of the Archbishop's Commissary, the Dean of Bocking. In
this year the parish was removed from the Archbishop's jurisdiction by Act of Parliament or Order in Council.

Coggeshall is in the Archdeaconry of Colchester, and was formerly in the Lexden Rural Deanery, but, on the 1st January, 1846,
it was transferred to a new Deanery, which comprises the parishes
of Coggeshall, Feering, Inworth, Messing, Easthorpe, Layer Marney, Layer Breton, Copford, Tiptree and Stanway, and is called

the Coggeshall Deanery. The two parishes were in Witham Union until its dissolution in 1880, when they were transferred to Braintree.

For legal purposes of a civil nature the inhabitants are within the Braintree County Court District, while the Justices of the Witham Division of the county exercise jurisdiction in criminal matters, and in such administrative affairs as come within the cognizance of magistrates. Coggeshall returns a member to the County Council. Wills and letters of administration to the effects of persons dying here are proved or taken out either in the Ipswich District Registry or in the Principal Registry of the Court of Probate.

The nearest Railway Station is at Kelvedon, about 2½ miles distant, and is easily accessible by ' Moore's Bus,' which travels to and fro three times daily.

The principal industries are the brewing of beer, the growing of garden seeds and the manufacture of gelatine and isinglass. Tambour lace is still made here, but the cloth trade which once flourished has become extinct. There are two Banks, the London and County and Messrs. Sparrow, Tufnell & Co.

A few ancient domestic buildings have escaped to some extent the vandalism of past generations, and the frieze of one in Church Street bears date 1565, another in East Street, 1585 ; while Paycocke's house, in West Street, was doubtless built between four and five centuries ago.

A local magazine was established, in 1870, under the name of the 'Coggeshall Parish Magazine,' and is continued to the present time, but its name was changed in 1875, when an extra sheet was introduced so as to embrace the news of the rural deanery, and the title is now 'The Coggeshall Ruri-Decanal Magazine.' The numbers should be kept and bound periodically, as also should the excellent ' Coggeshall Almanack,' first issued in 1883, by Mr. Edwin Potter, and containing much local information with a supplement of the principal events of the year preceding its issue.

Geological.

THE solid geological formation which underlies the parishes of Great and Little Coggeshall and extends for many miles in all directions, is known as the London clay, and consists of a very tenacious bluish grey clay, which near the surface weathers into a brownish colour. Few fossils are found in this district, and such as are to be obtained are very friable. The depth attained by the London clay in this neighbourhood varies of course with the contours of the surface and substratum. The well at Messrs. Swinborne's Gelatine Factory, about 120 ft. above Ordnance Datum, disclosed beneath about 2 ft. of soil a depth for the London clay of about 173 ft., of which 18 ft. was yellow clay, 130 ft. blue ditto, 5 ft. sand, and 20 ft. brown clay. Passing through these beds, the borers pierced 38 ft. of the Reading Beds and 31 ft. of Thanet sand, reaching chalk at 244 ft. below the surface, and boring into this for 16 ft., they obtained at a total depth of 260 ft. an abundant supply of water, which rose to within 14 ft. from the surface.

The well at Mr. Gardner's Brewery, in Bridge Street, situate about 90 feet above Ordnance Datum, disclosed 25 feet of gravel, 120 ft. of London clay, and 60 ft. of slate coloured sand, a greenish sand being reached at 205 ft.

The well at the Gravel Brewery, about 95 O.D., bored in 1887, and commenced at the bottom of the old bore hole, 110 ft. from the surface, showed Dead sand 7 ft., Running ditto 4 ft., Loamy ditto 2 ft., Dead ditto 8 ft., Pebbles and brown sand 5 ft., Brown running sand 16 ft., White sand 3 ft., Mottled clay 5 ft., Greensand 10 ft., Grey ditto 9 ft., Green ditto 6 ft., and Grey ditto 41 ft., Chalk being reached at 226 ft. from surface, and being bored to a further depth of 79 ft., water rose about 2 ft. above the surface and gave over 36 gallons per minute.

The preceding details have been thus fully set out, as they will doubtless be of service to any who may contemplate the luxury of an abundant supply of pure water from a depth of from 250 to 300 ft. The supply from the chalk bearing stratum has great advantages for brewing purposes, but for domestic requirements Coggeshall has an ample surface store of good water. This supply is furnished by the rains which are absorbed by the high level areas. Its reservoir is an extensive bed of glacial gravel, covered with the boulder-clay in part and the brick-earths in other part, these prevent evaporation, while the impervious London clay below arrests filtration.

The geological beds which are exposed to view in this district are those of the glacial series and the valley gravels, and brick-earths of later date. The Boulder-clay, which is the chief of the glacial series, is a heterogeneous collection of fragments of rocks from many parts of the kingdom, but mainly composed of London clay and chalk, with slabs of Kimmeridge clay containing innumerable fossils, pieces of the oolitic formation and of the lias limestones with belemnites and other remains of a former world, and here and there may be found rounded, polished and striated blocks of granite. It was deposited during an intensely cold period of time, when the whole of our district was submerged to a considerable depth in oceanic waters, the enormous blocks of foreign rocks being borne here by glaciers and icebergs. Passing upwards from the glacial series of deposits, we come upon the gravels and brick earths of later date. These were formed during the gradual re-elevation of the land from the depths of the sea. The coast line by degrees receded from the north-west, and we picture the waves of the ancient sea beating upon the uplands by Bourchiers Grange and Hovels, and again, some centuries later an enormous river sweeps in its pre-glacial course, denuding here and re-assorting there, gravel in one place, sand in another, and brick-earth elsewhere; and thus, and only thus, can we account for the road-mending material we now find 50 ft. or more above the present river, and the earth for the potter's wheel, near Fabians or Hill Farm, beyond the Church and elsewhere.

So far as the personal researches and enquiries of the writer have been pursued, no traces of palæolithic or neolithic man have been discovered in this district, but well polished flint implements of neolithic man have been found at Feering and at Inworth, and sooner or later the diligent observer will probably be rewarded with similar "finds." Fossil bones of the elephant and other mammals have been found in the gravel pit in the Vicarage Field and elsewhere, but they are generally so fragile that they can seldom be preserved entire.

Early History.

ALTHOUGH we have no traces of an early British occupation of this place, there is, nevertheless, satisfactory evidence that the Romans were for some time dwellers here. The road which we traverse every day when we pass along East Street and West Street is a remnant of one of the great works of this noble race, a race to whom England owes its mediæval and its modern greatness. Let the reader walk along this road, and although he cannot now gaze upon the barrow of British or Anglo-Saxon date, which probably occupied a place in the locality of the ' Mount,' yet, when he descends the gentle slope towards the town, he will find in the field opposite the western end of Starling Leeze, that a portion of the original road is still extant, and may be traced by the raised ground or highway.* The barbarians, who succeeded the Romans, it would seem at this point diverted the road a few yards to the north and on the ancient way built their miserable hovels, and so the original road is now lost beneath the houses which occupy the south side of the present highway. But the old road is again plainly seen opposite the Vicarage and the Hitcham School, and on its crown, Paycocke's House, the Fleece Inn, and other houses now stand.

Dr. Holland, in his translation of *Camden's Brit.*, p. 449, and Weever also, p. 619 (see also *Newcourt Rep.*, Vol. II., p. 158), tell us : " That in a place called Westfield, three-quarters of a mile from Coggeshall, and belonging to the Abbey, there was found by touching of a plough a great brazen pot ; the ploughman supposing it to have been hid treasure, sent for the Abbot of Coggeshall to see the taking of it up, and he going thither met with Sir Clement Harleston, and desired him also to accompany him thither. The mouth of the pot was closed with a white substance like past or clay, as hard as burnt brick ; when that by force was removed, there was found another pot but that was of earth, that being opened there was found in it a lesser pot of earth of the quantity of a gallon covered over with a matter like velvet and fastened at the mouth with a silk lace ; in it they found some whole bones and many pieces of small bones wrap'd up in fine silk of flesh color, which the Abbot took for the Reliques of some saint and laid up in his Vestiary."

If one refers to the ordnance map of Great Coggeshall, he will have no difficulty in finding the West Field of the government surveyors of 1875, for it appears in large type under the No. 314. It is doubtful whether there is any authority for calling

---

* From earliest times the principal roads appear to have been raised above the level of the adjoining ground ; thus in Numbers xx 19, the Israelites state that they will go by the raised road or highway, and in the 17th verse, it will be noticed, they call the road, the King's Highway, just as we do at the present day.

this field West Field, for in the title deeds it is not so called ; in the Morden College Survey of 1740, it is called Crow Barn Field, and in the tithe map its name is Lower Crop Barn ; one can therefore only conclude, that the surveyor having ascertained that many Roman remains had been .found in this field, set it down without further enquiry as the West Field of Camden. The Rev. Dr. Cutts, who knew Crow Barn Field well, when writing (1855) on the Roman remains of Coggeshall, evidently did not consider it possessed the name of West Field, for in quoting from Camden he parenthetically suggested that the place in question was near West Mill.*

A search at the Public Record Office among the rolls of the Duchy of Lancaster (Bundle 58, No. 726) enables me to produce the following from the Court Rolls of the Manor of Coggeshall Hall, dated 1517. " At this Court the Steward by command of the Lord granted out of the hands of the said Lord to John Aylward and Benedicte his wife, certain enclosures and crofts of land called Colvercroft, late in the tenure of John Aleward, his father, while living, lying between the way called Colmannes Lane, on the one part, and *enclosures of the Lord Abbot called Westfields* and Bawnes Shott, on the other part, one head thereof abutting upon land of the said Abbot called Bouneshott, and the other head upon the field called Westfield." The fields called Colvercroft or Cutlers Crofts are shown on the map of Coggeshall Hall manor and are the same as Nos. 79, 81, and 82 on the tithe map of Little Coggeshall. No. 109 in the same map is called Boonshots, and Colemans Lane is now called Cuthedge Lane. From these facts we may learn approximately the locality where the remarkable pot was found, which so delighted the Lord Abbot of Coggeshall.

The Rev. E. L. Cutts *(Essex Arch. Soc. Trans.)* says (1855) that in a couple of fields, called Crow Barn and Garden Fields, on the north of the road from Coggeshall to Braintree, a little distance west of the town, gravel has been excavated for some years back, and he was told that from time to time a considerable number of Roman urns had been discovered, a drawing of one of which he possessed. The dimensions of this urn were 10½ in. in height and about 8 in. in width, and he adds, several had more

---

* There are West Fields near West Mill, but they are at least a mile and a half from the town.

recently been discovered, and two of them, smaller ones, were preserved tolerably entire. One of these was enclosed within a larger vessel, whose impress he saw in the bank of earth, but its fragments had been thrown among the gravel and carted away; these urns were deposited as is usual in Roman sepulchral deposits on the top of the gravel which lies about 2 ft. beneath the surface of the soil; human bones had also been found here, and there were two plots of soil of some yards square, in each of which was a layer of black ashes, perhaps the trace of funeral pyres; and in the middle of Crow Barn Field was found a large quantity of Roman bricks, which were taken out and used to repair the farm premises. The space over which these urns were scattered is about three acres. Dr. Cutts continues—To the east of this cemetery, with one field intervening, is the park-like field in front of Highfield House; an avenue of fine elm trees extends from the house to the road, running from north to south; the easternmost row of trees is planted on the edge of an artificial dyke, in the hollow of which runs the drive up to the house. This bank and hollow way have very much the appearance of the agger and ditch of a Roman camp. From the southern extremity of this, another very similar ditch runs westward in the direction of the Roman cemetery; there are faint indications of a continuation of this along the western side; and the line of the hedge along the nothern side would complete a square enclosure of about an acre and a half in extent. Dr. Cutts says his attention was first called to the eastern and most conspicuous of these lines of embankment by hearing it spoken of as Roman; but there was not any general tradition of the kind, and the intimation may have been merely the echo of the opinion of some previous antiquary.

Weever *(Funeral Monuments)*, writing in 1631, makes the following observation:—"Adjoining to the Rode called Coccillway, which to this towne leadeth, was lately found an arched vault of brick, and therein a burning lampe of glasse covered with a Romane tyle some 14 in. square, and one urne with ashes and bones, besides two sacrificing dishes of smooth and polished red earth, having the bottom of one of them with faire Romane letters inscribed COCCILL. M. I may probably conjecture this to have been the sepulchrall monument of the Lord of this towne, who lived about the time of Antoninus Pius (as by the coyne there likewise found appeareth), the affinitie between his and the now towne's name being almost one and the same. These remain in the custody of that judicious great statesman, Sir Richard Weston, Knight, Baron Weston of Nealand, Lord Treasurer of England; and of the most honourable Order of the Garter Companion, who for his approved vertues and industrie, both under father and sonne doth to the publique good fully answere the place and dignitie."

As a detached portion of Coggeshall until recently adjoined the bridge at Blackwater, it should be mentioned that when that bridge was re-built between thirty and forty years back, the remains of several successive timber bridges were discovered, and planks were found at a considerable depth below the present bed of the river, having the darkness and heaviness characteristic of very old oak; and Mr. Murdock, the clerk of the works, entertained the idea that the river might have been paved with these planks to form a ford; for, as the soil is boggy at this particular spot, some such paving would have been necessary to make a ford passable on a road so much frequented. Mr. Cutts observed, after recording these facts *(Roman Remains at Coggeshall)*, that the Romans invariably bridged over the streams which were crossed by their great military roads ; the bridges over insignificant streams being sometimes composed of a horizontal roadway of planks laid upon abutments of piles. Among other interesting antiquities found at Blackwater, and, be it observed, at a considerable depth below the bed of the stream, were a portion of a glass vessel, described by Mr. Murdock as like in quality and appearance to Roman vessels of glass which he had seen; the upper part of an earthenware drain pipe, the upper orifice enlarged for the insertion of the next pipe, which resembled Roman aqueduct or drain pipes*; a portion of a brick, honeycombed with deep irregular holes like rustication ; a vertebra of a large ox ; and perhaps most important of all, an iron instrument, believed by antiquaries to be a horseshoe for a horse with a diseased hoof, having two tags of iron

---

* I have not seen this pipe, but it would seem to be similar to two I have in my possession, taken by me from a field (341 ordnance survey) on the Abbey Farm. These are 4 in. square at one end, tapering to about 3½ in. at the other, and measuring 2 ft. ½ in. in length, with circular bore of 1¾ in. in diameter. The pipes have sockets and enlarged orifices, and were disinterred from a disused clay pit. My own opinion is, they are of mediæval date and were used by the monks as conduits for the carrying of the pure water of the hill sides to the domestic offices of the monastery.

which may have been clasped over the hoof, and the shoe being further fastened by a rope attached to the hook at the hinder part of the shoe *(see illustration in Mr. Cutts' paper).*

Many Roman coins have been found in Coggeshall and the immediate neighbourhood, but, with the exception of one of the Emperor Vespasian, found in 1887 in Mr. Beaumont's orchard opposite the Church, and one of Constantinus (locality where found unknown), a second bronze of M. Aurelanus found on the Abbey Farm (1888), and some others in my possession which are illegible, it has not been found possible to add to the following list compiled by Dr. Cutts :—

M. Antoninus (31 B.C.), a denarius found at Curd Hall Farm ; Nero (A.D. 54-68), 2nd bronze ; two of Vespasian (69-79), 2nd bronze ; two of Domitian (81-96), 2nd bronze ; Trajan (98-117), 2nd bronze ; Hadrian (117-138), 2nd bronze ; ditto 3rd bronze, found in the field in front of Scrip's Farm ; Antoninus (138-161), mentioned by Weever ; ditto, second bronze ; Faustina (wife of Antoninus), 2nd bronze ; M. Aurelius (161-180), 2nd bronze ; Commodus (180-192), 2nd bronze ; Julia Domna, wife of Severus (193-211), a denarius ; Gallienus (253-268), 3rd bronze ; Victorinus (265-267), 3rd bronze ; Claudius Gothicus (268-270), 3rd bronze ; Tetricus (267-272), 3rd bronze ; Claudius Tacitus (275), 3rd bronze ; Diocletian, 284-305), 3rd bronze ; two of Carausius (287-293), 3rd bronze ; Maximinus (308-313), 3rd bronze ; seven of Constantine (323-337), 3rd bronze ; Magnentius (350-353), 3rd bronze ; Theodosius (379-395), 3rd bronze ; Head of Constantinopolis ; four undecypherable. Ancient urns have also been found at Bouchiers Grange, by the side of an old pond filled in some years ago, but the workmen did not preserve them.

As Hovels (otherwise Holfield, Holville or Oldfield) was the manor house of Great Coggeshall, it is probable that it is the site of a Roman villa, which, when its buildings had fallen into decay, and the population of the place had migrated to the Saxon *ham,* or home, where our town now is, became very properly known as the *old-ville,* afterwards corrupted into various forms. Whether Hovels Farm, or Holfield Grange, is the original Oldville it is impossible to say, but the road north of Holfield Grange should be noticed ; then there are the Vineyard, and the *Stock Street,* close by, and although the Vineyard may have been planted by the monks in later days, it is well known that the Romans intro-duced the vine into this country. The survival of the name, Stock Street, in a locality where there are only three or four houses, is decidedly indicative of former importance.

Scrips Farm, with its Church Field and Kitchen Field, in Little Coggeshall, may also be the site of a Roman villa, as to which it should be stated that, in addition to the Roman urn mentioned by Camden, several Roman coins have been found on this farm, and the reader is invited to compare the plan of its fields with the plan of a Roman holding, at Much Wymondley, given by Seebohm, in his *Village Community*. Coggeshall Hall is also a locality which should receive attention.

Let the reader glance at the ordnance map of Coggeshall, in the neighbourhood of Highfields Farm and some distance west-wards, and discover, if he can, why the field lines are not parallel with and at right angles to the ancient road from Colchester to Bishops Stortford, and say, was there an older way, a British or a Roman road from Aldham or from Halstead, which formed the base upon which the surveyor worked, when he divided the lands into separate enclosures.

It may be mentioned that Coggeshall has at different times been considered the site of one of the Roman stations mentioned in the *Itineraries* of *Antoninus*, some writers contending for Canonium, while others thought it Ad Ansum, and with regard to the latter station a recent writer,* though not placing it at Cog-geshall, fixes upon the neighbouring village of Kelvedon or Feering as its proper site.

Etymological.

THE word Coggeshall is of uncertain derivation. We first meet with the town's name in a grant in the time of Edward the Confessor, where it is rendered Coggashael; in the Domesday Book, 40 years later, viz. 1086, we have Cogheshal, and since then corruptions in nearly every form may be met with, thus, we have Cogshall, Coxal, Gogshall, Coggashael, and many others. We have seen in a previous page what Weever has to say

---

* Mr. H. F. Napper, *East Anglian Notes and Queries*, Vol. II, pp. 278, 304, 332, and Vol. III, p. 6.

upon the matter, and it will be remembered that this learned
writer found an affinity between the name of the person inscribed
upon the Roman *patera* and the name of the town, and to make
his conjecture the more apparent he speaks of the Coggeshall
road as the Coccil way (pronounced Cocksill), and so he concluded that the town belonged in Roman times to the Lord
Coccillus, whereas the inscription COCCILLI. M. means, as is now
well known, Coccilli manu, i.e. : by the hand of Coccillus the
potter.

Dunkin *(Monumenta Anglicana)* says that it has been
ingeniously conjectured that this name was compounded of two
Celtic words, Cor or Cau (enclosure), and Gafael (hold) ; or
otherwise was derived from Coed (wood), and Caer or Gaer
(camp), Coed-Gaer, Cogger, *i.e.* camp in a wood. The Saxon thane
might have occupied the Caer with the house and out-houses, and
the rustics would call it Coed-Gaer's Hall or Coggeshall. This
derivation seems almost too far-fetched.

The learned Essex historian, Morant, was of opinion that the
true and original name was Cocks-hall, and his view is supported
by the fact that the seal of the Abbey is charged with three cocks,
but he does not give any reason for the appropriation of this
name to our town.

The following suggestions are also offered, first, that it is just
possible that the earliest Christian Church here, was, as the present is, dedicated to Saint Peter, and on some part of it figured
prominently a cock (A.S. a Cog), not only as an indication of
the dedication, but also as a mark, warning the people against
the sin of denying their Redeemer, whence the building was
called by the inhabitants the Cog's-hall, and later on the parish
itself was distinguished by that name. Secondly, that Coggeshall
may mean nothing more nor less than North Hall, just as the
Welsh Prydain y Gogledd is equivalent to North Britain, and
this name it may have received from the position it occupied in
regard to Kelvedon or Feering, the Canonium of some antiquaries,
as at both these places Roman and Anglo-Saxon remains have
frequently been found.

It is worthy of note, that the Galatians in Asia Minor, who
spoke the same language as our ancient Gauls, had, as St. Jerome
says, a little shrub which they called Coccus, with which they
made a deep red or scarlet colour, and that very colour is at this

day called *Coch* in the British language. Camden observes, that in the names of all the ancient Britains there appears some intimation of a colour which without doubt arose from the custom of painting, and he fancied that this word Coch or Goch laid couched in such names as Cogidunus and Argentocoxus, and if his imagination served him aright, there would seem reason in tracing the same indication of colour in the word Coggeshall.

It may be remarked that whereas part of this parish is known as Crowland, on the other hand, part of the parish of Crowland, in Lincolnshire, is called Gogguslands.

There are several places which bear a similar appellation to that of our town, such as Uggeshall and Cockfield in Suffolk, Cogshull in Cheshire, Cogges in Oxfordshire, Cockley-Cley and Coxford in Norfolk, and Coxall Knoll in Herefordshire.

Sunnydon.

G REAT Coggeshall or some part of it appears to have been at one time called Sunnydon, and is mentioned by this name (Sunnedon) in the agreement between the Abbot of Coggeshall and the Vicar of the same place, in or about the year 1224, and Holman, speaking of the place early in the eighteenth century, thus quaintly puts it : "Tis scituated somewhat lowly, some part of it on the declivity of a hill, but so pleasant that part which leads to Colchester and Fering is called in old deeds Coggeshall *alias* Sunny Bank, as I am informed by that oracle of the law, John Cox, Esq."

ECCLESIASTICAL HISTORY.

F the early ecclesiastical history of this place very little is known, but it may be mentioned that, in 1851, when the recent restoration of the present church was commenced, pieces of brick were found in the walls, and among them were some fragments of scored and flanged tiles, which the Rev. E. L. Cutts pronounced to be undoubtedly of Roman date. This fact, however, tends to show nothing more than that there were Roman buildings in this locality, not necessarily ecclesiastical.

There was probably a Saxon church here, for the Great Domesday Book tells us that there was a Priest at Coggeshall at the time of the survey, and we may consequently not unreasonably infer that there was a building in which he ministered to his flock. The site of this Saxon building it is believed has never been suggested ; there was without doubt an earlier church in the same position as our present building, but that the earliest place of worship stood here appears improbable.

The origin of the town is apparently due to the convergence of minor roads to a point on the Roman road or Stane Street leading from Camulodunum (Colchester) to Verulamium (St. Albans). At this point our Saxon forefathers from divers villes and hamlets met and transacted their primitive sales and purchases. This eventually resulted in the establishment of a market, and around the place of mart, known as Market Hill, the rude houses of those who decided to settle here gradually grew up and formed a town. The market was held at regular intervals, and after the business of the day had been completed we can picture the homely traders and farmers with their wives, children, and dependents gathered round the missioner, who had been sent out by the Bishop of the Diocese to spread the doctrines of Christianity As the population of the place increased and the inhabitants became converted, a church, wherein they might assemble for worhip became necessary, and it is probable our Saxon forefathers erected one of their wooden buildings for the purpose.

We now come to consider the question, where did this church stand? It is improbable that it stood on the same site as the present one; a spot which, by reason of its distance from the market place, would have been most inconvenient; we must therefore look for a more suitable locality, and having found it consider the surrounding circumstances.

Our town, in early Saxon times, was probably nothing more than a hamlet or cluster of small houses on the Stane street. These houses in time extending northward formed the way called Stanham or Stoneham Street, above what we still call Market Hill, and running almost at right angles with the Roman Road. If this surmise be correct the site of the church was probably in Stoneham Street, above the market place just below Church Lane. For convenience the position is unequalled, and the following facts support the proposition :—There is a well near the corner formed by the junction of Church Lane with Stoneham Street, in the yard

at the rear of the cottage opposite the Congregational Chapel; it is said to have been called 'Peter's Well,'* and when it was repaired, about 50 years ago, a stone, with what was believed to be the head of St. Peter carved on it, was found embedded in the steaning. It is evidently the central boss of an arched portion of a church. It

CARVED HEAD FROM S. PETER'S WELL.

---

* Not to be confounded with the better known Peter's Well, near Wayne Lane, which would seem to be the old church pond reduced in size and enclosed in a circular brick wall. The enclosing of this pond appears to have been effected nearly two centuries ago and is referred to by Bufton thus :—
".1689—In June the Church Pond was cast, it cost 50s."

now belongs to Mr. Edward Catchpool, of Feering Bury. Beneath the boss was another stone with the cross keys carved on it in relief. This was removed when the well was repaired, but the stone with the carved head was allowed to remain till about 20 years ago, when Mr. William Smith, of Stoneham Street, assisted in removing it.

This is doubtless the well to which Bufton refers as follows :— " 1696, Sept.—Peter's Well was very well repaired by the Constables :"—and it is also the well in which Joseph Dor was drowned ; the fact being recorded in the Parish Register of Burials :—" 14th June, 1765, Joseph Dor, drowned in Peter's Well." He could hardly have been drowned in the shallow Church Pond.

The custom of giving names to wells is of the most remote antiquity, and it is not improbable that the well near Stoneham Street was dedicated to St. Peter shortly after the introduction of Christianity into this country, and it may be that this was the baptistery of our Saxon forefathers.*

Then again on the west of this site are the fields known as ' Crouches,' strongly indicating that a cross, possibly the church cross stood here ; and to the south west of Crouches are the lands which belong to the Vicarage as glebe, and have been so held for a certainty since 1223 (see the agreement between the Vicar of Coggeshall and the Abbot and convent), and probably long before that date.

And yet again, immediately above Saint Peter's Well (where the Congregational Chapel now stands) is a property which, in 1710, was known as ' Old Ales,† signifying that here was the old

---

* Staveley, in his *History of Churches*, says that "fonts were first set up in private houses, and subsequently in more peaceful times, at a little distance from the church or oratory; afterwards they were placed in the church porch, and lastly in the church itself near the entrance, on account of baptism being the sacrament of initiation or admittance into the church, and have ever since retained the name of font or fountain, from the primitive custom of immersion in rivers and fountains. Anciently there was but one font in a city and that in or near the principal church, which peculiarity still obtains in some cities in Italy. *Fonts were anciently adorned with the images of Saints and Holy men*, to the end that such as were baptised might have before their eyes the representations of those persons eminent for holiness and virtue, whose actions they were to imitate."

It is not suggested that the stone with the figure on it is more than from five to seven centuries old. It may have come from the demolished Abbey Church, and have been placed in the position where found between two and three centuries ago.   See also *Arch. Jour.*, Vol. xxxv. p. 86.

† Ale means a feast in its original sense. See Brand's *Pop. Antiq.* vol. i. 279.

Play Place, where the inhabitants of the past were wont to assemble on certain feast days and engage in dances, bowls, shooting at
butts and other sports. These play grounds generally adjoined or
were but a short distance from the church.*

It may be mentioned also that, in addition to the easy access
to this spot from the market place, there are two roads on the
north which converge just above it, and if we assume that Church
Lane and the footpath through the Vicarage Fields and Crouches
are ancient ways, then we also have approaches to the very site of
the church both on the east and on the west.

To recapitulate the evidence in support of the suggestion that
the church of our Saxon ancestors stood in Stoneham Street, on
the south of Church Lane, we have : (1) Proximity to the Market
Place. (2) A well, dedicated to St. Peter. (3) Crouches Fields
on the west and the Glebe Lands on the south west. (4) 'Old
Ales' on the north. (5) The convergence to this point of several
roads or ways.

Attention has been thus fully called to these coincidences in
the hope that when any excavations are being made in the locality
care may be taken to note the occurrence of any foundations of
an early character, and if any Saxon or other coins should be
found let the discoveries be duly recorded, as this is the one great
way to obtain more accurate knowledge of the distant past.

It has been estimated that, during the 12th century, no
fewer than eight thousand ecclesiastical buildings were erected
for public worship; and, bearing in mind the fact that in those
days our town was one of the most important in this county, we
may safely conjecture that our Norman ancestors, with the assistance of the conquered Saxons, early in this same century on the
site of the present structure erected a place of worship to which
for two centuries the townspeople of Coggeshall resorted. These
enthusiastic builders doubtless had the advantage of the advice
and guidance of the monks who had settled on the southern side
of the river, and were at the same time erecting the monastery-
church which they dedicated to the Blessed Virgin.

Evidences of an earlier church having existed on the same site
as the present building have been found on several occasions ;
thus, when the church was seated with benches, about 1863, there
were unmistakeable signs of a former church having a south aisle ;

* See post, under title, ' Fairs, Customs, and Folk-Lore.'

C

and, while the excavations were being made, in 1886, for the heating apparatus, the writer detected immediately beneath the north wall, the foundations of which are six feet deep, fragments of human bones, showing that a burial ground existed where the north aisle now stands. Some ancient tiling was also found in 1863 ; and in the early days of the present restoration of the nave, which commenced about 1851, fragments of masonry of later Norman or Early English character were found, and in the composition of the present building may now be seen pieces of brick of early date.

The church which immediately preceded the present appears to have been small, for its dimensions may to some extent now be traced on the tower, which also served the purposes of that earlier building. Thus, there can be seen the remains of the two diagonal buttresses which, until they were cut away, stood within the present building. There are also on the tower marks of the former roof, which was high pitched, and sprang from a height corresponding with the top of the arches of the present building. From these facts we gather that the nave of the former church was about the width of the tower and that there was no clerestory. There was probably a south aisle but no aisle on the north.

The Church of St. Peter-ad-Vincula.

THE present church is situate in the north-eastern corner of the town, about 50 feet above the River Blackwater, which flows in its winding channel through the fertile valley on the south. The position, though not so convenient as a more central one, has the advantage of a healthy elevation and possesses commanding views of the surrounding country. To the south, in years gone by, might be seen the grand old Abbey Church, dedicated to St. Mary, with the multifarious monastic buildings clustered around her ; beyond, in the distance a glimpse is caught of the tower of Feering Church, and in the farther distance, on the gentle slope towards Tiptree Heath, the massive tower of Inworth Church stands boldly out to view. The principal approaches are by way of Church Street and Church Lane, the latter being also known as Queen Street or Back Lane.

The present building is one of the few churches in this country whose dedication is to St. Peter-ad-Vincula, or St. Peter-in-Chains

Its dedication to Saint Peter is testified not only by tradition but by the symbols of that apostle—the cross keys—which figure prominently in many parts of the Church, notably on the shields on the outer side of the walls between the plinth and the ground line.

 The second corbel from the east wall of the chancel, in the north clerestory, is a figure of an angel bearing on an escutcheon a chain between two keys erect. The most satisfactory evidence, however, of the true dedication of the church is to be found in the will of William Goldwyer,* of Coggeshall, dated the 26th January, and proved 10th March, 1514-15. He directs " My body to be buried in the quere of Saint Peter-ad-Vincula—ther as the legende is redde [the lectern] by the sepulture of my wif." And the fact that the Fair, which the Abbot of Coggeshall was licensed to hold, under Letters Patent, granted in 34th year of King Henry III., was to last for eight days every year from the vigil and on the day of St. Peter-ad-Vincula and for six days following, is certainly confirmatory of the dedication ; for, it will be remembered, that the Latin *feria*, whence we derive fair, is the ecclesiastical term for saints' day. The Feast of Dedication is held on the 1st August, and not on St. Peter's Day, the 29th June. In the year 1500, there was in the chancel the image of St. Peter ; for we read in the will of Thomas Halle,† a resident of this town, directions that his body should be " Cofered and buried within the quere of the parish church of Coksale, near to the sepulture of my wife." He then bequeaths " Towarde makeyng of a tabernacle for the Image of Saint Peter the Apostle in the quere of the said Church of Coksale X marcs, if it be made within 3 years after my decease, else to be disposed in deeds of charity for my soul and my friends' souls." This will is dated 15th Jany, 1499-1500.

The church, which is almost as perfect as when first erected, was built in the reigns of Kings Henry IV., V. and VI., in other words in the first quarter of the 15th century. It is said, by an eminent authority on the subject [Hadfield *Eccl., &c. Architec. of Eng.*, 1848], to be one of the very best specimens in the county of the perpendicular period of Christian architecture; and he goes

---

* Essex Arch. Journal, Vol. 1, N.S. 177.   † Ib.

on to say that there are very few churches in the kingdom equal to it. It consists of a nave, with north and south aisles, from which it is divided by five bays or arches ; a chancel, with similar aisles separated therefrom by three bays. There is a tower at the west end, and on the south side is a porch, which is the principal entrance to the building, a turret on the north and another on the south side of the building.

The general plan of the church is convenient and architecturally good, but it has been suggested that it would have been improved by extending the internal length so that it might be exactly equal to twice its internal width, and by dividing it into nineteen equal parts, devoting fourteen to the nave and five to the chancel, that is to say, to make the nave seven bays in length and the chancel two and a half.

The size of the church is surpassed by few in the county, probably two only; viz., Saffron Walden, measuring 200 feet in length by 82 in breadth, and Thaxted, which is 183 ft. by 87 ft.

The dimensions (taken internally) of our building are as follows :—Total length (excluding tower), 120 ft. 7 in., total width, 62 ft. 9 in. The chancel, to the centre of the western arch, is 51 ft. 11 in. long and 28 ft. 3 in. wide. North chancel aisle, 51 ft. 11 in. long and 17 ft. 3 in. wide. South chancel aisle, 51 ft. 11 in. long 17 ft. 3 in. wide. The north aisle, 68 ft. 8 in. long 17 ft. 3 in. wide. The south aisle, 68 ft. 8 in. long 17 ft. 3 in. wide. The tower, 13 ft. 11 in. by 13 ft. 9 in. The nave is about 36 ft. in height at the sides, rising somewhat higher in the centre. The aisles by the arches are about 26 feet in height. The tower, from base to top of parapet, 66 feet, thence to top of turret, 6 feet. The chancel is elevated about 6 inches above the nave, from which it is separated by a fine arch of the width of 20 ft. 10 in. having a hood-moulding terminating with a floral decoration. The altar is approached by 3 steps. Each of the chancel aisles is separated from the nave aisle, of which it is a continuation, by a plain arch.

The tower, nave, and porch are composed for the most part of flint rubble, with some fragments of brick. The walls of the chancel and its aisles together with the north turret are of Kentish rag. The parapets, which surmount the north and south walls of the chancel, are of brick of more or less modern date. The parapets of the other parts of the church are in keeping with the walls upon which they are built.

The roof of the chancel is of pine and rests on oak rafters supported by plain oak brackets standing upon stone corbels carved in relief, most of them probably original but some of recent date.

The roof of the nave is far richer than that of the chancel and is entirely of oak. The beams are well moulded and have floral bosses. The corbels are chiefly modern, of Bath stone, carved in relief with figures of angels and saints. Most of these were inserted shortly after the commencement of the latter half of the present century when the restoration of the roof was effected. The canopied figures, beautifully carved in oak and resting upon the corbels, represent the twelve apostles, and were presented to the church by Mr. John Parkinson Hall, of Yarmouth, who for many years served the office of churchwarden of this parish. The roofs of the aisles are ornamented with bosses of various designs. The stone corbels are carved with heads of saints or grotesque figures.

Under the East window outside was formerly a carved representation of the Crucifixion, of which traces only now remain.

There is a stoup for holy water on the east of the priest's door, the basin has, however, been cut off flush with the wall.

The Porch.

THE Porch is of flint rubble with stone quoins and dressings and is supported by a diagonal buttress at its south-eastern and south-western corners. It is entered by a doorway of stone with a pointed arch, over which is a dripstone terminating with two heads crowned with a wreath. The doors are of oak. The north doorway of the porch is a depressed arch of stone within a rectangular frame, and over this there is a label, the spandrels being filled with a shield within a quatrefoil.

The double door is of massive oak, beautifully carved by Mr. Barleyman about 35 years ago, in a design of perpendicular character. [Mr. Barleyman afterwards went to New Zealand and became a barrister-at-law.] There is an east and a west window each of two lights. The floor is paved with inverted monumental slabs, and the ceiling is groined, and in the centre is a boss, a pelican in piety, but it is said that the original boss was the Virgin and Child.

The room over the porch, which is known as the Record

Room, has probably at different times been used for various purposes, and, from the fact that Thomas Howell, sexton, was buried in the porch in 1680 (April 15), it is just possible that in his day the room above was the private apartment of the sexton. This room is entered by a door in the north-east corner, access to which is gained by a narrow stone staircase approached from the interior of the Church. In the north-eastern corner is a modern fire-place; on the south is a window of two lights, and on the east and west a window of one light. The roof is supported by massive beams of oak. There is little of interest in this room save the old oak parish chest with three locks, but this is of no great size nor of handsomely designed character.

The Tower.

IN comparison with the body of Church the tower is low. It is of flint rubble with fragments of brick, and is supported by four diagonal buttresses, the eastern two being now built into the walls of the Church. The bells are rung from the ground floor, above which is a disused chamber, reached by a staircase in the turret at the south-eastern corner, and continued upwards to the belfry and thence to the leaden roof.

There are eight bells, which bear the following inscriptions :—

The 8th (Tenor) "Cast by John Warner & Sons, London, 1877. This bell, cast in the year 1692, was re-cast June, 1877. C. P. Greene, Vicar, J. S. Surridge and A. T. Warwicker, Churchwardens." The former inscription was "James Bartlet made me, 1692, Thomas Keble, Robert Townsend, Churchwardens."

The 7th—"Thos. Gardiner, fecit 1733, Isaac Potter, John Tayler, C.W's."

The 6th—"Tho. Gardiner, fecit 1757, William Moss, Churchwarden."

The 5th—"Thomas Gardiner, Sudbury, fecit 1733."

The 4th—"Miles Graye made me, 1681."

The 3rd—"John Bryant, Hertford, fecit 1806, W. Swinborn, T. Alleker, C.W's."

The 2nd—"Cast by John Warner & Sons, London, 1876, W. J. Dampier, Vicar; H. T. W. Eyre, Curate; J. S. Surridge, A. T. Warwicker, Churchwardens, 1876."

The Treble—"Cast by John Warner & Sons, London, 1876.

Through the exertions of the Rev. H. T. W. Eyre, Curate, this peal was augmented to eight bells, Easter, 1876."

Bufton has the following notes anent the bells :—"November 8th, 1681, three bells were run in Mr. Ennow's barn, and the other three, December 23rd, 1681."

"In September, 1682, the 6th bell and 3rd bell were new run at Colchester."

"In April, 1683, the 5th bell was carried to Colchester and there was made thereof a little bell less than the least before."

"In May, 1692, the great bell was carried to London to be new shot, and was brought home again in July."

"In June, 1693, the 4th bell was carried to Sudbury to be new shot, and the rest were chipped to make them tuneable."

"In Jan. 1693-4, the 4th bell was split and carried to Sudbury to be new shot and brought home about May 7, 1694. Then it was made too little, and was carried to Sudbury to be new shot and made bigger, and was brought home about June 18, 1694, and were first rung after that June 22, 1694."

The bells are in the key of F ; the tenor weighs 20 cwts., the treble 5¾ cwts.

The following items, concerning the bells, are said to have been in the churchwarden's accounts (Dale's *Annals of Coggeshall*), but these accounts have never been seen by the present churchwardens, nor have they any knowledge as to what has become of them. The only accounts and books kept by these officials which are now extant are those of more modern date :—

"1807—Sept. 10th. To Briant, for recasting bell, £17 10s.

"1808—April 17. To Thomas Hughes' bill for bells, £15 17s. 1¼d.

"1813—July 14. Paid the ringers for Lord Wellington, £1. July 22.—Ditto, Anniversary. Aug. 3—Battle of Vittoria. Aug. 12—Prince Regent's birthday. Sept. 22—King's Coronation. Nov. 4—Battle of Leipsic.

"1814—April 7th. Allies entering Paris. April 9—Buonaparte dethroned."

The Windows.

THE east window of the chancel is a splendid specimen of perpendicular work ; and, with regard to it, Hadfield says, "A finer example of the style perhaps is not to be found in

England, there is decidedly nothing to compare to it in the
county." The window is of seven lights, and measures from the
sill to the spring of the arch, 12 ft. 6 in., thence to the apex 11 ft.
10 in., making a total height of 24 ft. 4 in.; its width, from jamb
to jamb is 14 ft. 8 in., and each light is slightly over 1 ft. 8 in.

This window was re-glazed in 1848, the glass of it having been
painted by the vicar, the Rev. W. J. Dampier. In July, 1866, it
was replaced by the beautiful stained glass of Messrs. Clayton &
Bell, inserted (according to a note in one of the parish books) by
Osgood Hanbury, Esq., and Osgood Hanbury, Jun., Esq., in memory of Helen and William Hanbury, and it bears the following
inscription : " In memory of Helen Caroline Hanbury, wife of
Osgood Hanbury, Jun., died 5th April, 1865, aged 31, after giving
birth to her son, Osgood, who died, 14th May, 1865 ; also of S.
William D. Hanbury, H.M.S. 'Nerbudda,' lost off Simons Bay,
Africa, about 11th June, 1855."

The pictures are representative of the principal incidents in
the life of Christ, the tracery lights being filled with figures of the
saints.

In this window, Holman says, there was in his day, "an escutcheon Argent, 3 lions rampant, 2, 1, gules, within a border
engrailed azure."

The east window of the north chancel aisle represents 'The
Agony,' 'The Crucifixion,' 'The Resurrection,' and 'The Ascen-
sion,' and bears the following : " To the honor and glory of God,
this window is erected in affectionate remembrance of Richard
Townsend, who died, August 4, 1852, aged 80 years, and of Mary
Johnson Townsend, his second wife, who died, 4th December,
1858, aged 69 years, by their children, G. Gretton Townsend and
Mary Ann Gretton Townsend."

The east window of the south chancel aisle was presented by
Thomas Sadler, Esq. ; subject, "The History of David ; inscription, " Deo dedit et ecclesiæ, Thomas Sadler, Anno Domini,
1863."

The east windows of the chancel aisles, the three windows in
the south chancel wall, and the easternmost window of the north
chancel wall, have four lights and are of a pattern different to the
other principal windows of the Church which are of three lights.
The clerestory windows are of three lights, those in the chancel
being of later date than those in the nave.

Proceeding from the east end of the Church, and taking the north wall, the first window is at present plain, but will soon be replaced with stained glass by the Young Women's Help Society, a fund for which is being raised under the energetic secretaryship of Miss Margaret Gardner. The subject will probably be the life of St. Katherine, as this aisle is dedicated to that saint.

The next window is "To the memory of George Deeks Skingley, who died June 16th, 1888, erected by his widow, Mary Isabella Ellison Skingley," and contains in the central light, 'The Good Shepherd,' and in the side lights are quarries with the sacred monogram and other designs. There are also appropriate texts interspersed. This is the work of Messrs. Heaton, Butler & Co.

The third, a rich stained glass window, was inserted "In memory of Susan Bowles, the wife of Major G. D. Skingley, who died 19th October, 1878." [This is the date of her burial, she died 14th October, 1878.] The subject is 'The Sermon on the Mount.' In the centre is the figure of Our Blessed Lord in a sitting posture, uttering to the listening multitude the eight Beatitudes ; below are the words of the sixth Beatitude : "Blessed are the pure in heart for they shall see GOD." Among the multitude are men and women, young and old, listening to the words of the Saviour, whilst in the tracery lights are angels looking downwards and adoring Him ; at His feet among the wild flowers is a lily of thevalley, the emblem of purity. The window was designed and executed by Messrs. Meyer, of Munich.

Leaving the chancel, the first window in the nave on the north side is the gift of Osgood Hanbury, Esq., as a memorial to his deceased father and mother. This work, of Messrs. Clayton & Bell, represents 'The Presentation of our Saviour in the Temple;' a label from the mouth of S. Simeon has on it, "Mine eyes have seen Thy Salvation ;" and below is the inscription :—"In memory of Osgood Hanbury, died 4th November, 1873, aged 79, and of Eleanor Willet, his wife, died 26th March, 1870, aged 75."

The next window depicts 'The Adoration of the wise men,' and was presented—"To the Glory of GOD and in memory of William Appleford, who died 1874, and of Bithia, his wife, who died 1881 "—by their children. This is also the work of Messrs. Clayton & Bell, and is similar in design to the last described window, but of a more conventional character. In the centre light is the Virgin Mother with the Divine Infant in her arms, the side lights containing representations of the kings offering their gifts, and beneath :—"In Whom we have redemption through His blood."

The principal window of the tower was given by—"Ann Skingley, in memory of her daughter, Ellen Brown, who fell asleep in Jesus, October IV., MDCCCLII." Subject, the three Marys; one of whom bears a plate, another a lily, and the third a box of ointment.

The window at the nave end of the south chancel aisle is of four lights with several openings in the upper, or tracery, portion. The eight pictures illustrate as many incidents in the life of St. Peter, they are placed as follows; viz. in the upper row :—'The Call of St. Peter'—'The Gift of the Keys'—'St. Peter and Malchus' —'St. Peter's repentance.' Underneath these, 'St. Peter and St. John at the beautiful gate'—'St. Peter cast into prison'—'St. Peter released from prison'—'The martyrdom of St. Peter.' The spaces between are filled with canopy work. In the tracery openings four angels fill the four largest pieces and they hold a scroll upon which is inscribed the following lines :—"In this window is shown forth the life and martyrdom of St. Peter, a servant and an apostle of JESUS CHRIST." Between the upper and lower tiers is this text :—Peter was kept in prison but prayer was made without ceasing of the Church unto GOD for him." In the other four tracery lights are emblems of St. Peter. At the base of the window is the following :—"To the glory of GOD and in memory of Joseph Smith Surridge, 21 years churchwarden of this parish, who fell asleep, 23 July, 1888."

The window was designed and executed by Messrs. Lavers and Westlake, and cost about £200. It is certainly a work of great merit, and a most suitable memorial to one who, for so many years devoted such unceasing labour to the work of restoring and beautifying the Church.

The only window in the south wall of the nave, which is of stained glass, is the easternmost. This, the work of O'Connor, portrays 'The Transfiguration of Our Blessed Lord," with the superscription, "This is My beloved Son, hear Him ;" and an inscription records that the window was erected "To the Memory of Arthur Gardner, departed Jan. 7, 1867, aged 21."

Some old glass was found during the restoration, about 1851, under one of the benches, but it is not known what became of it.

The glass of the two westernmost windows of the north clerestory was painted by Mr. Charles Bonton. In the centre light of the westernmost window are the arms of the Diocese of Rochester. Arg., on a saltier gu., an escallop shell or., with the bishop's mitre above. The middle light of the other window contains the arms of the DuCane family, the patrons of the living. Arg., a lion ramp sa., ducally crowned or., on a canton az., a chevron of the 3rd between 3 acorns slipped and erect : Crest a demi lion ramp sa., ducally crowned or., supporting with the paws an anchor erect of the same.

Mural Decorations.

THE first mention, regarding the colouring of the walls, is in Bufton : "In the months of July and August, 1684, Coxall Church was whited and painted." And here, perhaps, the following from the same diarist may not be inappropriately quoted :— "In 1692-3, the new King's Arms and ye 10 commandments were set up in ye church."

From a paper read before the Royal Institute of British Architects, by the Rev. Edward L. Cutts, sometime Curate of this town, we learn that the walls of our church were not profusely decorated with paint. There was a line of red in the moulding round the edge of the window splays. The bell of the capitals of the pillars was coloured red. The arches across the chancel and its aisles had a few stripes of plain colour, chocolate, bright red and yellow. The east walls of the chancel and aisles were formerly painted over with a tapestry pattern of a character common about the reign of Henry VII., which pattern returned a short distance along the adjoining walls to form an enrichment above the altars. The simplicity of this decoration Mr. Cutts attributed to the desire of the decorators to give emphasis to the chief architectural features of the building, and to act as a foil to bring out the brilliant colouring of the windows, all of which were probably at one time filled with stained glass.

There were formerly eight consecration or dedication crosses painted on the walls, either in fresco or distemper, but these were destroyed or covered over in the early period of the present restoration. Two were under the windows of the north wall of the north chancel aisle, and one higher up on the right hand of the east window of that aisle, one under the east window of the south

chancel aisle and four others under the windows in the south wall.
They were all of the same character, namely a cross patée, dark
red within a circular rim of dirty grey or perhaps faded green.
Before each of these, on the anniversary of the dedication and at
certain other times there was probably burned a taper, candle or
lamp.

In 1882, the first portion of the polychromatic decoration
which now adorns the chancel was commenced, and consisted of
a dado of chocolate on the east wall and the return walls of the
sacrarium. The work was continued, at the latter end of 1886, as
far as the apex of the easternmost arch. Early in 1889, the
painting was finished through the munificence of an anonymous
donor. The whole design was by Messrs. Clayton & Bell, by
whom also the work was executed. On the north of the great
window Our Saviour's Resurrection is beautifully depicted in
various colours. At his feet are the holy women and among them
an angel bearing the legend :—" He is not here, but is risen."
Beneath this picture are the words :—" I am the Resurrection and
the Life." On the south side of the window is a very fine representation of the Ascension, with the inscription :—" I ascend unto
my Father." It is impossible to give any detailed description of
this decoration, but it may be shortly stated that the coloring is
chiefly chocolate, with gold, green, red, blue, and other tinctures,
harmoniously interspersed. Immediately below the string course,
is the text :—" Worthy is the Lamb   *   *   *   *   for ever
and ever," and beneath this are cameos containing an angel holding a scroll, thereon "Alleluia."

The Reredos.

THE first stone of the reredos, which preceded the present one,
was laid on the 26th August, 1843, immediately after the
2nd lesson at morning prayer, by William Dampier and Maria
Elizabeth Dampier, two of the children of the vicar. The reredos
of 1843 was of stone in five bays, in the centre panel, I.H.S., the
other panels being filled with the Creed, Lord's Prayer, and Ten
Commandments. At the date of its erection it was an ornament
to the dilapidated church, but, with the vast improvements effected
under the zeal and guidance of Mr. Dampier, it was considered
that its place should be supplied with one of nobler character and
richer design.

On the 20th November, 1878, at Ramsgate, the Rev. William James Dampier entered into his "long home." He had often expressed a wish to see a new reredos in our church ; and, although the wish was not consummated in his lifetime, his desire was not forgotten, and, under the honorary secretaryship of the Rev. E. Hall, rector of Myland, about £300 was collected, with the result that on the 18th October, 1880, the new reredos was unveiled. The framework of the reredos, including the rich floriated cornice and canopies, is of alabaster; the figures being in Caen stone, carved in high relief. There are three principal panels, the central one of which contains a representation of the Crucifixion of our Lord, with Mary His mother, and Mary the wife of Cleopas, on either side, and Mary Magdalene at His feet. In the left panel, the sacrifice of Isaac is portrayed, while the right contains the Feast of the Passover. Each of the four minor panels contains the figure of an Archangel beneath a trefoliated canopy. The whole work is beautifully designed and remarkably well executed. A brass plate with these words inscribed was afterwards affixed : "To the Glory of GOD, and in memory of William James Dampier, vicar of this parish, 1841-1876, by his brother priests, friends and parishioners."

The Font.

THE font is of early English date, and was originally in Pattiswick Church, from which it was removed, and for some time used as a horse trough, and afterwards as a flower stand in the garden of Mr. William Mayhew, who gave it to Mr. Dampier in 1841, by whom it was set upon new pillars and completely restored, and presented to the church in 1852. It was temporarily fixed in the south chancel aisle, but afterwards removed to the position it now occupies in the nave. In 1871, the shafts which support the basin, were reduced a few inches in height, and the brick steps were replaced by a stone base.

The Piscina

IS an arched niche of stone in the south wall, under the easternmost window. The drain consists of four holes; the projecting part of the basin has been cut off flush with the wall. In each spandrel there is a thistle.

The Screens.

THERE was, until comparatively recent times, a handsome screen in the chancel arch, and in the arches between the chancel and the north and south chancel aisles. These were within the remembrance of Mrs. White, of West Street, whom Mr. Dampier, in 1863, interviewed with reference to the internal state of the church when she first knew it in her youth. Mr. Dampier states in his note, that this lady was then nearly 100 years old. Mrs. White did not remember any screen filling the western arches of the chancel aisles, but the carved oakwork found in 1863, serving as joists of the pew flooring, seemed to Mr. Dampier to be the screen work of those western arches.

The rood loft was reached by the turret, on the north side of the church, the opening for the doorway on a level with the loft being still plainly visible from the inside of the turret. Behind the door leading from the church into the turret, may be seen a small recess, the use of which is not quite apparent, but it may have served as a stoup for holy water.

Pulpit.

THE pulpit, which immediately preceded the one now in use and which can be recalled by most of us, was painfully plain and totally unworthy of a place in the fine old church. It is almost unnecessary to say that it was not the pulpit of pre-Reformation days, but was of 18th century date, as we find from the entry of the burial of its builder, which appears in the parish register thus:—"1775, April 7th, John Morton, Carptr. & Joyner, he made the pulpitt."

In August, 1871, the old pulpit was replaced by the present structure, which is of oak, carved by Mr. W. B. Polley, of this town. The central panel contains the figure of Saint Peter, with the cross keys in his right hand, and a volume in his left; and the panels on the right and left are respectively occupied by the effigies of St. John with a cup, and St. James with a sword. The projecting cornice is handsomely carved with a flowing conventional thorn. The woodwork rests on a stone base, whereon is carved a wreath of geranium.

Organ.

THE Organ, which was built in 1819, stood in the gallery at the west end of the Church. It was replaced, in 1839, by one given by Henry Skingley, Charles J. Skingley, Esqrs., and Major George Deeks Skingley, in compliance with the wish of their deceased father, Henry Skingley, Esq. It remained in the gallery till about 1852, when, on the demolition of its resting place, it was removed and was afterwards placed in the position in the south chancel aisle, in the rear of the middle bay, where the present instrument stands. The fine instrument now in use, was built by Messrs. Holditch. The subscription list was opened by Mr. Joseph Beaumont, in 1865, but nothing further was done until 1870; in this and the following years great activity was displayed, with the result that, on the 18th December, 1873, the organ was opened, Mr. C. Warwick Jordan, Mus. Bac., Oxon, presiding at the instrument.

The Organ consists of three complete manuals, with a compass of CC to F, 54 notes, and an independent pedal organ, from CCC, 16 ft. to E, 29 notes.

The Great organ contains	10 stops	...	648 pipes.
The Swell organ	„ 8 „	...	540 „
The Choir organ	„ 6 „	...	312 „
The Pedal organ	„ 3 „	...	87 „
Couplers	6 „		—
Total ...	33		1,587

The case of the organ is of pine, ornamented with a conventional pattern in chocolate. The pipes are partly diapered.

The Seats.

WE have no record of the earliest sitting accommodation of the Church, but Bufton tells us something of the pews of two hundred years back, thus :—"In 1678, betwixt Michaelmas and Christmas, 2 new pews were set up in our Church—one for Counsellor Cox, ye other for Mr. Thomas Stafford. In July, 1679, there was a new pew, very fine and large, set up in our Church by John Thorne and George Abbot, and was pulled down againe in Aprill, 1680. In November, 1684, a new pew was set up in the chancel, near ye door, by Samuell Sparhawk and Samuel Smith. In November, 1685, a new pew was set up againe in our Church, where there was one set up before in 1679, and pulled down in 1680."

The nave of the Church was re-seated in 1863, the old pews,

which were then removed, had existed for at least a century, and were about 3 ft. 8 in. in height and constructed of deal.

The nave and its aisles are now seated with comfortable benches of oak, the ends by the centre passage being carved with heraldic shields, alternating with some floral or other suitable design. The shields represent, among others, the arms of the Sees of Canterbury, and Rochester, and of the families of DuCane, Hanbury, Dampier, Martin-Leake, Townsend, Sadler, Drummond, Honywood, but they in no manner indicate that the seats to which they are attached are appropriated to, or were ever even occupied by the families bearing those arms.

The following notes, in the handwriting of the Rev. W. J. Dampier, may be quoted here:—" 1842—two old chairs presented and placed within the altar rails, having high carved backs. 1843, Passion week—two benches substituted for the Vicarage pew, at private cost, and with the Bishop's sanction. 1847—the free pews extending from the chancel door, westward, to the arch, which were high and of various sizes, &c., were taken down and replaced by three rows of open sittings of the ancient pattern, low, uniform, and looking north; this was done with the sanction of the Incumbent, the Churchwardens, and the Archdeacon."

The chancel is seated with handsome benches of carved oak, adorned with figures of angels. The carving of all the benches was done by Mr. W. B. Polley.

The Sedilia

ARE three in number, cut in the south wall of the sacrarium, and are all of the same elevation.

Ornaments and Smaller Furniture.

THERE are two chalices or Communion cups of silver, 6½ in. in height, and bowl, 3 in. in diameter, one inscribed, "Sacred to GOD and the Church of S. Peter, Coggeshall, 1783, Richard White, William Walford, Chwns." Three patens of silver, one 9 in. in diameter, inscribed, "Sacred to GOD and the Church of S. Peter, Coggeshall, 1783;" another, 8½ in. in diameter, inscribed, "In Mem., John Doane Forster, MDCCCLVII," and the third, 6 in. in diameter, inscribed, "S. Peter, Coggeshall, sacred to the memory of Arthur Gardner, 7th June, 1867." One flagon or cruet of silver, 13 in. in height, inscribed, "Given to S. Peter's

Church, Coggeshall, by Georgiana Ann Barnard, in memory of her father, Abraham Lawkin Barnard, who died at White Notley, July 17th, 1857." An alms bason of silver, measuring 9 in. in circumference, and inscribed, "Sacred to GOD and the Church of S. Peter, Coggeshall, 1783."

There are six altar frontals and five super frontals, fair linen cloths, two brass and two oak candlesticks, moveable brass desk, a credence table, two glass cruets for wine and water, a silver spoon and a shell for baptisms.

The survey or inventory of church plate, jewels, vestments and other ornaments, which was ordered to be made early in the reign of Edward VI., is, so far as it concerned Coggeshall, believed to be lost. After the Reformation, many of the valuable ornaments of our Church were sold, and the proceeds expended in the general restoration of the building. In the sixth year of Edward VI. a further survey was taken, and, though in many cases it furnishes a mine of information upon the subject of church furniture and goods, yet, in the case of Coggeshall, we only learn that the certificate, as it was called, was made on 3rd November, 1547, by Anthony Waynflet and Thomas Baker, Churchwardens; who state that they had sold, by the assent of the town, so much plate as cometh to the sum of £10, whereof they had received £6, and had bestowed the same, some in the reparation of the Church and the highways next adjoining, and the other £4 remained in the hands of Master Thomas Playter, Esquire.

ꝶestoration.

SOME idea of the magnificence of our Church in pre-reformation days, is to be gathered from the Paycocke wills, extracts from which appear on another page. It will be seen that in the early part of the sixteenth century, there were, besides the High Altar, an Altar of Saint Katherine, a Tabernacle of the Trinity at the High Altar, and another of Saint Margaret in Saint Katherine's aisle. Mr. H. W. King, the learned secretary of the Essex Archæological Society, who has made considerable extracts from the Paycocke's Wills,* thus writes, "I, for one, do not doubt that Coggeshall Church owes its architectural grandeur as largely to the piety and zeal of the clothworkers of the town, as perhaps, to

---

* Paper read before the Essex Arch. Soc. at Coggeshall, on 19th October, 1888.

the benevolence of the Cistercian fathers. We can only imagine, we cannot realise, the ancient splendour of its internal decoration ; the value of the sacred vessels and other ornaments of metal work ; the richness of the woven and embroidered fabrics used in the services, for the English embroidery excelled all other ; but we do get just a gleam of light in the dedication, by Thomas Paycocke, of the two tabernacles with sculptures of the Holy Trinity and Saint Margaret, for which he bestowed, for the carving and gilding of them, one hundred marks ; all else we must suppose to be conformable in gilding and color." Mr. King has explained * that the Tabernacle of the Trinity was a niche, with probably a lofty canopy or spire, containing a sculptured representation of the Holy Trinity ; the Almighty Father or Ancient of Days, in the form of an aged person, seated and holding a crucifix upon which the emblem of the Holy Spirit is alighting ; these tabernacles were often so lofty that the spire reached nearly to the roof. We have read elsewhere of the gift by Thomas Halle of ten marks towards the making of a tabernacle for the Image of Saint Peter, the apostle, in the choir of the Coggeshall Church.

But though so magnificent in the past, our Church, by reason of the destruction wrought during the reign of Edward VI. and in the days of the Commonwealth, and through the indifference of the clergy and laity of later years, presented such an appearance that Holman, in the beginning of the 17th century, was doubtless justified in saying, "The inside has nothing of that beauty and ornament which its outside promises to the transient spectator, but is ill-kept and runs to decay." This running to decay was not arrested until the late Rev. William James Dampier was presented to the Vicarage in 1841. No sooner was he inducted than he determined to—"Gather of all Israel, money to repair the House of your GOD,"† and, by Divine Grace, after thirty-five years of patience, perseverance, and unceasing labour, he might in his last hours have added,—"And the work was perfected, and they set the House of GOD in His state and strengthened it." ‡ The restoration of the Church of S. Peter-ad-Vincula, Coggeshall, is a standing memorial of the never-to-be-forgotten

WILLIAM JAMES DAMPIER.

Among the notes he made in one of the Church books, we trace some of his early works, and learn that, during Advent of 1842, the altar rails were fresh painted [carved oak rails with angels, now take the place of the old rails], and in December following, two of the tower windows were brought out to view and repaired, at the cost of two individuals. On 26th August, 1843, the first stone of the reredos [not the present one] was laid, and in the following year, on 4th October, two open benches of oak with a front of open work, were placed in the chancel as his gift. Then, in 1845, we find our great benefactor making memoranda of "Things which I have projected to do if GOD bless me in them *(inter alia)*: Have the Church re-seated (open if possible) for the better accommodation of the parishioners, especially the poor. Have the south porch restored to its former state. Restore the pinnacles and 4 crosses on the tower, the cross at the east end, the west window of the tower, the entrance at the west and open the tower arch."

In 1847, the chancel had been repaired by the lay-rectors, Mr. Western and Mr. Skingley, the improvements comprising a new roof and the opening of three north clerestory windows, and the raising of the pavement 9 in., to the level of the floors of the aisles.

On 9th January, 1848, Mr. Dampier notes that "a high wind (the east window being still unglazed) blew down the woodwork in the chancel, put to protect the reredos, breaking the lectern to pieces and utterly destroying the old communion table, which was very unworthy of its purpose and made of common deal, the fragments of which were reverently burnt in the Church the next day by the curates with the churchwarden's sanction."

The restoration of the nave commenced about 1851, and, from the appeal issued by the committee and its most energetic honorary secretary, the Rev. Edward L. Cutts, then curate of Coggeshall, we gather that the roof of the nave was defective in principle and its timbers insufficient permanently to support the weight discharged upon them; and it was considered that any further settlements would cause the tie-beams to be drawn from the walls and fall inevitably into the church, hence a new roof was found to be indispensable. The roofs of the aisles were also unsafe, some of the buttresses and the clerestory walls of the nave required rebuilding, and new mullions, tracery, jambs, and arches were necessary for the repair of the windows, and, such was the general state of the building, that for substantial repairs alone, it was estimated a sum of £4,000 was required.

In 1863, the work of restoration had so far progressed, that the committee could report that the fabric of the nave and aisles had, under the directions of Mr. Ewan Christian, the architect, been substantially restored, but there remained to be done the benching of the nave and nave aisles, the lighting and warming of the Church, to say nothing of a new organ, and the general decoration of the building.

In 1875, it was estimated that no less than £7,460 had been expended upon the church, independently of the outlay upon the chancel, which had been substantially repaired at the cost of the lay-rectors. Since 1875, many additions and improvements have been made, and upwards of £1,040 has been spent by the Restoration Committee, to which must be added the private gifts of many benevolent individuals, most of which gifts have already been mentioned under their proper headings.

The Registers.

THE earliest book is of parchment, in part a transcript, and commences as to baptisms, in April, 1584; as to marriages, in October, 1561; and as to burials, in December, 1558. Each page, up to the year 1599, is signed at its foot by "Laur Newman" who was vicar, and "Richard Constantyne, * and Nicholas Gray, churchwardens." Among the burials is the following note, —"1597, May 15, Helen Robson, see the '*former* register for her end and manner of death.'" This volume was rebound in 1885. The entries on many of the pages are totally obliterated, but otherwise the book is in fairly good condition. The *former* register referred to above, has not been among the parish books for many years, and nothing is known about it.

Registers were first ordered to be kept by Lord Cromwell, Vicar-General, in the year 1538, but many parishes did not comply with the order until some years later. A further order was issued in 1558, in the reign of Queen Elizabeth, but the first of the now existing registers, is the result of a mandate issued in 1597, when the clergy of Canterbury, in convocation, with the approval of

---

* A house on Market Hill is called 'Constantines.'

Queen Elizabeth, commanded that every minister, at his institution, should declare that he would keep the register book according to the queen's injunctions. The 70th canon of 1603, directed that every parish should provide itself with a parchment book, and that the entries from the old paper books should be transcribed therein, each page being authenticated by the signature of the minister and churchwardens, so far as the ancient books thereof could be procured, but especially since the beginning of the reign of Queen Elizabeth ; and that the parchment book should be kept in a " sure coffer with three locks ;" and that for further security against loss a true copy of the names of all persons christened, married, or buried in the year before should be transmitted every year to the bishop of the diocese within a month after Easter, to be preserved in the episcopal archives. This latter injunction was in very many, if not most cases totally disregarded.

The other volumes are in a fair state of preservation, but, as continuity has not been observed in keeping the books, space does not allow the contents of each volume to be set forth here, but it may be mentioned that particulars as to the dates, condition and number of the registers should be found in a Blue-book, published in 1833, and also in a return made to the Archdeacon of Colchester, in 1887. This latter return, however, is not quite accurate.

Beside being a record of births, deaths, and marriages, the registers frequently contain items of a quaint or noteworthy character ; a perusal of the various books enables one to reproduce the following entries :—

" 1558—Dec. 17. Robert Whelpsted, Undertaker " (Buried).

" 1558—Dec. 28. Jo. Lawrence, Sexton, of Coggeshall " (Buried).

The above are the first two entries in the burial register—the undertaker and the sexton !

" 1578—Aug. 10. Lore, the wife of Jo. Smith (buried).

" This Lore Smith was ye instrument the Lord used to bring the infecon of the plague into this towne. She was the first y^t dyed of that infectious sicknes, and the most of theise that followed dyed of the same, until the cold winter time came, when the Lord in m^{r}cie stayed the same. The woman was commonlie noted to be a notable harlot."

" 1580—Dec. 28. Thom. Paycocke, who gave ii^{cli} [£200] to buy lands for the use of the poor of Cogshall for ever " (buried).

"1590—March 24. Nic. Coma, slaine in the stocke of ·the fulling mill" (buried).

"1591—May 13. ✱ Wm. Trewe [bur ᵈ.] This Wm· Trewe and all hereafter noted with this mark ✱ with mennie others dyed of an extraordinarie . . . . which disease the more the phisitions labore to cure the more sharpe and vehement it grewe."

There are 74 persons marked ✱ buried between 25th Nov. 1597 and 1st May, 1598.

"1592—Aug. 1st. Thomas Warner found murthered with a knife in his throate in standing wheat in Great Windmill Fields, for which murther Geor. Haven (?) of Coxall was executed."

"1600—June 3. Peter Marcant was slain in campinge on Sunday" [buried].

"1603—Dec. 1st. { Between these dates the names of 7 persons
"1604—March 26. { buried are followed by the remark—
 { "*ex peste.*'

"1606—Feb. 22. Robert Ennow, church clarke" [buried].

"1608—May 30. Father Brewer" [buried].

"1608—July 16. Mother Bruer" [buried].

"1612—Oct. 22. Henry Vane and William Wentworth, slaine both by the fall of a barne in a wynde."

"1613—Aug. 24. Robert Clench [buried] *eod* [*i.e.* same day] *ux* George Tailor dying exc. [excommunicate] was violently brought and cast into the grave made for Clench."

At the end of Vol. I. "A true record of al such apprentices which have been bound by Indenture according to law. Henry Oliver bound with Francis Page by Indenture for the terme of seven years, beginning at St. Michael, the Archangel, 1623, and to expire 1630." "Daniel Byeby, bound with the sayd Francis Page 7 years, beginning the 22nd day of May, 1626, and then 2 year of King (Kater?)" "Abigail Lennard taken as a Covenant Servant by James . . . . of St. James' Parish, in St. Edmund's Bury, for a year this 7th day of August, the sayd Lennard giving three pence to the said Abigail for a covenant to tye her, the said Abigail, to him the said Lennard and his wife, for a yeare, in ye presence of Nehemiah Dodd and Nicholas Northey. Dated the aforesaid 7th day of August, 1634, and the 10th yeare of King Charles."

In Vol. II. are the following entries :—

"Persons who received certificates to be touch'd by his Majestye for the Evill.

"1683—March 21.   Mary, daughter of John and Hesther Tayler.

24.   Mary, daughter of Daniel and Katharine Emmin.

25.   Elizabeth, daughter of Mr. David Batty, ye second time."

"1707—April 15.   Margaret Harrington, daughter of Jane Clifte."

Among the marriages in this volume :—

"1753—June 24.   Thomas Coker, widower, and Susanna Nicholls, spinster.   These were the first couple married at the Communion Rail."

"Marriages—I doe approve and allow of ye choice made by ye major part of ye inhabitants of Coggeshalls Greate and Little of John Brightwen being elected by them to be their parish Register, according to a late Act of Pliament in that case made and provided, and accordingly I have given him his oath, this 30th of September, 1653.

(Signed)   D. WAKERINGE."

Marriages, between 1653 and 1656, were contracted in the presence of either Jeremy Aylett, Esq., J. P., William Harlackenden, of Earls Colne, Esq., J.P., or Dionysius Wakeringe, Esq., J.P.   In 1657, before Herbert Pelham, Esq., J.P.

Monumental Inscriptions.

"IN the Floor of this Church and Chancell have been several fair Grave stones with portraitures and inscriptions in Brasse, which are torne off by sacrilegious hands or worn out by frequent calcation, so that the remembrance of the persons interrd had utterly perished if it had not been for some remains preserved by Mr. Weever and Mr. Symonds in their collections."   Thus wrote Holman, and since his day how many more of these memorials have either perished or been destroyed?   Weever, speaking of some of the tombs, says, "I have not seen such rich monuments for so meane persons."

The following memorials in *italics* are no longer extant.   The others still remain.

The Guyons.

A LARGE tomb of black marble, which formerly stood on the south side of the present entrance from the vestry to the chancel, was some years ago moved further east to its present

position. On the western end of the tomb are the arms of the Guyon family. Ar., three bendlets az., on a canton sa., a lion passant guard or. Crest a demi lion ramp guard or., gorged with a collar per pale az., and sa., but the tinctures are not depicted on the tomb, they were, however, on a hatchment in the church many years ago. On the

ARMS OF THE GUYON FAMILY.

south face are these words :

> "Hic jacet corpus Thomæ Guyon Gener, qui obiit 24º. Novembris Aº. Dom. 1664. Ætatis suæ 72. He bequeathed two hundred pounds to be laid out in land, for a weekely allowance of bread to the poore for ever."

In the south chancel aisle near the door was a grave-stone of gray marble, at the head the Guyon arms, with this inscription beneath :—"*Here lieth the body of Thomas Guyon, eldest son of George Guyon, Gent., son of Thomas Guyon, Gent., he was borne the 15th of June, 1652, and departed this life the 13th of June, 1673.*"

> *Epitaphium.*
> *Died he so young, then learn we all by this*
> *To think of death and to prepare for bliss.*
> *He died so we are sure and now injoies*
> *The fruits of labore everlasting joyes.*"

A stone within the chancel, near the easternmost arch of the south side, was covered by the new pavement in 1865, it bore the Guyon arms and the following inscription :—

> "*Here lieth the body of Matthew Guyon, Gent., who died the 3rd day of March, 1678, and in the forty-sixth year of his age.*"

Holman described the position as on the south side of the chancel by the *partition*, and says the gravestone was of black marble enclosed with iron rails.

There is also another stone in the centre of the chancel, but now covered by the pavement. It bears the following inscription :

" Here lyeth Sr. Mark Guyon, Knight.
Anno Domini, 1690."

Beneath the altar is a large black marble slab thus inscribed :

" Another Dorcas, or the remains of Dame Dorcas Guyon,
who departed this life October ye 2nd, 1714, aged 58
years, waiting the happy summons of ' Tabitha, arise.'
On her left hand lyeth Dorcas Boys, her daughter, who
dyed November ye 2nd, 1714, aged 20 years."

On the wall of the south chancel aisle is a marble tablet
bearing the following :—

" In a vault in the middle aisle of this church are deposited
the remains of Mr. Mark Guyon, late of White Colne,
who died May 31st, 1839, aged 47 years. This tablet
was erected by his beloved wife."

𝕿𝖍𝖊 𝕻𝖆𝖞𝖈𝖔𝖈𝖐𝖘.

THERE were formerly several memorial slabs of the Paycocke
family in the north chancel aisle, but two only, and one in
part destroyed, now remain. One is to the memory of Thomas
Paycocke, who was buried in the north
chancel aisle, his place of sepulture being
marked by a stone bearing the figure of
a man in a long civil gown, his hands
folded in the posture of devotion ; from
his mouth there was formerly a scroll
bearing the words, " Only fayth justifyeth,"
and round the edge of the stone was the
following legend engraved in brass, which,
except the italicised part may still be read :
" Here lyeth buried Thomas Peaycocke,
the sonne of Robert Peaycocke, who departed this lyfe the xxvith day of December, 1580, and left behinde hym two
daughters, Johan and *Anne, wᶜʰ Thomas*
Peaycocke Dydd gyve CC pounds to buy
land for the continuall relief of the poore
of Coxall for ever." At the feet of the
effigy are the following lines : —

THOMAS PAYCOCKE.

" Thou mortall man yt wouldest attayne
The happie haven of heavenly rest,

Prepare thyself : of graces all
Fayth and repentance are the best."

At each corner of this stone was an escutcheon, long since toi n off, and above the figure was a merchant's mark, which showed him to be a clothier.

There is no account of this tomb-stone in Weever's *Funeral Monuments ;* the next four inscriptions are recorded therein, but the stones bearing the inscriptions are either covered over or destroyed :

" *Hic jacet Thomas Paycocke quondam Carnifex (i.e.* butcher) *de Coggeshal, qui obiit 21 Maii, 1461, et Christiana uxor ejus quorum animabus."*

There was another large grave-stone of gray marble in the north chancel aisle, which had engraved in brass this inscription :

" *Prey for the soul of Robert Paycock, of Coggeshall, Clothmaker, for Elizabeth, and Joan his wyfs, who died 21 Oct., 1520, on whos soul · . . . "*

JOHN PAYCOCK.   JOAN PAYCOCK.

In the north chancel aisle is a large grave-stone of grey marble that had inlaid round the ledge a large fillet of brass, thereon the Creed in Latin curiously insculpt, " *Credo in Deum Patrem*," &c., but this is gone. In the middle the effigies of a man and woman, their hands folded in an attitude of devotion, still remaining. The matrix shows that there were labels out of the mouths of the two effigies. At the head of the stone the effigy of our Saviour; at each corner an escutcheon. Underneath, on a plate of brass inlaid, was this inscription in Gothic letters :—

> " *Orate pro anima Johannis Paycock et Johanne uxoris ejus qui quidem Johannes, obiit 2 Aprilis, 1533.*

And beneath that a kneeling group on one side and a figure kneeling on the other, and labels over them.

Another stone had on it :—

> "*Here lyeth Thomas Paycock, Cloth-worker, Margaret and Ann hys wyfs: which Tho. died the 4 of September, 1518.*"

Aylet.

A BRASS plate of diamond shape was many years ago found in the Aylet vault, at the east end of the north chancel aisle. It formed a coffin plate and was taken out of the vault by Mr. Mathews, when he was vicar here. It is now fixed to the south chancel wall, but was formerly on the north wall. It bears in the centre the arms of the Aylet family : A fesse embattled between three unicorn's heads erased ; Crest, a demi unicorn reguardant issuing out of a helmet and beneath the following inscriptions :—

> "Primogenito suo Pr Chariseimo Thoma Aylet Hospiti Lincolis Armigero Posuit Thoma Pater superetes."

> "Ab hac migravit Luci Clariori, the 4th August, Anno Domi, 1638."

> "With ynch of time hee to ye best impous
> Of greater hopes, free loving and belovid:
> His lose so soon us leaves all ful of sorow
> Hee sets tonight, we follow him tomoroo
> Who thus his couse doth finish in his prime
> Runs through much bisnis in litel time.
>   Anno Domi 1638."

On a grave stone of blue marble there was formerly the following :—

"*Here lyeth buried the body of Thomas Aylett, Gent., Lord of the Manor of Coggeshall, who departed this life the 19th day of October, 1650, in the 81st year of his age.*"

Goldwyre.

O N the south side of the chancel there was formerly a slab with the figures of a man and two females. On another stone were the figures of a man and his two wives with two groups of children below and a saint above ; scrolls proceeding from the mouths of the females, and a horizontal scroll over the head of the man, and this inscription at their feet :—

"*Orate pro anima Gulielmi Goldwyre et Isabelle et Christiane uxorum qui quidem Gulielmus obiit** . . . . *1514.*

"*Mary Moder mayden clere
Prey for me William Goldwyre
And for me Isabel his wyf
Lady for thy joyes fyf†
Hav mercy on Christian his second wyf
Swete Jesu for thy wowndys fyf. ‡*

In his will, dated 26th January, 1514-15 and proved on 10th March following, he directs " my body to be buried in the quere of Saint Peter-ad-Vincula, there as the legende is redde by the sepulture of my wif."

This is, probably the William Goldwer to whom, in 1488 (3 Henry VII) the Lord of the Manor of Coggeshall granted " a tenement and garden in Church Street, called Cachpoles, to hold by the rodde at the Lord's will, paying to the Lord yearly 12s. rent Fyne 2 capons."

Farrington.

I N Symond's collection is recorded a memorial, which was in the chancel in the seventeenth century :—

"*Orate p. aia Rici Farrington Quoadum vicarii istius eccli qui obiit 8 die Octob. 1479.*

---

* The month and day of the month are blank in Weever, edit. A.D. — 1631, and in Holman.

† The five joys and five wounds, not joyes *syf* as in Dale.

‡ Weever.

Which may be translated—
Pray for the soul of Richard Farrington, sometime vicar of this church, who died 8th day of October, 1479.

Oldam and Brewninge.

ON a brass plate, now in the chamber over the porch but formerly embedded in a stone of grey marble, is the following :—

"For the memorye of John Oldam, of East Tilburye, Gent. who dyed the 24 day of August in the yeare of our Lord 1599 and of his age the XXXth. Frances ye daughter of Richard Brewninge, of Wimeringe in the County of Southampton Esqvire and his late wife mother to one only davghter by him named Marye, hath set this to remayne.

Grimes and Carter.

ON the north wall of the north chancel aisle is a large marble monument, bearing the following inscriptions beneath arms, or., a chief sable charged with 3 escollops : crest, a lion's head erased or.

ARMS OF THE CARTER FAMILY.

"In memory of The Honble Lieutenant Colonel John Grime, Esqr. (late of this town) who served in several campaigns in Flanders and the Spanish Netherlands with His Grace the late Duke of Ormond. He was a brave and experienced soldier, and King William III. of Glorious Memory at his return from abroad gave him a pension for his Life for his bravery and courage which he enjoyed till his Death, which happened the 2nd day of Novr. 1714, in the 74th year of his age.

"Also in memory of Samuel Carter, his Grandson, Esq. (late of this town) who died the 24th day of October, 1773, aged 73 years."

The Grimes family resided in the house in Church Street, known as 'Plumbers,' belonging to Mr. E. T. Scott, midway between Swan Lane and Bird-in-Hand Lane.

Col. Grime was baptised at Coggeshall, "4th Aug., 1640, John sonne of Wm. Griem and Joane his wife," and buried here on 7th Nov., 1714.

Fuller.

WITHIN the chancel on the south pier of the large arch, which divides the nave from the chancel, is a marble tablet with this inscription :

" Memoriæ Sacrum Gulielmi Fuller, Hujus Parochiæ
Generosi, cujus animi probitas, morumque integritas,
In Deum pietas, erga socios, æquitas, omnibus, qui
Illum reapse norint, clarissime effulserunt. Has
virtutes fervidas (quod ipse maluisset) non flaminam
sed lucem eficientes, nos visuros Credite posteri.

Morti cessit Die May 15th Anno $\begin{cases} \text{Domini 1748} \\ \text{Ætatis 68} \end{cases}$

Hoc Marmor nitidum tam charo capiti, grates
persolvens dignas Henricus Fuller, Filius ejus
superstes, humillime Dat. Dicat. Dedicat.

The Skingleys.

ON a marble tablet, in the north-western corner of the chancel, is a monument—

" In memory of Henry Skingley who departed this life Aug.
3rd, 1793 aged 53 years, also of Mary his wife who departed this life November 30th 1815 aged 75 years."

On the south wall of the sacrarium is a marble slab bearing

the Skingley arms :—Az., on a cross engr ar., between 4 garbs or., an oakslip fructed ppr between as many roses gu barbed and seeded also ppr ; a chief indented of the second, thereon three lions ramp. of the fourth : crest :—Between two branches of oak a demi lion ppr charged with a bend ar., thereon two roses as in the arms holding be-

ARMS OF THE SKINGLEY FAMILY.

tween the paws an escutcheon gu., charged with a garb or., [Mr. Probert, '*Arms and Epitaphs of Essex*,' Vol. i, Brit. Mus. 33,520-29, says that Windsor Herald told him these arms were granted by the College in 1827], and the following inscription :—

" Sacred to the memory of Henry Skingley, Esqr. who died
July 5th, 1837, aged 68 years, and of Ann, his widow, who
after surviving him 23 years died August 14th, 1860, aged

79.   Her remains rest in the vault of her family in this
churchyard.   Blessed are the dead that die in the Lord."

On another tablet, below the last—

" Sacred to the memory of Henry Skingley, son of Henry and
Catherine Skingley of Wakes Hall in this County who
died April 1st, 1839, aged 1 year and 10 months."

On the north wall of the sacrarium is a marble slab with the
Skingley arms and the following lines :—

" In memory of Charles Joseph Skingley, Esqr., second son
of the late Henry Skingley, Esqr., and Ann his wife, of
this parish, who departed this life on the 9th March, 1853,
aged 43 years.   His remains are deposited in the chancel
of this church.   This tablet is erected by his two surviving
brothers."

Another stone placed on the north wall of the sacrarium is :—

" In memory of Susan Bowles, the beloved wife of Major G.
D. Skingley, who died, 14th Oct., 1878, aged 47."

also of

" Major G. D. Skingley, who died, 16th June, 1888, aged 76.
Buried at Kensal Green."

Duddell and Skingley.

A MURAL slab of marble in the north chancel aisle bears the
following inscription :—

" Sacred to the memory of the Rev. John Duddell, Rector of
Wormington, Gloucestershire, and for thirty-three years
Curate of this town, who died, January 8th, 1826, aged 82
years.   And also to Margaret his widow, who died the first
day of November, 1833, aged 85 years ; by whose daughter
Ann, the wife of Henry Skingley, Esq,, this monument
was erected."

The Townsends.

B ENEATH the arms of this family, (which were granted on 5th
June, 1718, Ar., on a chevron between three escalops az., as
many estoiles of the first : crest, on a mount vert a buck sejant
ppr attired or., supporting with the dexter foot, a lance erect gu.,
headed of the third,) is a large marble monument on the north
wall of the church :—

"Sacred to the memory of the Honourable Robert Townsend, Esq., son of Robert Townsend, in this town, Gentleman. He was an officer in the seven ever-memorable campaigns under the late Glorious Duke of Marlborough, and at the time of his death Colonel in the King's first Reg-

ARMS OF THE TOWNSEND FAMILY.

iment of Foot Guards—In which posts, from faithful and appoved services he merited the valuable character of a brave and experienced soldier. The distinguishing qualities of a gentlemen he possessed in so eminent a degree that the esteem he justly deserved all who knew him liberally gave, and if any were wanting in that esteem to them he was not known.

Reader, may the particulars of his good character (as he himself would desire) live rather in thy imitation than his extraordinary praises, and be thou an instance of his laudable worth and goodness. He died, Nov. 26th, 1728, aged 46, lamented by many friends by none more than by his only surviving brother, Mr. William Townsend, who erected this monument."

On the south wall, beneath the Townsend arms :—

"Sacred to the memory of William Townsend, Esq., Attorney, who died, March 8th, 1789, in the 65th year of his age. Also his brother, Charles Townsend, Gent., who died May 5th, 1777, in the 52nd year of his age. Also William Townsend, Esq., son of Charles Townsend, who died, March 2nd, 1806, in the 48th year of his age; by whose desire this monument is erected."

Also on the south wall is another monument to this family, bearing the arms with a crescent, indicating that the deceased was a second son or of the second house. The shield is also charged with an inescutcheon bearing the Townsend arms :

"Sacred to the memory of Richard White Townsend, who died July 7th, 1823, aged 32 years; also of Helen Emm Townsend, who died Septmbr. 30th, 1818, aged 8 months, and of his son Arthur Townsend, died Novr. 3rd, 1879, aged 63 years, Buried at Shalstone, Bucks."

On the same wall :—

"This Tablet is placed as a small tribute of respect, esteem, and regard to the memory of Mary Ann, the beloved and affectionate wife of the Revd. N. R. Dennis, M.A., Chaplain to His Majesty's Forces, and eldest daughter of Mr. Townsend, of Ferriers. She died near Villa de Conde in Portugal, on the 8th March, 1827, aged 38 years."

𝔚𝔥𝔦𝔱𝔢.

THERE is a marble slab on the north wall, inscribed :—

"Sacred to the memory of Richard White, who died, March 22nd, 1806, aged 44 years.

God the supreme disposer of events,
In judgment ever righteous will'd it so,
His will be done.

This unadorned monument is erected by his widow, as a small token of affection."

Beneath the above, on another stone :—

"Richard Meredith White, died January 3rd, 1796, aged 58 years."

"He that hath pity upon the poor, lendeth unto the Lord, &c."

𝔄𝔫𝔡𝔯𝔢𝔴.

ON the wall of the north chancel aisle, is a slab :—

"Sacred to the memory of Thomas Andrew, Esqr., of this town, Solicitor, whose mortal remains lie deposited in a vault near this spot."

"He was removed from the midst of health, enjoyment and prosperity, by an instantaneous death, without one previous fear or moment's warning, on the 27th June, A.D. 1826, in the 53rd year of his age."

"Be ye also ready, for in such an hour as ye think not, the Son of man cometh."

𝔗𝔥𝔢 𝔅𝔬𝔶𝔰 𝔉𝔞𝔪𝔦𝔩𝔶.

IN the chancel, beneath the Communion table, on a large black marble slab, bearing arms, a winged griffin rampant, passant within a border :—

"Exuvias hic deposuit Reverendus Vir Jacobus Boys, A.M., Hujus Ecclesiæ per XLIV. Annos Vigilantissimus Pastor,

E

Qui per totum sui Ministerii cursum vestigia premens
Apostolica assiduo conatus est.
' To give no offence in anything that the ministry be not blamed.'
—II Cor. vi. 3. [In Greek]
Nat. VIIIᵛᵒ Martii MDCL. Obᵗ Xᵐᵒ Octobris MDCCXXV."

On the north wall of the sacrarium is a marble tablet which
records quite a family history :—

" Here lies (near the remains of his ancestors) the body of
Mr. William Boys, Gent., eldest son of the Revd. Mr. James
Boys, late Vicar of this parish. He married Hester, the youngest
daughter of John Cox, Esq., and Ann, his wife, who was the
daughter of Major-General Haynes, of Copford Hall, in this
county. John Cox, was of Emmanuel College, in Cambridge,
and of Grays Inn, London, Barrister-at-law, and (late) of Mount
Hall, in this parish. A gentleman justly esteemed and respected
as an eminent and able Councellour, an Honest and Upright man
and a good Christian. Hester, wife of the said Mr. William
Boys, departed this life, May 30th, 1742, aged 53 years and was
buried in this chancel, where by his own desire his remains are
also interred, after a long life spent in piety and good works ; his
great care and study in particular was to instruct the poor and
ignorant in the knowledge of their Christian duty. Witness the
many good books he dispersed for that purpose. Witness that
charitable donation to the parish of Great Bardfield, to perpetuate
the same pious design to the end of the world. Thus lived this
good man, and thus he died, July 25th, 1768, aged 83 years.

" Beatus servus ille, quem quum venerit Dominus ejus invene-
rit ita facientem.

"The Revd. Mr. John Harrison, Nephew and Executor of the
deceased, to testify his respect to his memory caused this monument to be erected."

Boeßm.

Near the chancel, on the north of the central passage, is a
stone with the following inscription :—

" Jane Boehm born ye 8th of August, 1737, died ye 19th of
May, 1738; she was daughter of Charles Boehm, of
London, and Jane, his wife, daughter of Richard DuCane
Esq., of Coggeshall.

Elizabeth, twin sister of the above Jane, died 26 September, 1738.

Jane Boehm, the second, born ye 4th December, 1738, died 13th April, 1740.

Richarda Boehm, sister of the above, born 26 June, died 27th September, 1742."

𝔏awrence.

THERE is a stone of gray marble, in the north chancel aisle, with the deceased's merchant's mark, and the following memorial inscription :—

"Here lyeth buryed the body of George Lawrence, the sonne of John Lawrence, sometyme Clothier of this towne, which George died the xiii daye of November, in the yeare of our Lorde God, 1594.

𝔊ladwin.

ON the floor of the north chancel aisle, partly concealed by a pew, is a stone inscribed :—

"In memory of Elizabeth, wife of John Gladwin, Gent., who died, Feb. 8th, 1771, aged 73 years.

"Also in memory of John Gladwin,,who died, Septbr 1st, 1773, aged 77 years.

"The hour . . . . and . . . .
As Flower fadeth so man dieth
O man be wise, consider now your latter end,
pray do."

𝔐athew.

ON a marble slab on the wall of the south chancel aisle is this inscription :—

"Hoc marmor, memoriam filioli hocce in templo conditi, Edwardi Coldham Mathew, nati, Jul. 26, mortui, Dec. 21, 1820 ; in æternum proferre voluit pater hujus parochiæ vicarius. Necnon patruelis carissimæ Helenes Mariæ Mathew quæ a parentibus multum desiderata annos quindecim apud Anglos commorata in patriam tandem reversa ; vix prius visa quam extincta, heu vitæ nimia brevitas. Anno ætatis undevicesimo, Calcuttæ, Feb. 10, 1822, animam efflavit.

"Germen flosque, novo subsecti tempore veris :
    Cælo vos numen fronde virere sinat."

Among other memorials no longer extant are the following :—

Coggeshall.

. . . . *Coggeshal* . . . . *Coggeshal* . . . . *mil MCCC."*

Weever says " For which of the name this broken inscription should be engraven I cannot learne, but I find that these Coggeshals, in foregoing ages were gentlemen of exemplarie regard and knightly degree, whose ancient habitation was in this towne, one of which familie was knighted by King Edward the 3rd, the same day that he created Edward his eldest son Earl of Chester and Duke of Cornwall, Anno, 1336."

Kebul.

" *ORATE pro animabus Johannis Kebul et Isabelle et Johanne ux ejus Quorum, &c.* About the verge of the stone in brasse a Paternoster inlaid :—*Pater Noster qui es in celis sanctificetur nomen tuum*, and so forth to the end of the praier. · Upon the middest of the marble this Ave Maria :—*Ave Maria gratia plena ; Dominus tecum ; Benedicta tu in mulieribus ; et benedictus sit fructus ventris tui Jesus. Amen."* †

Worseter.

" *ORATE p. aiabj Petri Worseter de Coggeshall, Mercer, obyt 8 Sept., 1471."* (Symonds).

Sandford.

"*Here under lyeth the body of Thomas Sandford, late of this parish, Gent., whoe departed this life ye eight day of May, Anno Domini, 1636."*

In the church of Horndon on-the-Hill there is a slab recording the death, in 1633, of Susan Sandford, daughter of Thomas Sandford, late of Coggeshall.

In the north aisle there were formerly divers grave-stones with the inscriptions gone. The clerk in Holman's time had it by relation that they belonged to the Coleman's, who were clothiers.

---

* Weever.   See further under the family of Coggeshall.   † Weever.

THE LYCH GATE.

The Churchyard.

THE Churchyard is entered through a handsome lych-gate, presented by Messrs. Charles and William Bonton, as a memorial to their mother. It was designed by Mr. Edwin J. Dampier, a son of the late vicar, and is of 15th century character. It is of oak and is covered with tiles; on the south side is the text : —"Through the grave and gate of death we pass to our joyful resurrection."

The principal tombstones now remaining in the churchyard are those to the memory of the Buxton family, ancestors of Sir Thomas Fowell Buxton, and of Edward North Buxton, Esq., High Sheriff of this County, in 1888. The name occurs among the earliest entries in our parish registers, the first record of the family being that of the marriage of William Buckston with Katherine Roche, on the 14 Dec., 1561, and from that day, if not earlier, down to the present time the family has been connected with this town either by residence or as owners of property. Their arms are argent; a lion rampant, tail elevated and turned over the head sable, between 2 mullets of the second, and were confirmed to them by the Herald's College, in 1634. Their crest is a buck's head couped gules, attired or., gorged with a collar of the last, therefrom pendent an escutcheon argent charged with an *African's head*, sable. The African's head upon the pendent escutcheon is doubtless commemorative of the philanthropic exertions of Thomas Fowell Buxton for the abolition of the slave trade. For his great services in this respect he was created a baronet, on 6th July, 1840. He died in 1845 [A Memoir with the correspondence of T. F. Buxton, was edited by his son, Charles Buxton, in 1848].

To revert to the tombstones and their inscriptions, there are the following in the churchyard. A marble slab covering a brick tomb with this inscription :—

" Here lyeth the body of Thomas Buxton, of Great Coggeshall, Cloathier" [The Clothiers or cloth manufacturers of those days may be compared with the wealthy brewers of the present time. In these districts their position was little below the rank of the squire.] "Who departed this life the 16th of October, 1713, and in the 70th year of his age.

Here also lyeth the body of Elizabeth Buxton, the wife of Isaac Buxton, of Coggeshall, Cloathier, who departed this life the 12th of December, 1713, in the 40th year of her age.

Here also lyeth the body of John Buxton, Esq., who departed this life the 22nd of July, 1751, aged 49.

Also

Thomas Buxton, Esq., who died the 5th February, 1777, aged 82 years.

Also

Ann Buxton, his 3rd wife, obt. Sept. 5th, 1782, æt. 63."

A tomb of obelisk form, about 7 feet in height, has on it :—

" In memory of Charles Buxton, Esq., of Great Braxted, in
this County, Citizen and Lace Merchant, of London, fourth
son of Isaac and Elizabeth Buxton. He died, 22nd Sept.,
1777, in the 74th year of his age."

On another marble stone over a brick pedestal :

" Here lieth the body of Judith, wife of Thomas Buxton,
Clothier, who died the 16th of September, 1719, aged 78.
As also the body of Isaac Buxton, Clothier, her son, who
departed this life, the 26th of December, 1732, aged 60."

On another similar tomb :—

" Here lieth the body of Samuel Buxton, son of Isaac Buxton,
who was buried under the stone adjacent. He died, September the 15th, 1737, aged 26.

Here also lieth the body of Sarah, wife of John Buxton,
who died, February the 7th, 1736, aged 34.

Here also lieth the body of Miss Mary Buxton, daughter
of John Buxton, Esq., who departed this life the 19th of
June, 1750, in the 21st year of her age.

Also John Buxton, Esq., of Highbury Place, in the
County of Middlesex, who departed this life, May 16th,
1802, aged 69."

There are also the following inscriptions :—

" Sarah Buxton, daughter of the late John Buxton, Esq., died
at Camberwell, in the County of Surrey, January the 15th,
1815, aged 41 years.

Also the remains of Mary Buxton, Relict of John Buxton, Esq., and mother of the above Sarah Buxton, who
died, at Camberwell, December 29th, 1838, in the 95th
year of her age."

" Hannah Buxton, daughter of Charles Buxton, Esq., whose
remains by her desire were here deposited, died February
28th, 1780, aged 37. To her memory this monument, at
her request, was erected by Anna Unwin.

Why are friends ravisht from us ? 'Tis to bind
By soft affection ties on human hearts
The thot of death which reason too surpine
Or misemployed so rarely fastens there.

Here

Are deposited the remains of Anna, the daughter of Thomas Buxton, Esq., late of this town, the wife of Jacob Unwin Brewer, who died, 1763, she was born in the year 1737, married in 1761 and died in 1798.

Also are deposited the remains of John Buxton, Esq., of Denmark Hill, Camberwell, in the County of Surrey, who died, Nov. 16th, 1843, aged 72.

Also the remains of Hannah Buxton, Relict of the above John Buxton, Esq., of Denmark Hill, who died, Nov. 25, 1861, aged 95.

Also here was interred the body of Anne, daughter of Josh. Bentley, of Leicester, and 2nd wife of Thomas Buxton, Esq., who died, Aug. 19, 1747, aged 44 years.

This memorial was inscribed by her daughter, Anna Unwin, 1780."

Another tomb has inscribed :—

" Deposited in this vault are the remains of William Forbes, Esq., of Camberwell, in the County of Surrey. He was married at Coggeshall Church, on the 1st of July, 1778, and died there while on a visit, on the 20th of Sept., A.D., 1818, in the 65th year of his age.

Also the remains of Elizabeth Forbes, widow of the above William Forbes and daughter of Thomas Buxton, late of this town. She was born at Coggeshall, on the 22nd day of January, A.D., 1751, and died at Camberwell, on the 23rd day of August, A.D., 1825."

There were also either in the church or the churchyard the following inscriptions :—

Carter.

" *HERE lyeth the body of William Carter, Gent., who died 12th Nov 178 (5?) aged 72 years. Also the body of Mary his wife, who died 8th July, 1795, aged 80 years.*"

Sutton.

" *HERE lyeth ye body of Mr. Ambrose Sutton, who departed this life, the 15th day of May, A.D. 1688, aged 63.*"

Mullings.

. . . " *Body of James Mullings, who dyed the 7th of Jan., 1726, aged 40 years.*"

Chignell.

. . . . . . *" the body of Mr. John Chignell, who departed this life the 10th day of October, 1720, in the 32nd year of his age."*

Cockerell.

" HERE lyeth the body of Thomas Cockerell, Yeoman, who died 20th September, 1564" (Symonds).

There are also tombs of the families of Abbot, Appleford, Bonton, Cable, Cox, Fuller, Gardner, Godfrey, Hall, Iegon, Richardson, Richmond, Sach, Tupper, and many others.

There are a few quaint epitaphs but of no particular merit.

A stone is still extant with these lines on it :—

" Lord, Thy grace is free,
Why not for me ?
Death is to me no gloomy shade
While JESUS is in view.
Oh, may my ashes then persuade
Others to love him too."

This stone is to the memory of one Thomas Hance, a clothier, who *(The Excursion for Essex,* dated 1818, says) died a bankrupt, and on his tomb one of his creditors wrote a reply to the query contained in the first two lines :—

" And the Lord answered and said—
Because thy debts ain't paid."

In 1819, the churchyard was enlarged by taking in a piece of Church Green, and the Parish Register has this entry, " 1819, June 20, Hannah Birles 1st interred in ye new ground, consecrated ye 17th of June, 1819, by William, Lord Bishop of London, age 51." A sketch of the ceremony is in the possession of Mr. Thomas Simpson, whose wife's grandfather, Mr. William Swinborne, one of the Churchwardens, is a prominent figure in the picture.

By an Order in Council, dated 21st July, 1855, burials were discontinued in the churchyard as from the 1st February, 1856, an exemption being made in favor of the existing family vaults on condition that such vaults should be opened without digging up the soil of the churchyard, and that each coffin be embedded in a layer of powdered charcoal, 4 inches at the least in thickness, and be covered over with brickwork properly cemented.

In this year about 3 acres, part of Pitt or Overchurch Field, was bought by the Burial Board, since which, with very few exceptions, interments have taken place in the cemetery.

𝕿𝖍𝖊 𝕮𝖑𝖊𝖗𝖌𝖞.

THE first mention we find of the Vicars of Coggeshall, is in the taxation of the Borough of Colchester, 24, Edw. I. A.D. 1296.

"JOHN, THE VICAR OF COGGESHALL, has on the day aforesaid, 3 quarters and a half of oats, price per quar., 2s., sum 7s. Out of that the 7th,/12d." *Rol. Parl.* Vol. I. p. 228.

RUSHENDEN, * Richard de, presented Ides, June, 1330.

SEWALE, William, diac 6 Ides, May, 1333.

GALFRIDUS, dictus Chappell de Bury.

BROOKS, Stephen, Id. Oct., 1362, on resignation of Galfridus.

WEADLINGBURGH, John de, 12 Kal. May, 1369, on resignation of Brooks.

BELTESFORD, John.

HYDE, Richard, 6 Feb., 1384, on resignation of Beltesford.

PHILPOTT, Roger.

BURGERSETH or BURGHWASH, Henry, 22nd Sept., 1425, on resignation of Philpott.

WHITE, Robert, 18th Oct., 1426, on resignation of Burgerseth.

HUBERT, Nicholas, 8th Oct., 1450, on resignation of White.

SPROTBURGH, Richard, presented Nov., 1456, on death of last vicar.

SOUTHYN. John, 3rd July, 1461, on resignation of Sprotburgh.

FARRINGDON, Richard, 26th July, 1475, on resignation of Southyn. Buried at Coggeshall, see memorial inscription.

GYFFREY, John, presented 14th Oct., 1479, on death of Farringdon.

BULGEN, John, A.M., 27th April, 1510, on death of Gyffrey.

MYTTON, Stephen, L.B., 5th Aug., 1534, on death of Bulgen.

VAUGHAN, Hugo, L.B., 20th July, 1545, on death of Mytton. Presented by Bishop Bonner, Vicar of Great Bardfield, 1533; Rector of Gestingthorpe, in 1537; and Vicar of Halstead, 1537-40.

---

* A reference to Newcourt's *Repertorium* will in most instances disclose the name of the previous cure held by the incumbents.

STOCKTON, Robert, 6th May, 1558, on resignation of Vaughan.

NEWMAN, Lawrence, A.M., 10th Feb., 1575, on death of Stockton. Fellow of Emmanuel Coll., Camb., B.D. of Oxford in 1610, afterwards D.D. Buried at Coggeshall, 1st March, 1599. He was vicar here when the transcript of the earliest register was made. His daughter, Martha, was baptised here, 13th July, 1588, and Elizabeth, 31st Jany., 1590. In the Register at Dr. William's Library, Somerset House, is recorded the burial on 20th June, 1585, of his daughter, Rebecca ; while the Parish Registers here record the following burials : 1621, July 23, Nathaniel Newman, son of Mr. Lawrence Newman ; and 1621, Jany. . . . Newman, widow of Mr. Lawrence Newman, sometime vicar of Coggeshall.

DYKE, William, was preacher here at the time of Aylmer's Visitation, but he is not mentioned in Newcourt's Rep. Brook, in his *Lives of the Puritans,* in reference to this man, who in error he calls Daniel (Neal, 1284), says, " Because he continued a deacon and did not enter into priests' orders, which the Bishop supposed he accounted Popish, and because he refused to wear the surplice, and troubled his auditory as his grace signified with notions which thwarted the established religion, he was suspended and at last deprived in the year 1589." The distressed parishioners being concerned for the loss of their minister, petitioned the Lord Treasurer Burleigh to intercede with the bishop in their behalf, but the Treasurer did not meet with success. Dyke died in 1614. He had a son baptised here, as appears from one of the earliest entries in the Register : " 1584, Oct. 13, Hieremy, son of Wm. Dike, Preacher of Coggeshall."

TUKE, George, was a preacher here in 1587, as appears from an entry in the Register of baptisms : " 1587, Aug. 20, Elizabeth, daughter of George Tuke, Preacher."

STOUGHTON, Thomas, presented 12th Dec., 1600, on death of Lawrence Newman. He was deprived in 1606.

CUDWORTH, Ralph. S.T.B., presented 4th April, 1606, on deprivation of Stoughton. Fellow of Emmanuel Coll., Cambs. He died, 1624.

HEYLEY, John, presented 8th March, 1607, on resignation of Cudworth. Resigned, 1609.

DODD, John, presented 5th May, 1609, on resignation of Hey-

ley. On the cover of one of Bufton's Books in my possession, is the following note :—"I have often heard it reported
of holy Mr. Dodd, yt. when one, inraged at his close convincing doctrine, pick't a quarrell with him, smote him on ye
face and dashed out two of his teeth, this meek servant of
CHRIST spat out the teeth into his hand and said, 'See here
you have knocked out two of my teeth and that without any
just provocation, but on condition that I might do your soul
good, I would give you leave to dash out all the rest.'"

The Baptismal Register for Coggeshall has :—

"1612—June 11, Elizabeth, daughter of Mr. John Dodd,
Vicar. 1625—Dec. 4, John, son of Mr. Nehemiah Dodd
and Elizabeth his wife. 1628—Sept. 21, Nehemiah, son of
Nehemiah Dodd and Elizabeth his wife. 1632—May 13,
Robert, son of Nehemiah Dodd and Elizabeth his wife.
1635—Sept. 29, Elizabeth, daughter of Mr. Nehemiah Dodd
and Elizabeth his wife." And in the Burial Register we find:—
"1630—July 25th, Martha, wife of John Dodd, Vicar; and
1639—April 18, Mr. John Dodd, Vicar of Coggeshall."

SEDGWICK, Obadiah, S.T.B., presented 6th July, 1639, on the
death of Dodd. Born at Marlborough, Wilts, 1600; educated at Queen's College, Oxford, afterwards tutor of Magda-
len Hall; at a later period he was preacher to the inhabitants
of St. Mildred's parish in Bread Street. He preached before
parliament on several occasions. A print of one of his sermons in my possession is thus entitled :—"England's Preservation, or a Sermon discovering the only way to prevent
destroying Judgements. Preached to the Honourable House
of Commons at their last Solemn Fast, being on May 25,
1642, by Obadiah Sedgewick, Batchalour in Divinity, and
Minister of Coggeshall, in Essex. Published by order of that
House." His induction is recorded in the Parish Register of
Burials, anno 1639, the entry, however, is much obliterated
by damp :—

"Obadiah Sedgwicke . . . . Vicarius de Coggeshall,
Julie 15, Anno Dm. 1639, presentibus Nobilitiam . . .
doio & patron . . . . Robert . . . . Warwick
Nehemiah Sedg . . . doio, Tho. Aylet, &c. . . .
Articules relig Anglian & . . . public —— Testibus
Neh. Dod, Tho. Aylet, Rob. Crane, William Gladwine,

Tho. Coxe, Guliel Tanner, Richard Shortland, Johi Allis-
ton, Johi Sparhawke, Benjamin Hawes, Jacob Aylet, Sam
Crane, Tho. Guyon, Ric. Shepheard, Joseph Scot, Jo. Pick-
ard (? Pickeld); and from the Register we also find that he
and his wife Priscilla had the following children baptised
here :—Francis, on 2 July, 1640; Robert, on 19 October,
1641; Susannah, on 17 January, 1642; and Priscilla, on 7
Sept., 1645; and one child buried, viz :—Robert, on 30 Oct.
1641.

OWEN, John, not mentioned in Newcourt's *Repertorium*, but,
it appears from the Journals of the House of Lords, that an
order was made by that House, on the 18th August, 1646,
authorising and requiring Dr. Aylett, or his lawful deputy, to
institute and induct Mr. Owen, clerk to the Vicarage of Coggeshall, in the Diocese of London, void by the resignation of
Mr. Obadiah Sedgwick, late vicar there, upon Mr. Owen producing the presentation thereto under the hand and seal of
the Right Honble. Robert, Earl of Warwick, and others.
John Owen was the second son of Henry Owen, Vicar of
Stadham in Oxfordshire, and was born at the Vicarage, in
1616. Educated at Queen's Coll., Oxford. In his 19th year
he took his M.A. degree; was a staunch puritan and an able
preacher; was Vicar of Fordham, Essex. Married Mary
Rook, by whom he had eleven children, of whom one only,
a daughter, lived beyond childhood. His son, John, was baptised at Fordham, on 20 December, 1644, and his daughters,
Mary, Elizabeth, and Mary, were baptised at Coggeshall, on
18th July, 1647, 10th Feb., 1649, and 18th Feb. 1649, respectively; and one daughter (probably Mary, for the register
here is illegible in parts) was buried on 25th July, 1646 or 7.
He wrote several works, and on more than one occasion
preached before the House of Commons. He became Chaplain to Cromwell, retaining at the same time the Vicarage of
Coggeshall, from the dutes of which he appears to have absented himself, in favour of the apparently more congenial
companionship of Cromwell during his visits to Ireland and
Scotland. On the 18 March, 1651, Owen was made Dean of
Christ Church, Oxford, and ceased to be Vicar of Coggeshall.
He held very many different offices, and in 1654, sat in the
House of Commons as member for the University. His first

wife died in 1676, and shortly afterwards he married Michal, widow of Thomas D'Oyly, of Chiselhampton, near Stadham, by which alliance he received a considerable fortune, and this, with his own property and a legacy that was left him about the same time by his cousin, made his condition easy and even affluent, so that he was able to keep a carriage during his remaining years, and also a country house at Ealing, in Middlesex, where he died, on 24th August, 1683. He was buried in Burnhill Fields. (See very full account of this Puritan Divine in Davids' *Nonconformity in Essex*.)

JESSOP, Constantine, not mentioned by Newcourt, nor is the date of his presentation known, but Anthony Wood, in his MS. says, that "He closed with the Covenanters and succeeded Owen in the ministry of that factious town in Essex, called Coggeshall."

SAMES, John, not mentioned in Newcourt, but as Vicar of Coggeshall, in April, 1654, he was appointed a trustee of Gooday's Charity. In 1656, Cromwell appointed him a Commissioner of Religion. On 11th July, 1656 "Deborah, daughter of Jo. and Anne Sames, Vicar," was baptised. On 16 Dec., 1672, "Mr. John Sames" was buried. Coggeshall Register.

LOWRYE, Thomas, not mentioned in Newcourt, but in the Parish Register are these baptismal entries :—

"1661—May 18th, Obadiah, son of Thomas and Bridgett Lowrye, Vicar. 1662—Sept. 28th, Robert, son of Thomas Lowrye, Vicar;" and these burials :—"1662—Sept. 28, wife of Mr. Thomas Lowyre. 1664—Sept. 29, Abigail, daughter of Mr. Lowyre, Minister of Coggeshall."

RANEW, Nathaniel, 1st. March, 1660.

JESSOP, Thomas, 3rd Oct., 1662. Bufton has preserved notes of many of the occasions on which Mr. Jessop preached funeral sermons, as also the greater part of many of the sermons themselves, and these are now in my possession; extracts from them will be found in a subsequent page. He was buried at Coggeshall, 31st January, 1679, without a sermon, (Bufton). His first wife was buried at Coggeshall, 14th Jany., 1672, "Mrs. Mary Jessop, wife of Mr. Tho. Jessop, Minister of Coggeshall." On 10th March, 167¾, he married Elizabeth Calandrine, of Marks Hall, (Marks Hall Register). On 21st Feb., 1674, their daughter Esther was baptised at

Coggeshall. Mr. Thomas Jessop, citizen of London, who was buried at Coggeshall, 6th April, 1670, was doubtless the father of Thomas, the Vicar.

BOYS, James, M.A-, 16 Feb. 1679, on death of Jessop. He is the last vicar mentioned in *Newcourt's Rep.*, published 1710 ; by mistake he is called John Boys. He was a son of the Rev. John Boys, Dean of Canterbury, whose family is said to have come over with the Conqueror and settled in Kent. The Rev. James Boys had a son, James, who was a barrister-at-law, and the father of Lucy Boys, who married the Rev. Charles Ley, Rector of Layer Marney, great grandson of the Rev. Philip Ley ; descended from James Ley, of Westbury, Wilts, created Lord Ley of Ley, in Devonshire, 22 James, and Earl of Marlborough, 1 Charles [See Benton's *Rochford Hundred*, 417]. Bufton's notes of several sermons preached by Mr. Boys are in my possession.

The following entries relating to this family are to be found in the Coggeshall Marriage Registers : " 1683—Sept. 5, Mr. James Boys and Mrs. Martha Bennett. 1688—Sept. 21, Mr. John White and Mrs. Ann Boys. 1697—March 3, Richard Boys and Mary White. 162⅞—January 4, Mr. William Boys and Hester Cox." And the Coggeshall Baptismal Register has, "1681—Dec. 4, Rebecca, daughter of William and Jane Boys. 1684—Aug. 3, William, son of James and Martha Boys. 1693—March 24, James, son of James and Dorchas Dame Guyon, born ye 21st Feb. 1694—Aug. 9, Dorcas, daur. of James Boys and Dorcas Dame Guyon. 1696—March 29, Martha, daur. of James Boys and Dorcas Dame Guyon." And the Coggeshall Burial Register contains :— " 1725—Oct.13, The Rev. Mr. Boys, late Vicar of Coggeshall. 1768—July 30, Mr. William Boys, interred in the chancel within the communion rails, son of the Rev. Mr. James Boys, vicar 44 years."

Bufton has the following notes concerning this family :—

" 1682—Nov. 26, Mr. Boy's brother's son of 11 years' old died at the vicarage, of the small pox, and was carried to Colchester to be buried. 1683—Sept. 5. Mr. Boys was married to a kinswoman of Mr. Thomas Keeble's; her name was Bennet. Her father was a poulterer in London. 1685—Nov. 11, Mr. Boys had a son buried three days' old.

1685—Nov. 18, the first wife of Mr. Boys was buried ; 6 gentlewomen carried up ye pale with white hoods and white veils, and Mr. Livermore preached at her funeral, and I was gone to London. 1688—Sept. Mr. John White was married to Mrs. Ann Boys. 1692—April 5, Mr. Boys was married to the Lady Guyon.

BURNET, Gilbert, 1725, on the death of Boys. He was for some time Minister of St. James's, Clerkenwell. Died at Coggeshall, 28th January, 1746.

GULLIFER, Joseph, M.A., 1746, on death of Burnet. He appears to have been Curate here many years prior to his presentation to the Vicarage, for on 1st April, 1739, he records in the register, that Sacheverall, the son of Ernal and Mary Dullen was "the first infant baptised by Jos. Gullifer, Curate." The following entry is in Vol. II. of the Registers, "The Rev. Joseph Gullifer, A.M., Corpus Christi College, in Cambridge, was inducted into the Vicarage of Coggeshall, June the 27th, 1746, at the presentation of Peter Du Cane, Esq. He was inducted to the Vicarage of Burnham, February 16, 1749, at the presentation of the Right Hon Benjamin, Earl of Fitzwalter, and one of his lordship's chaplains." Whose son Joseph Gullifer was does not appear, but the family of that name seems to have been connected with this place as early as 1679, as on 22, 23, 24 March, 1679-80, a great many persons were baptised the entry concluding with these words, "by Mr. Gulliford baptised." The names of the god-parents' are set opposite the several entries, an addition which is exceptional. On 11th July, 1682, Ann, daughter, of Josiah and Ann Gulliver, was baptised here; and the following burials are entered in the Registers, "1713, Oct. 8, Mr. Joseph Gulliver. 1754, Nov. 6, interred in the vestry about 1 in the morning, Mrs. Rachel Gullifer, wife of the Rev. Mr. Jos. Gullifer, Vicar, who died of the small pox, Nov. 3, 1754, ætatis 41. 1767, March 22, The Rev. Mr. Joseph Gullifer, Vicar, interred in the vestry, died 13 March, 1767."

Josiah Gullifer, who was Vicar of Messing, died 1704.

· COTT, John, was Vicar in 1768 (See Baptismal Register)

DU CANE, Henry, son of Peter Du Cane, Esq., by his marriage with Mary, only daughter of Henry Norris, Esq., of Hackney. He married Louisa Desmadrille, and had issue the Rev.

Henry Du Cane, of Witham Grove, Richard, Charles, Louisa, Anna Maria, and Sarah, all of whom were baptised at Coggeshall. He lived at the Home Grange, but died at Witham; He does not appear to have taken active duty at Coggeshall, but to have left the care of the parish with

DUDDELL, John, who was Curate here for 33 years (see Memorial inscription); and afterwards with

BULL, John. He had a son, baptised here on 24th Nov., 1807, by name Elijah Serle. His daughter, Susanna, was buried in the churchyard here, and on her tomb was this inscription : "In memory of Susanna, daughter of the Rev. John Bull, sometime Curate of this parish, and Mary, his wife, who died, 31st March, 1810, aged 7 years."

MANT, Richard, M.A., was inducted on 2nd May, 1810. Born on 12th Feb. 1766, at Southampton, where his father was Rector of All Saints; educated at Trinity Coll., Oxford; Fellow and Tutor of Oriel ; ordained, 1802 ; Bampton Lecturer, 1812. In 1813, he and Dr. D'Oyley were commissioned by the Christian Knowledge Society to prepare the 'Family Bible with Notes,' which was first published in 1817. In 1820, he was made Bishop of Killaloe and Kilfenora, and was, on 22nd March, 1823, translated to the See of Down and Connor. He died, 2 Nov., 1848. A memoir of his life was published by Archdeacon Berens, in 1849.

STEVENS, B. B., was Curate about 1813 ; he was afterwards Chaplain to His Majesty's Forces.

MATHEW, Edward William, was instituted to the vicarage about the year 1815, on the resignation of Dr. Mant; he was afterwards Reader at St. James's, Bury St. Edmunds, and is said to have been of a most amiable disposition, and celebrated for his extraordinarily beautiful reading. Died, 1834. He was a grandson of James Mathew, of Bury St. Edmunds, and a son of Colonel William Mathew (Norfolk Light Dragoons), by his marriage with Elizabeth Maria, daughter of Edward Coldham, Esq., of Bury St. Edmunds ; whose wife was a daughter of Joshua Brise, of Cavendish, of the family of Ruggles-Brise, of Spains Hall, Finchingfield. The Rev. Edw. Wm. Mathew was born about 1790, married in 1815, Charlotte Olivia, eldest daughter of Oliver Johnson, Esq., of Hay House, Earls Colne, a descendant of Benjamin Johnson, Governor of Ports-

F

mouth, *temp.* Charles II. By this marriage, there was issue several children, of whom was Edward Fisher Ruggles Mathew, architect of the Cathedral of St. George, Basseterre, in the West Indies, who died, in 1858, at St. Kitts, leaving a son, Edward Jermyn Mathew, who is now of St. Edmund Hall, Oxford. Emily Brise Mathew, another child of the Vicar, married in 1856, her first cousin, Oliver Johnson, Esq., eldest son of Richard Oliver Johnson, Esq., doubtless the same person as Richard Oliver Johnson, who, on 14th Aug., 1828, married at Coggeshall, Mary Ann, daughter of Henry Skingley, Esq., and Ann, his wife, *née* Deeks. The arms of the family are : Az., 3 lions ramp arg., on a chief of the second, as many cross crosslets sa., crest a lion's jambe erect, holding a cross crosslet sa. The Mathew family became possessed of estates at Pentloe, Clare and Cavendish, through the marriage of the Rev. E. W. Mathew with Miss Coldham.

FREELAND, William Coyte, was Curate 1830-4, during which time he appears to have had sole charge of the parish.

SMITH, Percy, was presented to the living in 1834. He was a son of Mary (the daughter of Peter Du Cane, Esq.), by her marriage with Edward, son of William Smith, Esq., of Horsham, Sussex. In 1835, he became Rector of Pattiswick. A tombstone in Pattiswick churchyard has this inscription : " Percy Smith, 41 years priest of this parish, fell asleep, 21 Feb., 1876.

WALLACE, Arthur Capel Job, M.A., was presented, on the resignation of Mr. Smith, in 1835, and remained here till 1838, when he removed to Monks Eleigh, in Suffolk. He was a son of the Rev.' Job Wallace, of Braxted, and was of Corpus Christi Coll. Camb.

ARMSTRONG, William, was Curate in 1838.

ELEY, Henry, was originally engaged in commercial pursuits, but afterwards went to Cambridge, graduated and was ordained to the curacy of West Ham ; removed to High Beech, near Epping ; vicar of Coggeshall, 1838-40, removed to Broomfield, in 1841. On leaving Broomfield he took no more clerical work. Was the author of " Geology in the Garden," and one or two other minor works. He died at Brighton.

BENTLEY, Robert Henry was Curate, 1839-41.

DAMPIER, William James, was born at Hackney, on the 9th

May, 1803, and was the youngest son of Edward Dampier, Esq., of Chase Gate House, Enfield, by his marriage with Elizabeth Norris [Peter Du Cane, formerly patron of the living, married a daughter of Henry Norris, Esq., of Hackney]. At the age of 17 he went to the West Indies (Dominica and Trinidad) to study for the Bar, during which time he served in the militia of the country, this being compulsory on all above a certain age. After an absence of seven years he returned to England and entered himself at the Inner Temple, and kept all his terms but one. About this time he was impressed with an irresistible desire to devote himself to the ministry, he accordingly relinquished the profession of the law for that of the church. He at once set himself to learn Greek, of which he was at that time quite ignorant, and made such progress with the language that shortly afterwards he entered at Christ's College, Cambridge, graduated and received ordination at the hands of the Bishop of Winchester, in the year 1831. His first curacy was at Catherington, afterwards he went to Ware as curate, and here he was mainly instrumental in erecting the District Church of Saint Mary. In 1839, he accepted the sole charge of Great Yeldham during the incapacity of the rector.

In 1841, he was presented to the Vicarage of Coggeshall, into which he was inducted, as he recorded in his own handwriting in the parish register, "on the 6th of August, by the Rev. Charles Dalton, Vicar of Kelvedon, and Rural Dean, in the presence of Charles Skingley and William Swinborne, Churchwardens."

He married, in 1837, Elizabeth Isabella, only child of John Martin-Leake, Esq., R.N., of High Cross, younger son of the Rector of Wivenhoe, by whom he had two sons and five daughters.

Mr. Dampier's early legal training was applied by him in after life to many useful purposes. He had not been long inducted here before he set himself the fulfilment of several important works, an entry of which he made in one of the parish books, and before he left Coggeshall he had the satisfaction of writing opposite each resolution, "Done." Few of us can properly realize the immense good that Mr. Dampier did in this parish; he was often misunderstood, but, persevering in what he believed to be right, he was in the later years of his ministry deeply loved and respected by his parishioners.

Mr. Dampier was the author of a 'Memoir of John Carter,' and 'The Sympathy of Christ.' He resigned the living of Coggeshall, in March, 1876, after holding the benefice for five-and-thirty years. For more than a year previously he had, through failing health, become incapacitated.

He died, at Ramsgate, on the 20th November, 1878, but was buried at Coggeshall ; his place of sepulture being marked by a yew-tree, planted many years ago beside the grave of his wife. The stones, beneath the shade cast by the perpetual verdure of this emblem of the Resurrection, bear the following inscriptions :—

" In loving memory of William James Dampier, thirty-three (it should be thirty-five) years vicar of this parish, died 20 Nov., 1878, aged 75."

" Elizabeth Isabella, the wife of William James Dampier, M.A., Vicar of this parish, 21st December, 1858, in peace, aged 49 years."

" Elizabeth Maria, widow of John Martin-Leake, R.N., died at Honfleur, in France, 11th January, 1862, aged 75 years."

The following were Curates here during Mr. Dampier's incumbency :—

Wigson, William, 1841-44.

Griffinhooff, Thomas John, 1844, B.A., Oxford ; married Henrietta Sophia, daughter of Henry Skingley, Esq., on 2nd July, 1846.

Iremonger, Frederick Assheton, 1845.

Sutton, John, 1846.

Brown, James William, 1847-8 ; married Ellen, daughter of Henry Skingley, Esq., on 25th January, 1849.

Hill, Thomas Smyth, 1847-9, B.C.L., M.A., Oxford ; now Rector of Thorington, Halesworth.

Jackson, William, 1849.

Cutts, Edward Lewes, 1850-7, B.A., Cam., Hon. D.D. of the Univ. of South, U.S.A. Many years hon. sec. of the Essex Arch. Society, and was for some time, hon. sec. of the committee for the restoration of Coggeshall Church, a work in which he took a deep interest and rendered much valuable service and advice, which he was so well able to do, by reason of his extended knowledge of ecclesiastical architecture and church furniture and decoration. He is the author of very many works, including 'Turning Points of English Church History,' 'Turning Points of General Church History,' 'A Dictionary of the Church of England,' 'Constantine the Great,' 'Charlemagne,' 'St. Jerome,' 'St. Augustine,' 'Monks of the Middle Ages,' 'A History of Colchester,' &c., &c. He is now Vicar of Holy Trinity, Haverstock Hill.

FRASER, William Francis, 1857-9, M.A. Cam.; late of Hillgrove, Stonehouse, Gloucester; now of Westbere Rectory, Canterbury.

BROWN, James William, 1859.

WALLER, Robert Plume, 1863, M.A. Cam.; now Vicar of Nazing, Essex.

HORROCKS, George, 1864.

PERTWEE, Arthur, 1864, M.A. Oxon.; now Vicar of Brightlingsea.

ALLEN, John, 1864, B.A. Oxford; died 26 May, 1867, buried at Coggeshall.

RAYMOND, Charles Andrewes, 1867; now Rector of St. Mary-le-More, Wallingford.

COX, Cecil Walker, 1868, B.A. Oxford; now Rector of Atherstone-on-Stour, Stratford-on-Avon.

CLARKE, D. L., 1871.

EAREE, Robert Brisco, 1871; now Chaplain at Sigismunderstrasse, Berlin.

WHITTINGTON, Richard Thomas, 1872, M.A. Oxford; now Hon: Canon of St. Alban's and Rector of Orsett.

EYRE, Henry Taylor Williamson, 1873-7, M.A. Oxford; now Vicar of Great Totham.

GREENE, Charles Philip, instituted, 14 May, 1876. Born 2nd Oct., 1840, at Cotton House, Cotton, County Louth, Ireland; son of William Pomeroy Greene, Esq., of the Royal Navy, by his marriage with Anne Griffith, sister of Sir Richard Griffith, Bart., well known as the author of 'Griffith's Valuation.' In 1842, Mr. Greene with his wife and family went to Port Philip (now Victoria), the family then consisting of six sons and one daughter, Mary Frances, who afterwards became the wife of the late Sir William Foster Stawell, K.C.M.G., Lieutenant-Governor of Victoria, and formerly Chief-Justice of that colony. Of the six sons, Charles Philip was the youngest. He graduated at Melbourne University in 1862, came to England in 1864 ; was at Cuddesdon College for a year, returned to Australia in 1867 ; Curate at the Cathedral, Hobart, Tasmania, in 1868 ; Incumbent of Avoca in 1872 ; Incumbent of St. John's, Hobart, 1873-5 ; Vicar of Coggeshall, 1876 to 1885 ; now Rector of Clapham.

Curates during Mr. Greene's Incumbency :—

Eyre, H. T. W., 1873-7.

Bowers, John Philips Allcot, 1877-8, M.A. Cam. ; now Canon designate of Gloucester, Missioner for the Diocese of Gloucester and Bristol, and Domestic and Examining Chaplain to the Bishop of that Diocese. He married, 18th Feb., 1879, Mary Louisa, daughter of Joseph Beaumont, Esq., of The Lawn, Coggeshall.

Morton, Henry James (1878-9), M.A., L.L.B., Cam. ; now Vicar of Cricklade, Wilts.

Ley, Gerald Henry Lewis, 1880-5, M.A., Oxon. ; now Rector of Chagford, Devon.

Evans, Arthur Fitzgerald, 1880-5, M.A., Oxon ; now vicar of Great Maplestead.

Patch, Hubert Mornington, inducted 27th Nov. 1885. Educated at Clare Coll. Cam., where he took the degree of B.A. in 1862 and M.A. in 1865 ; ordained deacon, 1864, priest, 1865. His first curacy was at Lower Brixham, in the Diocese of Exeter. In 1866-7, he was Curate of St. Luke's, Torquay ; from 1867-9, Curate of Hungerford ; from 1869 to 1885, he was Curate-in-charge of the poor district of St. Michael, Torquay, where he won much love and respect from all those with whom he came in contact.

During Mr. Patch's Incumbency :—

Scott, Frederick George, M.A., was Curate, 1885-6 ; he is now Rector of Drummondsville, in the Diocese of Quebec. On his resignation, Dec. 1887,

White, Charles Lechmere, B.A., Oxon., from S. Peter's, London Docks, was appointed Curate.

JOHN OWEN 1646-51.

WILLIAM JAMES DAMPIER 1841-76.

COGGESHALL CHURCH.
1889.

CHARLES PHILIP GREENE 1876-85.

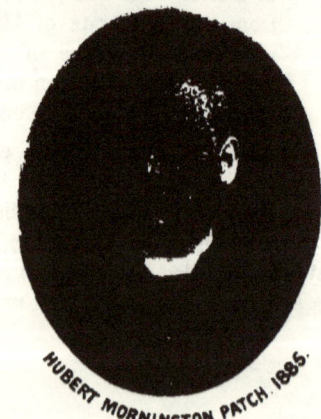

HUBERT MORNINGTON PATCH. 1885.

The Rectory and Vicarage.

THE Rectory of Coggeshall, in early times, belonged to the Abbot and Convent of Coggeshall, and although the evidence is not conclusive, it supports the opinion that originally there were two Churches at Coggeshall ; one in the larger parish, and another in the smaller. Be this as it may, the Rectory or Rectories became vested in the Abbey about the same time as the Manors were conveyed to it, and so remained until the dissolution of the Abbey in 1538.

The abbots, as the possessors of the emoluments of the church, discharged certain of the duties and obligations incumbent upon them, such as the entertainment of strangers and the doling out of charity to the poor, but the cure of the souls of the parishioners, they remitted to a vicar, (*vicarius*—a substitute) and for his services he was allowed some small portion of the rectorial profits. All went well for a time, but in the first quarter of the thirteenth century a controversy arose about the Church, between Eustace de Fauconbergh, Bishop of London, and his Chapter on the one part, and the Abbot and Convent of Coggeshall on the other part. This dispute was, by unanimous consent, referred to John de Fontibus, Bishop of Ely, the Abbot and Convent first resigning all their right in the Church into the hands of the Bishop of London. The Bishop of Ely, in 1223, made a final determination of the controversy, and ordained that the Monks of Coggeshall should possess for the sustenance of the poor and strangers, in perpetual right, all the tithes of corn of the whole parish of the Church of Coggeshall (which in this document is called the Church of Sunnedon), with all the land belonging to it, except the chief mansion and nineteen acres in North Field adjoining the same, and one acre in West field on the east side, as far as the meadow, and all the meadow beyond the water-course on the north side, and except the tenements which were held of the same Church by Walter de Rustylford, John Gallicus, William de Fonte, William Bore, John Delbroch, Widow Edith, with their farmers, which, with all their tithes, obventions, and all other things to the same Church belonging, the Vicar, who for the time being should minister in the same Church, should receive by the name of the Vicarage, and that he should sustain all burdens, debts, and customs, and that the appointment and collation should belong to the Bishop of London and their successors in perpetuity.

From this time (1223), the Rectory of Coggeshall was appropriated to the Abbot and Convent, and the Bishop of London became patron of the Vicarage, and so continued till Dr. Nicholas Ridley, Bishop of that See, on the 12th April, 4 Edw. VI., granted the perpetual Advowson of this Vicarage to the King and to his heirs and successors; notwithstanding which, on the next vacancy, Bishop Bonner, after he had been restored to the Bishopric, taking no notice of his predecessor's grant, collated Robert Stockton to this Vicarage in 1558. The advowson or right of presentation was subsequently confirmed to Lord Riche, who died, possessed of it in 1566, but without male issue, whereupon it devolved upon his co-heiresses. Afterwards the advowson was possessed by Sir Henry St. John, Bart., who was raised to the peerage as Viscount St. John. He and his eldest son, Henry, Earl of Bolingbroke, conveyed the right of presentation to Nehemiah Lyde, Esq., whose only daughter married Richd. DuCane, Esq., and in the DuCane family it remains to the present day.

The Rectories of Great and Little Coggeshall, and the Vicarage of Little Coggeshall, with all tithes and appurtenances in those parishes, were, in the 33rd year of Queen Elizabeth, granted to John Wells, of London, Scrivener and Hercules Wytham, of London, Gentlemen, who, on 8th Jany., 34 Elizth., sold them to Richard Bettenson, of Coggeshall, Gentleman. He sold them in the 2nd year of James I., to Richard Benyon, who died, 17th Nov., in the 7th year of the same reign, leaving Richard his son and heir, aged 4 years and 6 months. In the inquiry taken about this time, the property is described as the Rectories of Great Coggeshall and Little Coggeshall, with the Vicarage of Little Coggeshall, held of the King, as of his Manor of East Greenwich, by fealty as in free and common socage, and not *in capite*, nor by Knight Service, and valued at £8 per annum clear.

Richard Benyan settled this estate, in 1629, on himself and Margaret his wife for their lives. He, by will, dated 13th May, 1659, gave to Henry, his eldest son, all tithes of land in the Hamlet of Little Coggeshall, part great and part small, and the tithes of those grounds belonging to the Abbey, lying in Great Coggeshall, and the barn and ground in the Abbey Lane.

Henry Benyan, by his will, dated 18th Sept., 1673, gave his

brother Charles, in lieu of a legacy left him by his father, his tithes in Little Coggeshall, except from a field called Horsepasture. The residue of the tithes he gave to Thomas Stafford, Gentleman, with a direction to sell them and his other estates for the payment of his debts; the balance he gave to Thomas Stafford for the maintenance of the Chancel. A law suit arose about this gift, and on the sale of the property by the sisters of Henry Benyan or Benion, Thomas Cudmore became the purchaser of one moiety or half part, and Henry Abbot of the other moiety.

Jones Raymond bought Cudmore's moiety, which afterwards passed to Mr. Caswell and Mr. Thoyts, and it is now, and for many years past has been, in the Western family.

Henry Abbot devised his moiety to his son Joseph, whose devisees sold it to Samuel Carter; it was afterwards in the possession of Ezekiel Wood and William Potter, then of Thomas Andrews, by whom it was sold to Henry Skingley, Esq., and in this family it continues to the present day.

Augustin Mayhew, of Great Coggeshall, Gent., in 1661, purchased of Henry Benyan, the tithes issuing out of Hovels, formerly the estate of Thomas Aylet, Gent. ; the tithes of a Farm, formerly the estate of John Gurdon, Esq. (query Potash Farm); the tithes of Thomas Guyon's, Stock Street Farm; and of a farm at Stock Street, formerly Robert Aylet's, afterwards his son's, Thomas Aylet; of another farm at Stock Street, belonging to Robert Crane; of a field containing 5 acres in Blackwater Field, near the bridge; of a house called the Vyne, in the same locality; of Crowlands Farm, belonging to Nicholas Foster; and of Monk Wood, and several other properties.

Augustin Mayhew, in 1675, when he is described as of Boreham, settled these tithes on the marriage of his son and heir, William Mayhew with Elizabeth Harrison, the only daughter of Bridget Onge, of Colchester, Widow. In 1695, William and Elizabeth Mayhew sold these tithes, or some of them, to George Nicholls.

𝕿𝖍𝖊 𝕮𝖔𝖒𝖒𝖚𝖙𝖆𝖙𝖎𝖔𝖓 𝖔𝖋 𝖙𝖍𝖊 𝕿𝖎𝖙𝖍𝖊𝖘.

IN 1836, the Tithe Commutation Act was passed, but the tithes of Great Coggeshall and Little Coggeshall were not commuted until 1851. Prior to this year the tithe was liable to be rendered in kind, and the following records bearing upon the subject are taken from the cover of Vol. II. of the Registers :—

"May 14, 1680—Memorandum that I, James Boys, Vicar of Coxall, did, on the day and year above sayd, tith out 400 of faggots in Monk Wood, in that part that belong to Hovels, it being sold by Mr. Plum standing. Peter Harvey, of Coxall, John Ellis, Richard Putner, of Sticestead, Henry Boltwood, of Passak (Pattiswick), assuring that they can sware that Mr. Sedgwick and Mr. Owen had tith there formerly."

"April 18, 1681—Memorandum that I, James Boys, Vicar of Coggeshall, did on the day and year above written tith out 350 tilts and 124 hop poles in Monk Wood, in that part that belong to Hovells, it being sold by Mr. Plum standing, Mr. Wilkins, of Patteswick, being with me and Mr. Ellis. April the 20th, 1681, then did Housin Dale . . . . fetch home the 350 tilts and 50 of the poles."

The commissioner, who made the commutation award, found that certain lands were by prescription totally exempt from the payment of tithes, that the tithes of other lands were merged, that no tithes were payable in respect of certain lands when in the manurance or occupation of the owners, as such lands were part of the possessions of the dissolved Abbey of Coggeshall, and were so held discharged at the time of the dissolution of the monastery; that other lands were exempt from the payment of all tithes, except tithes of corn, grain and hay, when in the manurance or occupation of the owners.

The following are the principal properties in Great Coggeshall which enjoy the Cistercian privilege, either of partial or total exemption from the payment of tithes when occupied by their owners : Raincrofts, Horse Pasture, Cowlees, Vincents Close, the Monk Woods, the Gate House Farm, Grange Wood, Bowers Grange, Bullocks Cross Farm and Monkdowns Farm. In Little Coggeshall there are only two small properties which enjoy total exemption from tithe when in the owner's occupation; these are Tye Mill Pightle, and the houses and gardens on the south side of the river by Long Bridge.

The total amount of the tithes of Great Coggeshall as commuted, is £1,136 18s. 6d., of which the Vicar receives £350 only, the rest being payable to the Lay Impropriators ; in Little Coggeshall, the tithes are commuted at £355 17s. 2d., the vicar's proportion being £28. The amount payable to the vicar from both parishes when the tithe is at par thus amounts to £378. This sum fluctuates with the price of corn, and, in the year 1889, yields only about £300 gross; and, as several of the lands which enjoy the Cistercian privilege are in the manurance of the owners, this sum is reduced to about £200, which is further reduced by rates, taxes and costs of collection to about £160 per annum.

In Newcourt's time, there was a terrier dated 1610, which set the property of the vicarage down as follows: "A vicarage house, a barn, an orchard, and a garden, and about 19 acres-and-a-half and three roods of glebe land." In addition to this there is near the river, and about a mile from the town towards West Mill, a field, No. 320 on the Ordnance Survey and containing 3a. 2r. 15p. which belongs to the vicarage.

The Vicarage House.

THE first stone, south-east corner, of the present residence was laid on the 10th June, 1869, by Isabella, second daughter of the Rev. William James Dampier, Vicar; and a record of the fact on parchment, with a piece of the current coin of the realm, was deposited beneath the stone. The house was completed and ready for occupation on the 9th April following. On the mantle-piece in one of the rooms are the arms of the Dampier family: or., a lion ramp sa., crowned gu., a label of five points of the same. The residence including the outbuildings cost about £1,000. This sum was advanced by the governors of Queen Anne's Bounty, and is secured by a mortgage of the glebe, tithes, and other profits of the living, and was originally repayable by 30 yearly instalments with interest at £4 per cent. The period of repayment has recently been extended; the instalment with interest for the year 1889 amounts to £41.

Augmentation of the Living.

BY his will, proved on the 19th July, 1888, Major George Deeks Skingley, directed his executors after the death of his wife to invest £3,333 6s. 8d. in consols or securities of a like nature in the names of the vicar and churchwardens for the time being of the parish of Great Coggeshall; the income arising from this fund, when invested, will be payable to the vicar for the time being of the parish for his own use and benefit in perpetuity.

The gift is to be free of legacy duty and expenses. It is hoped that Major Skingley's munificent gift will remind others that the Vicarage of Coggeshall is not yet endowed as fully as it ought to be considering the size of the parish and the work which a faithful minister finds absolutely necessary to be done.

Chantries and Obits.

CHANTRIES were certain portions of the church in which wealthy people set up and endowed additional altars for masses in propitiation for the sins of the departed. A separate aisle or transept was often added to the church for the purpose, and this would be dedicated to the favourite saint of the founder.

An Obit was a service kept on the anniversary of the death of some individual, and on the occasion of it, the endowment for its maintenance was distributed among the priest, the sexton, and such poor persons as were in attendance at the service, to pray for the soul of the deceased. The money was generally secured by a charge in favor of the churchwardens, upon a house or land belonging to the founder.

It is probable that the north chancel aisle of our church was erected by the Paycock family, as their wills * have frequent reference to Saint Katherine's Aisle; thus, John Pecok of Coggeshall, who made his will, on 20th January, 1505-6 (proved 7th April, 1506), directs that his body shall be buried in the parish church of Saint Peter, in the north aisle, before the image of Saint Katherine. He then orders a month's mind to be kept with lights and other observances, "as belongeth to a dead corpse to be done;" a priest to say mass, when disposed for the space of five years, for the deceased, his father and mother and all Christian souls, having for his salary, 10 marks. He makes a bequest for the maintenance of St. Katherine's light, for his name to be put upon the Bede-roll of the church, and for his obit for five years.

THOMAS PAYCOCKE, of Coggeshall, (third son of John Pecok) made his will, 3rd Sept., 1518 (proved 16th Feby., 1518-19). He thereby directs that his body shall be buried in the Church of Coxhall, before the altar of Saint Katherine; he bequeaths to the High Altar of Coggeshall Church, in recompense of tithes and of all other things forgotten, £4; he bequeaths to a tabernacle of the

---

* See ante page 33.

Trinity at the high altar, and another of Saint Margaret in Saint Katherine's Aisle, "there as the greate lady stonds," for the carving and gilding of them, 100 marks [13/4 each]; for the reparations of the Church and bells, and for his lying in the Church, 100 nobles [6/8 each]. He gives 500 marks to a chantry, for the priest to pray for him and his wife, his father and mother, John and Eme, and for his father-in-law, Thomas Arrold, of Clare, and for his friends' souls that he was bound to pray for, the purchasing and mortessing * [query mortifying] to the King and also to the same chantry, 6 poor men to keep the same mass 3 days in the week, viz: Monday, Wednesday and Friday, to pray for the souls before rehearsed, and therefor to have 18 pence among them every week to fulfil this, and also every year, 100 wood apiece, and his priest to sing in Coxhall Church, afore Saint Katherine's altar. He willed that his executors should bestow upon his burying, 7th day and month day, after this manner :—At his burial to have "a tryntal of prests and to be at dirige lawdes commendations, as many of them as may be purveyed that day at service, the tryntall, and if any lack to make it up the 7th day, and at the month day another tryntall to be purveyed hoole of mine executors and to keep dirige lawdes and commendations as is afore rehearsed, with 3 high masses be note, one of the Holy Ghost, another of Our Lady, and another of Requiem, both burial and 7th day and month day, and priests being at this observance and singing of their tryntals, to have -/12d. every time, and other priests being there and not singing the tryntalls, to have -/4d., and every other man being at this observance -/4d. every time, and children at every time -/2d. ; with torches at the burial -/12d., and -/6d. at the 7th day, and -/12d. at the month day, with 24 or 12 small children in rochets (surplices with short sleeves) with tapers in their hands, as many as there be of them let them be my godchildren, and they to have 6s./8d. apiece, and every other child -/4d. apiece, and every man that holdeth torches at every, he to have -/2d| apiece, and every man, woman, and child that holdeth up hand at every of these 3 days, to have -/1d. apiece, and also every godchild beside 6s./8d. apiece, and to the ringers for all 3 days,

---

* A License from the Crown was requisite before property could be conveyed to charitable uses; for, by such conveyance, the estate became vested in a corporation, with perpetual succession, and so the feudal rights of the lord of the fee were seriously prejudiced.

10s./; and for meat, drink, and 2 sermons of a Doctor [*i.e.* of
Divinity], and also to have a dirige at home, or I be borne to the
church, £50." He then wills that his lord abbot and convent
should have a broad cloth, £4 in money for to have a dirige and
mass and then bells ringing at his burial when it was done; at
church likewise, the 7th day and month day with 3 trentalls upon
the same days, if they could serve them, or else when they could
at more leisure, £10.   There are several other bequests for trentalls and other objects, including £40 to the foulways in West
Street, from Haresbridge to a field of unmentionable name near
the 1st milestone on the Braintree road, and a like sum for the
foulways between Coxhall and Blackwater.

SIR THOMAS MONTGOMERY, Knt., by his will dated 28th July,
1489, gave to the vicary of Coggeshall and to the vicars of other
places in this neighbourhood 8s./4d. each, "so that they or their
deputies remembre to pray for my soule and my wife's, ev'ry Son-
day two yere after my deceasse, at the *bedys bydding*, and to pray
for me and my wifes oon day in the weke aftre the custome is."

The bedys bydding or bidding of the beads was the reading
of the Roll of names of persons living and dead, whose souls
were to be particularly borne in mind by the congregation, during
the prayers which followed.   A bead means something bid or
prayer for, in its original sense.

JOHN FABYAN, who was a citizen and draper of London, made
his will on the 7th May, 1477, and directed that if certain of his
children died before they were of age or married, part of the
monies which he bequeathed to them should be employed by his
executors to sustain and find an honest priest to sing and pray for
his soul, and for the souls of his father and mother, and all his
children, and good doers, and all Christian souls in the parish
Church of Coggeshall, wherein his father laid buried, in the county
of Essex, by the space of 20 years next ensuing after the death
of that child of his said children that last died.   He also bequeathed one hundred marks therewith to ordain, sustain, and find
an honest priest to sing and pray for his soul and for the souls
aforesaid in the parish Church of Coggeshall for 10 years next
ensuing his own decease.   He gave to William Heysand, his servant, for to pray for his soul £20, or he was to have a tenement
with the appurtenances in the town of Coggeshall, in which the
widow Sterling then dwelt.   It was doubtless from this family of

Sterling that the name of the pastures on the north side of East
Street had its origin. .

In the 37th year of Henry VIII. the collegiate and chantry
endowments of the kingdom were, by Act of Parliament, declared
to belong to the King. They were, however, only partially appropriated in this reign, but, in the first year of King Edwd. VI.,
another statute was passed which granted to the crown the reve-
nues of all chantries, fraternities, hospitals and colleges still remaining.

The following certificate shows to some extent what properties
were possessed by the church or the abbey for religious purposes :
"CERTIFICATE of Chantry Lands, 2 Ed. VI., for Essex.

" Coggeshall, in Lexden Hundred.

" Lands and tenements there put in feoffment by divers and
sundry persons to the maintenance of a priest for ever, the said
priest to sing mass in Coggeshall aforesaid, and also to help serve
the cure. And one, Sir Thomas Francys, Clerke, of the age of
56 years, having no other promotion, and teacheth a school there,
of good usage and conversation, is now Incumbent thereof. And
the said Incumbent celebrateth in the said Church of Coggeshall.
The yearly value of the same doth amount to the sum of £7.
Rent resolute null. Goods and chattels none. Memorandum : it
is to be considered that the same town of Coggeshall is a populous
towne, and having in it to the number of 1,000 of howseling
people, and have no more but the Vicar and the said Chantry
Priest to minister there, who is not able to serve the same without
help.

" One tenement given by one HAMPSER for one yearly obite
for ever, in the tenure of Robert Miles, worth by the yere 2s. 9d.
whereof to the poor, 8d. Remainder clear, 12d.

" Vere, widow, holdeth 5 crofts of land with one meadow for
2 obites, one of PEACOCK and the other of COLDWIRES, worth by
the year 16s., whereof to the poor, 4s. Rem. clear, 12s.

" 7 crofts of land and one meadow for the obite of ROB. PEA-
COCK, in the tenure of John Hilles, worth by the year 16s., whereof to the poor, 6s. 8d. Rem. clear, 9s. 4d.

" One garden called *Godard's Garden*, given by one NESFIELD,
for one obite for ever, in the tenure of John Gooddaie, 2s. 6d.,
whereof to the poor, 11d. Rem. clear, 19d.

"—CLARKE, Taylor, gave one tenement for one obite for ever in the tenure of John Amye by Indenture, worth by the year, 3s. 2d.

"THOS. RANDOLPH gave a tenement with certain lands, called *Roodes* land, for the obite of the same Thomas, in the tenure of Thomas Clerke, and payeth by the year for the same 11s. 4d., whereof to the poor people, 3s. 4d.   Rem. clear, 8s.

"One tenement given to the finding of one obite for ever, in the tenure of Wm. Lawrence, worth by the year, 3s., whereof to the poor, 12d.   Rem. clear, 2s.

"One tenement given by one, WIMBORNE, for one yearly obite for ever, worth by the year, 3s., whereof to the poor, 12d.   Rem. clear, 2s.

"One tenement given by one GRANGER, for one yearly obite for ever, in the tenure of John Heyward, worth by the year, 20d., whereof to the poor, 8d.   Rem. clear, 12d.

"One messuage and a garden given by one OLD TRUE, to the maintenance of the *lamp light* for ever, in the tenure of Henry Warde, by Indenture for term of 80 years yet to come, worth by the year, 3s.

"Given out of a tenement with a cottage and a croft of land, called *Vincents*, in the tenure of John Peacock for one yearly obite for ever, by Indenture for term of 100 years yet to come, by the year, 6s.

" Item. *one old Chaple* in the street there, with a little garden, which is worth by the year, 4s.

"Item, one house there called the *Geildhall*, and is worth by the year, 5s.

" Item, one tenement decayed, called the *Priest's Chamber*, with one orchard, worth yearly 5s."

From a Particular of divers lands granted by Letters Patent to several persons in fee farm, in the reigns of Queen Elizabeth and King James I., further information may be gained with regard to properties held for religious purposes at the time of the reformation.

The following estates were granted to Jeffery Morley, on 18th March, in the 18th year of Queen Elizabeth (A.D. 1576), at the fee farm rents set opposite thereto respectively :—

" An acre of land in *Nether Church Field* [being the greater part of the garden known as 'The Lawn,' occupied by Mr. Joseph Beaumont]. Rent, 3s. 9d.

"A farm called *Stockman's*, and a tenement called *Tripps* [now part of the Hanbury Estate]. Rent, £2 13s. 4d.

"A house called *Sorell* [east of Windmill or Highfield's Lane in West Street]. Rent, 1s. 4d.

"A house called *Drapers* [in East Street, now belonging to Mrs. John Sach and in the occupation of Mr. Richard Browning Smith, Butcher]. Rent, 3s. 4d.

"A house called *Plummers* [in Church Street, owned and occupied by Mr. E. T. Scott]. Rent, 1s. 4d.

"*Cowlees or Horselees*, containing 7a. 2r. 0r. [No. 331, Ordnance Survey; belongs to Messrs. Pfander Swinborne, situate in West Street, bounded on the south by the Back Ditch]. Rent, 5s.

"*Pope's Lees, or Horsepasture*, containing 2 acres [situate in East Street, belongs to Mrs. Mayhew, No. 334, Ordnance Survey]. Rent, 4s. 8d."

The undermentioned properties were granted to Ralph Wolley, citizen and Merchant Tailor of London, and Thomas Dodd, citizen and Grocer of London, on 20th Oct., in the 2nd year of King James I. (A.D. 1604) :—

"*The Dairy House* at the Holme Grange in Little Coggeshall, then in the occupation of John Cowell, with the *Shepenhouse* nigh the Gatehouse on the north side of the King's Highway. Rent,. £24 6s. 8d. [This property comprises the lands between Curd Hall Lane and the river, and was purchased by Nehemiah Lyde, of Hackney, Merchant, in 1701, from Edward Bullock, Esq., of Faulkborne Hall, who at the same time sold to Mr. Lyde the fee farm rent of £24 6s. 8d. charged upon it.]

"The Watermill and Chambers to the same, and the garden called *Love's Garden*, and one other garden called *Sandford* garden, and the waste ground within the Monastery. Rent, £5. [Love and Sampford were Abbots shortly before the dissolution, and these properties were probably part of their possessions. This rent is not now payable, having probably become merged by unity of ownership.]

"The *Mansion House* within the Monastery, formerly demised to Mathew Bacon. Rent, £2 2s. 2d. [This is doubtless the Abbey Farm].

G

"The land and marsh called *Coggeshall Hay*, formerly demised to Richard Poulter. Rent, £3 13s. 4d. [These lands form part of the Hanbury Estate and lie near Pattiswick.]

"A croft called *Buskett*, with the rest of the premises formerly demised to William Enewe. Rent, £1 11s. 8d. [This property contains, according to the Morden College Survey of 1740, about 37 acres of land, lying between Tilkey Road and Tilkey Brook, and now belongs to various owners.]

"The woods, called *Monkwood* and *Little Monkwood*, late demised to Thomas Dockwray. Rent, £2.

"One tenement, one garden and shop, late demised to Richard Todd. Rent, 7s. o¾d. [Now belong to Mrs. John Sach, situate in Church Street, abutting west upon the Bull Inn, and north upon Back Lane.]

"Two pieces of land demised to William Trewe. Rent, -/8d. [In Church Street, and now belongs to Mr. Thomas Simpson; one of the houses thereon being used as a surgery.]

"The tenement called *Through-Inn*, late demised to George and John Ansell. Rent, 12s. and a pound of pepper. [The lb. of pepper is compounded for at 1s. 6d. Now called the Bird-in-Hand, and situate between Church Street and East Street.]

"A tenement demised to Richard Constantine. Rent, 11s. [At the corner formed by the juncture of Church Street with East Street.]

"A farm called *Griggs Farm*. Rent, £5 15s. [Still so called and situate on the south side of Braintree Road.]

"Two tenements in Stoneham Street. Rent, 1s. 8d. [Known as *The Limes*, belongs to Mr. Doubleday, occupied by Mrs. Gorbell.]

"The house called the *Brewhouse*, with the pasturage for 2 cows in the Old Park. Rent, 8s. [Houses and gardens adjoining the river towards the north, and the road leading to Kelvedon towards the west. This property belongs to Messrs. Green and Hart.]

"One tenement on the north side of *Longbridge*, together with the meadow containing 3 roods. Rent, 4s.

"A piece of land called *Pound* Pasture in Little Coggeshall, on the north side of the Grange Barn. Rent, 2s. [Evidently so named from the Pound which formerly stood on the west side of Grange Hill.]

"A tenement in East Street, late in the occupation of William Gray. Rent, 3s. 4d.

"Three tenements with the close called *Vincents* Close, with a dovehouse late in the occupation of John Gray. Rent, 6s. 8d. [Now the property of Messrs. Pfander Swinborne and situate on south side of West Street.]

"Two tenements in Church Street, late in the occupation of William Rodley. Rent, 8s. [On the south side of Church Street.]

"One tenement in West Street, late in the tenure of Elizabeth Richold. Rent, 4s. [Belongs to White's Trustees.]

"Three acres called *Butt's* Pasture near the Church Yard, late in the tenure of Joane Rivers, widow. Rent, 3s. 4d. [No. 364, Ordnance Survey.]

"One tenement with a messuage in West Street, and two gardens, and one croft, called *King's* Croft, at the west end of West Street. Rent, 18s. 6d. [Now belongs to Messrs. Pfander-Swinborne.]

"Lands and pasture in *Windmill Field*, late in the tenure of Jeremy Arnold. Rent, £1. [Part of Highfield's Farm.]

"Land, called *Pope's Lees* and *Pope's Meadow*, otherwise Horse pasture, late in the tenure of Thomas Guyon, containing 4 acres. Rent, 4s. 8d. [No. 333, Ord. Survey.]

"A messuage with a garden, called *Gotiers*, and one croft adjoining to a tenement called *Brookemans*, at Bissing Gutter, in the West Street ; one parcel of land in *Earleswell*, in Windmil Gate Lane, containing half-an-acre ; and one parcel of land, called *Church Pond*,* with a little cottage thereupon built, late in the tenure of Robert Litherland. Rent, 10s. 4d. [This comprises the gelatine factory of Messrs. Swinborne and other property to the east of it.]

"Two parcels of land called *Litleyards*, late in the tenure of the said Robert Litherland. Rent, 5s. 4d. [This is the Rood House, abutting west upon Long Bridge and south upon the river.]

"A tenement in Church Street, called *Algors*, with an orchard and two other tenements, and two gardens to the same lying against Coggeshall Church, late in the occupation of John Gray.

---

* The names ' Earles Well ' and ' Church-pond,' are interesting in connection with the Roman Cemetery, referred to on p. 7.

Rent, 5s. 11d. [Part of Mr. Beaumont's orchard opposite the Church.]

"A tenement in Church Lane, late in the tenure of Doctor Giggens or Joane Rivers, widow. Rent, 2s. 6d. [This property is situate east of Wayne Lane and north of the cloth factory, which stands on the north side of Church Street. Here was the residence, if not the birth-place of Dr. John Jegon, afterwards Bishop of Norwich, a short biography of whom will be given in a subsequent page.]

"One messuage with 2 crofts in Little Coggeshall, in Pointell Street, late in the tenure of John Leazwell. Rent 4s. [At the Hamlet.]

"Two tenements at *Starling Lees Stile*, late in the occupation of William Fuller. Rent, 2s. [The south east corner of Starling Lees].

"One tenement, called *Kemmers*, in East Street, late in the occupation of William Lawrence. Rent, 4s. [On the east of the Swan Yard, and now belongs to Mr. Marten.]

"Two tenements in Church Street, late in the occupation of Daniel Larke. Rent 8s. [Nearly opposite the Mechanic's Institute.]

"Two other tenements in Church Street, in the tenure of Henry Stedman. Rent, 1s. [Now a cloth factory, north of Church Street and east of Wayne Lane; has projecting upper floors, and is ornamented with carved woodwork, the frieze in Wayne Lane having on it 'Richard White, 1736.']

"Two acres in Pointell Street, in Little Coggeshall, late in the tenure of Nicholas Merrill. Rent 6s. [Hamlet House is built upon part of this property, now occupied by Mrs. Sheldrake.]

"One tenement, called a *Mill-house*, in Church Lane, containing one acre with a dove-house and pond, late in the tenure of Thomas . . . and William Sanders. Rent, 8d. [Belongs to Mrs. E. V. Gardner, and is situate in Church Street and Back Lane].

"One parcel of land called *Clappers*, lying on the west side of Stoneham Street, adjoining upon the west side of the *Cocks*, late in the tenure of Robert Fuller. Rent, 6s. 6d. [Now belongs to Messrs. Durant.]

"One tenement called *Frances*, with the appurtenances, late in the tenure of John Mann. Rent, 3s. 4d. [In East Street.]

"One little tenement containing one acre called *Scriveners barne*, in East Street, late in the occupation of Thomas Bridges. Rent, 4d. [Abbey View House, abutting east upon Starling Lees.]

"One parcel of land, called *Le Pond Garden*, in Church Street, late in the occupation of Joan Rivers, widow. Rent, 1d. [Abuts east on Wayne Lane, north on Back Lane, and west upon a pass age leading to St. Peter's Well.]

"All that land or pasture, parcel of the Grange or farm called *Hovells*. Rent, £1. [No. 53, Ordnance Survey.]

"A parcel of land called *Crowchers*, behind Stoneham Street, late in the tenure of William Fuller. Rent, 6d." [Nos. 294 & 295, Ordnance Survey.]

The following property was granted to Edward Newport and John Crompton on 25th March, 5 James I. (A.D. 1608) :—

"The Grange called *Coggeshall Grange*, and the buildings belonging thereto, lying on the south part of the Holme or Holme Grange, and all those fields called *Culies Beninshether Westfield* and *Further Westfield*, and all those 16 acres of meadow near Bradwell. Rent, £24 3s. 4d." [This property now belongs to the Du Cane family, and comprises Home Grange and Curd Hall. The Rent was purchased by Nehemiah Lyde (subject to the life interest therein of the Dowager Queen Katherine) of Sir John Banks, Bart., in 1694.]

The following properties were granted to Sir Edward Phillips and John Seward, on the 26th January, 5 King James I. (A.D. 1608) :—

"One parcel of land within the field called *Monkdowne*, lying near Colchester Highway on the south part, containing by estimation, 30 acres. Rent, £1 13s. od.

"Another parcel within the said field, containing by estimation, 27 acres. Rent, £1 7s.

"One other parcel of land in the said field, containing 20 acres. Rent, £1 10s.

"One parcel of land in Great Coggeshall, containing 7 acres . . [a word or two illegible] . . of land belonging to the Manor of Coggeshall aforesaid. Rent, £1 5s. 1od.

"One parcel of land, called *Jackletts Hawkes*, containing 20 acres. Rent, £1.

[The above are now known as Great Monk Downs.]

"One other parcel of land, called *Little Monkdowne*, containing 51 acres. Rent, £2 7s. 1½d.

"One croft of land, called *Raine Croft*, containing 32 acres. Rent, £1 12s." [Nos. 401, 402 & 403, Ordnance Survey.]

On the 29th April, 7 James I. (A.D. 1610), a tenement called the *Cocke*, in Coggeshall, was granted to Peregrine Gastrell and Ralph Lownds, with other property. Rent, £1 13s. 4d. This is probably part of the property belonging to Mrs. J. K. King, situate on the Gravel, and the land in the rear upon part of which Messrs. Durant's factory stands. It is still called Cock Orchard. The Courts for the Manor of Great Coggeshall appear to have been formerly held here. Opposite the Cock was the butcher's shambles.

On the 10th July, 21 James I. (A.D. 1624), the *Manor of Great Coggeshall and Little Coggeshall*, with the appurtenances, was granted to Sir James Fullerton, Knt., and James Maxwell, Esqr. Rent, £42 6s. 8¼d. This property belongs to the Du Cane family. The rent of £42 6s. 8½d. charged thereon, was purchased by their ancestor, Nehemiah Lyde, in 1694, subject to the life interest therein of the Dowager Queen Katherine.

Most of the foregoing rents, with others, were, on 13th Sept., 1672, conveyed by the Right Hon. Francis, Lord Hawley, Sir Charles Harbord, Knt., Surveyor to His Majesty King Charles II.; Sir William Hayward, Knt.; Sir John Talbot, Knt.; and Sir William Harbord, the Trustees thereof for the Crown, to Sir John Banks, Bart., and others. These rents afterwards belonged to Sir John Morden, of Ricklemarsh, Kent, Bart., who, by his will, dated 15th Oct., 1702, gave them to his trustees, for the sustenance of poor, honest, sober and distressed merchants of not less than 50 years of age, and such as had lost their estates by accidents, damages and perils of the seas, and otherwise; each of them was to have £20 a year, with right of residence in the College he had already built at Charlton, near Blackheath, in Kent.

THE ABBEY.

THE monks that settled in Coggeshall, sometime between the years 1137 and 1142, were of the Cistercian Order, and not of the Cluniac, as stated by Weever, whose error is quoted but not rectified by Newcouıt. The Clunies were black monks, whereas the Cistercians wore a white gown and hood over a white cassock, and it is pointed out in *Dugdale's Monasticon* that there is such evidence as cannot be shaken that the Monks of Coggeshall were of the Cistercian order.

This order was esteemed so highly, and received such support from the people of this country, and especially from Queen Matilda, that within three years after their first settlement no less than eighteen houses were established, founded, endowed and peopled, and of these it is said the Abbey of Coggeshall was fifth in order of time. Among their other houses were the magnificent piles of Tintern, Netley, Kirkstall, and Furness, the extensive remains of which throw some light upon the situation of the various departments of our abbey here.

The exact date of the foundation is uncertain. Parco Lude speaks of 1137; Weever, from the Book of St. Austin, in Canterbury, says 1140; Leland, 1141; while Tanner mentions 1142 as the date, and in this he is followed by Dugdale, who quotes from a chronicle of Coggeshall in the Cottonian Library (sub effigie Neronis, D 2) to the following effect :—" In year 1142, the Abbey of Coggeshall was founded by King Stephen and Matilda his Queen, who also founded the abbeys of Furness, Lungvillars and Favresham, where their bodies were interred. In the same year the convent came together at Coggeshall III Nones of August."

The greatest benefactor of the abbey was Queen Matilda, who endowed it with the Manor of Coggeshall, one of the estates she inherited as heiress of the house of Boulogne. This Manor, at the time of the Domesday Survey belonged to Earl Eustace, and was held by him in demesne having been held in the time of King Edward the Confessor by Colo, a freeman, for one manor, and for three and a half hides and thirty-three acres. The survey continues, " Always iii teams in the demesne, and when he got possession i team ; then (*i.e. temp.* Edw. the Confessor) xvi teams of the homagers afterwards and now (circa 1086, A.D.) xiv; then xi villeins, afterwards and now ix; then xxii bordars now xxxi ; now iv serfs ; then wood for dc swine now for d ; xxxviii acres of meadow. As much pasture as is worth x pence. Always i mill, i horse, xv swine, iv goats, iv hives of bees. To this manor belong xi socmen, and i priest, and i swineheard, and i hired servant. To this manor have been added xxxviii acres which i freeman holds of the king. Then this manor was worth x pounds, now xiv; but yet it yields xx pounds and the above-mentioned xxxviii acres are worth x shillings."

Such is probably the estate which passed to the abbey, as in the charter or deed of gift the manor is granted to the abbot and convent of Coggeshall, as freely and peaceably as "Count Eustace, my father, and we afterwards more freely and peaceably held it free from scots, aids, shires, hundreds, Dane gelt, and all things of the army and horsemen, from work of the park, from work and custody of the castle, from all other works and all kinds of service, from murder and all other things, and all fines, with sacha and socha, and toll and team, and power to punish crime, and all customs and liberties."

The grant was confirmed at Coggeshall by King Stephen in the presence of his Queen, their son, Eustace, Count of Boulogne, and others, and was subsequently further confirmed by William, Earl of Boulogne and Warren, another son of Stephen and Matilda.

Matilda also granted to the monks at Coggeshall an exemption from toll and other customs throughout all the lands belonging to her and her son, Eustace, both in England and at Boulogne.

King Henry II. confirmed to GOD and to the Holy Mother of GOD, Mary, and to the Cistercian monks "all the Manor of Coke-shale, where the abbey is situated, and to the same church what they have at Toleshunt of· the fee of Geofry de Tregoz, of the fee of Geofry de Magnaville, at Neweshales; of the fee of Baldwin de Rouet, and what they possess in the lands of Moldeburne, and in the marshes of Hely." This grant was confirmed by Henry II., in the eighteenth year of his reign.

William Filiol, with the consent of Emme his wife, and Baldwin his son, gave to the Abbey of Coggeshall, and the monks there serving GOD, in pure and perpetual eleemosinary for the souls of his son Ralph, and of his own heirs, one acre, one rood, and four perches of pasture on this side of the rivulet, from the spring of Stokewelle on the east of the abbey, for which, before the death of his son Ralph, they were accustomed to pay 12 pence per annum. The name of Filiol, or Foliole, occurs on the Roll of Battle Abbey, 1066, among the names of the warriors who fought under the banner of the Conqueror.

On the seal of the grant by William Filiol to Coggeshall Abbey, is a representation of a font, with a king on one side, and a bishop on the other, holding a child as in the ceremony of baptism, from which it is supposed that the family had a tradition of this surname (*fileul*, a godson) having been given at the time of baptism to one of their ancestors, by one of the kings of England. Baldwin Filiol had an estate at Kelvedon, in or about the reign of King Stephen, and it continued in the family of that name for several generations, and from Filiols Hall it is supposed that the present name of the property, Felix Hall, is corrupted, but it is possible that Felix Hall is associated with much earlier, namely, Roman times.

King Richard I., by charter, commanded that the brethren of this abbey, and all their men and things, be quit at fairs and sea-port, from toll and passage, portage and pedage, and every other custom and secular exaction, for all things which they should buy or sell, or cause to be carried away, throughout every place under the king's authority, by land or by water, to their proper use; and no one was to vex or disturb them, for the king acknowledged

that he held them and theirs in his protection and custody, and
any who should vex or injure them or theirs could not look for
his Majesty's protection.

Ralph the Vintner, between the years 1154-89, gave to the
Abbey of Coggeshall, and to the monks there serving GOD, an
annual rent of half a mark, which they were to receive from the
rent of the cellar next to the chapel of Saint Thomas the Martyr,
in London, namely: forty pence at the Feast of the Passover, and
forty pence at the Feast of St. Michael. This rent he gave, and
by his charter confirmed to them, to buy wine for saying masses
for the souls of all his ancestors, and for the welfare of himself,
his wife, his children, and all his benefactors. Shortly afterwards,
William, the son of Ralph the Vintner, by charter confirmed the
gift of his father. Later on, we read that Ralph, Abbot of Coggeshall and the convent of Coggeshall, sold to the Abbot and
convent of St. Peter, Gloucester, all the rent which they formerly
held of the gift of Ralph the Vintner, arising from a certain cellar
near the Church of Saint Martin of Bermanchurch, in London,
and for this sale the Abbot and convent of Gloucester gave to
the Abbey of Coggeshall, five marks sterling. (See the *Car-
tulary of the Monastery of St. Peter, Gloucester; M.R. Series,
Vol. 1, p. 390.*)

King John, on 10th January, 1243, gave the monks of Coggeshall leave to enclose their wood in the Manor of Coggeshall
(doubtless the same as is now called Monk Wood), with a ditch
and hedge of pales, and with gates, and to convert it into a park,
with liberty to fell therein whatever they wished, and of having
their dogs, and the dogs of their men unbound for which they
paid the king an acknowledgment of forty marks.

Robert Hovel, and Margaret, his wife, in 1249, gave to the
Abbot and monks of Coggeshall the advowson of Childerditch,
and they presented to it, as a rectory, till 1370.

King Henry III., in 1251, granted a license for the monks to
enclose their woods and heaths at Tolleshunt Mayer (Major),
Tolleshunt Tregoz, Inneworth, Chiltenditch, and Warlegh Setmoll,
with a small ditch and low hedge, according to the rule of the
forest, so that the deer with their young, might have free ingress
and egress, and that the foresters, both horsemen and footmen,
might also have ingress and egress to survey and keep the deer
there abiding; but the commoners were not to be deprived of their

rights of common, by reason of the grant. This King also confirmed, in 1247, to the Abbot and convent of Coggeshall, that they might have *free warren* in all their demesne lands at Coggeshall, so that none might enter their lands to hunt in them, or to take anything which belonged to free warren, without the license of the abbot and convent, upon forfeiture of £10. Three years afterwards (1250), King Henry granted to the Abbot and convent that they might have *one fair* for their Manor of Coggeshall every year, to continue for eight days, on the eve and on the day of *St. Peter ad Vincula* and six days following unless that fair was prejudicial to neighbouring fairs.

It will be noticed that the fair commenced on the feast day of *St. Peter ad Vincula* (1st August), the patron saint of the parish church. The annual fair, in 1728, was held on Friday in Whit-week; it is now held on Whit-Tuesday. Then again, Henry III., in 1256, granted to the Abbot and convent of Coggeshall the right to hold a *market* at Coggeshall every week, on Saturday, with all liberties and free customs belonging to such market, unless that market were damaging to neighbouring markets.

The market, such as it is, is now held on Thursday, the day having been probably changed on account of the presentment, in the 10th year of Edward II., that the abbot held a market on Saturdays, at the village of Coggeshall, to the detriment of that at Colchester.

In 1270, Herbert de Markeshall received a license from the crown to give 60 acres of arable land in his Manor of Markeshall to the monastery here. He died at Markeshall about 1274.

In 1276, Ralph de Coggeshall also gave the monks here, 60 acres of arable land.

Ralph, the son of Laurence, of Coggeshall, gave to the Church of St. Mary, of Coggeshall, and to the monks there serving GOD, a tenement which the same Ralph had in the town of Markeshall, of the gift of Herbert de Markeshall, and this gift was confirmed by King Edward I., in 1279.

In the 19th year of his reign, the charters of the Abbey were confirmed by King Edward II.

King Edward III., in 1344, in consideration of a promise by the Abbot and convent of Coggeshall to find a monk as Chaplain to celebrate divine service each day in their conventual church, in honour of GOD and of the Blessed Virgin Mary, and for the safety of the king and queen, and of their children while they lived, and for their souls when they died, granted to the same Abbot and convent, *one pipe of red wine* to be received each year at London, at Easter, by the hands of the Gentlemen of the Wine Cellar.

In the 10th year of Edward III., John de Kelvedon and others gave to the Abbot of Coggeshall, 3 messuages and 2 tofts, in Coggeshall. Eighteen years later, Galfridus de Stocktone gave to the Abbey one messuage and certain lands in Coggeshall, Stisted, Feering and Pattiswick. In the 34th year of the same reign, Matilda, the wife of John Cachpol, gave to the Abbot and convent of Coggeshall, one messuage and half an acre of land, with the appurtenances, in the town of Coggeshall.

William de Hamberstane, with other persons, in the 51st year of Edward III., gave to the monastery here, the Manor of Tillingham Hall, in Childerditch, Dodingherst and Southwelde, to support a light before the principal altar of the church of the convent, when high mass was celebrated.

From a license, granted by King Hen. IV., on the 27th January, 1407, it appears that a chantry was founded here by Joan de Bohun, Countess of Hereford, Margaret, the wife of Sir Hugh de Badew, William Bourchier, William Marney, Nicholas Hunt, Robert Rikedon, Edmund Peverell, Henry Frank, clerk, Geoffry Colvill, and John Norman, chaplain, for one monk to pray daily for the souls of Hugh Badew, and Margaret, his wife, and Thomas Coggeshall; the endowment, consisting of a rent-charge of £10 per annum, issuing out of two messuages, a fulling mill, 240 acres of arable, 11 acres of meadow, 46 of pasture, and 2 acres of wood, in Springfield and Sandon, called Springfield Barnes and Sandford Barnes.

The value of the estates of the Abbey, in 1291, appears from a taxation of Pope Nicholas, to have been £116 10s. per annum —a very large sum in those days—derived from the following sources :—In Berkewye de redd, £8 : In Alflameston de red, 8s. 6d. : In Northon, 4s. : In Springesfend, £2. : In Lega Magna, 1s. 10d. : In Chelmersford, 1s. : In Parva Waltham, 5s. : In Borham, 1s. : In Muslesham, 10s. : In Estorp, £1 18s. : In Birithe Magna, 1s. : In Messing, 15s. 6d. : In Inneworth, £6 13s. 4d. : In Coggishale, £67 11s. 10d. : In Markishale, £1 1s. 11d. : In Feringge, £3 5s. 4d. : In Goldhangre, £5 9s. : In Tholishunte Mangers, £14 3s. 2d. : In Tholishunte Trogoz, £3 3s. 4d. : In

Bracstead Magna, 4s. : In Colcestria, £1 3s 2d.—Total, £116 10s. 11d.

Unfortunately, the Ecclesiastical Survey, which was made in the 26th year of King Henry VIII. is lost, so far as it concerned the county of Essex, but the *Liber Valorum* gives the clear value at £251 2s. ; although Speed, who doubtless was referring to the gross value, gives the income at £298 8s.

The abbey was surrended on the 5th February, 29 Henry VIII., and in the *History of the Reformation* it is thus mentioned "Coxhall, Cisterc the Abbot, Essex, 5th February, Regni, 29 ; but Newcourt gives the 18th March as the date.

The seal of the abbey, attached to the surrender in the Augmentation Office, is round, and bears the Virgin seated in a

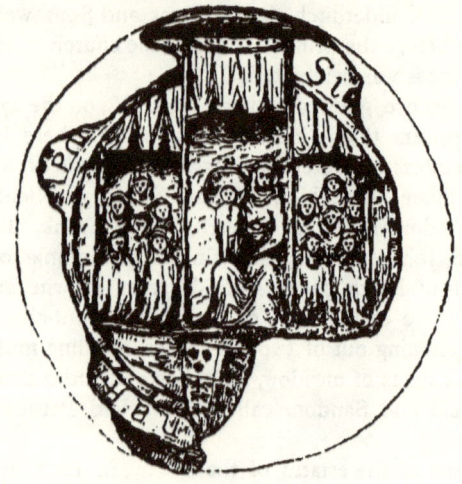

THE SEAL OF THE ABBEY.

canopied niche with crown, the Child with nimbus, on her right knee. In a smaller canopied niche, on each side, a group of six kneeling monks. In base, under an arch on the left, a shield of arms : quarterly, 1.4, France modern ; 2, 3, England. The corresponding shield on the right, is broken away ; in an impression referred to by Dugdale, *Mon. Angl. Vol. V., p. 452*, it bears : three cocks Coggeshall Abbey, SIGILLVM COMVNE ECCL'IE MONASTER DE COGGESHALE. [Catalogue of seals in British Museum,

No. 2972, [15 century] Sulph cast from imperfect impression, 2⅛ in. [lxiii., 5].

Among the MS. notes at the end of Salmon's *History of Essex*, presented to the Colchester Museum by the Revd. Jenkins, is a copy of the seal of Coggeshall Abbey, *temp.* Henry IV. :—the Virgin bearing the Child, at her feet are two cocks, but the armorial shields are not added.

The Cistercian order is generally considered to owe its reputation, in some degree, to Stephen Harding, an Englishman, but more especially to St. Bernard, who joined it in 1113. The name of the order is derived from Citeaux, (Latin, Cistercium), about 14 miles north-east of Beaune, in France, the place where the foundation was first established in 1098. The founder is said to have been St. Robert, Abbot of Molesme, sometimes known as Robert de Thierry. The manner of life of this reformed order was of the simplest possible character, their fare consisting generally of only one substantial meal a day, while their labor was manual rather than mental, their chief occupation being the cultivation of the soil and the manufacture of woollen articles. When not so engaged, the brethren would be employed in prayer and contemplation.

The picture which lay before the monks as they entered their new abode, whether by the ancient way from Verulamium to Camulodunum or by a detour from the London Road, must have been a pleasant one. At their feet were the fertile pastures bordering the ancient little river Blackwater, soon to be diverted into another channel for their milling operations,* while on the north, extending far afield, were the arbor clad slopes which to this day are known as Monk Woods and Monk Downs.

Their monastic buildings, as was the rule of this order, they erected on the low ground adjoining the river. The general plan of most of the Cistercian monasteries was of the same design, varied only by the peculiar circumstances of the situation, and,

* In the days of Edward the Confessor and William the Conqueror, there was a mill at Coggeshall, and it is probable that it occupied the site of the Tye Mill, the heading of water for which was derived from the Marks Hall watershed.

such being the case, we may to some extent learn the ichnography of the conventual buildings here.

The Abbey is reached by the road leading from the town of Coggeshall to Kelvedon and the lane which at the top of Grange Hill strikes out at right angles to the east. At the end of this lane the gatehouse doubtless stood, with the almonry and chamber above for the lower class of guests on the south side, while on the north was, and still is, the little chapel dedicated to St. Nicholas, and described in detail later on.

Forming the north side of the plan was the church, dedicated to the Blessed Virgin Mary, the western façade of which presented itself to the traveller as he passed along the abbey lane. This magnificient building was opened for divine service in 1167, for the Chronicle of Ralph, Abbot of Coggeshall, tells us that in this year, at Coggeshall, the great altar was dedicated in honor of the Blessed Virgin Mary, by Gilbert Foliol, Bishop of London, who, on the same day on that altar, solemnly celebrated mass; Simon de Toni being abbot of that place.

Although no fragment remains of this great building, its foundation lines may be easily traced in a dry summer, and were plainly visible in 1888. It was stepped by the Rev. W. J. Dampier, on 29th June, 1865, and he estimated the nave to be 141 feet by 24 feet; the chancel, 34 feet by 24 feet; and the north and south transepts, 31 feet by 24 feet each; and the lady chapel beyond the chancel, 31 feet by 24 feet. Mr. Dampier conjectured that there was a lean-to on the north and south sides, measuring about 10 feet internally. The foundation walls were about 5 feet wide. I have in my possession a large brick found on the Abbey Farm, and having a circular face; if this brick formed part of a pillar of the church, it gives the columns a diameter of about 4 feet. The tower was probably a central one, low, and without turrets and pinnacles. There was a crucifix, but no other carvings or representations of saints were allowed, the windows were of plain glass, and the candlesticks of iron; precious metal and ornamentation being avoided by this order as far as possible.

After the dissolution of the monastery, St. Mary's Church was pulled down, and tradition, in Holman's time (nearly two centuries ago) said that the bells were carried to Kelvedon. The materials of this grand building, even to the foundations, were doubtless utilized for road mending and similar purposes.

On the north side of the church the graveyard was generally located; a fact which demonstrates that the superstition as to burial on the north side, which prevailed among the ignorant classes, did not extend to the inmates of the convent.

On the south side of the church was the cloister, around which were clustered the buildings connected with the daily routine of the monastic life. One of the most important of these buildings was the chapter house, which invariably was entered from the east walk of the cloister, in a line with the south transept, and was a square building, generally divided by pillars and arches. South of the chapter house was usually the calefactory or apartment, warmed with flues, and forming the undercroft of the dormitory or sleeping chamber of the brethren. The dormitory was generally a long apartment running over the calefactory and chapter house, and had an approach at the north end by a flight of steps, into the church. At the south end of the calefactory were the lavatories and the other necessary houses of the establishment, built with scrupulous regard to health and cleanliness. The supply of fresh water was doubtless obtained from the hill sides on the east of the river, as these abound with an inexhaustible store of the purest quality, and it would seem that it was conveyed to the conventual buildings through socket and spigot pipes of red brick earth, 4 inches square tapering to $3\frac{1}{2}$ inches at the spigot end, and having a circular bore $1\frac{1}{2}$ inches in diameter. Some pipes (two in the writer's possession) of this description were found in Claypit Field (No. 341, Ord. Survey), during the drainage operations which were effected in 1887, and it may be that here was the "spring of Stokewell on the east of the abbey," referred to in the grant by William Filiol, mentioned in a previous page. On the south side of the cloisters, running north to south, was the refectory or dining hall, while along the entire length of the west side of the cloister quadrangle ran the cellars and storehouses, with the long dormitory above for the lay brethren. The abbot's house was usually detached from the other monastic buildings, as also were the mill, farm buildings, workshops and outhouses.

Such then were the general arrangements of the buildings of the Cistercian houses, and an admirable arrangement it was; the neighbouring land and buildings served for the purposes of the monks as cultivators of the soil, grinders of corn, manufacturers of clothes, shoes and other articles of a domestic nature. Nearer home were the buildings devoted to hospitality and storage, while beneath the shadow of the church, were clustered the apartments connected with the spiritual life and discipline of the order, and those used for refection and repose.

The monastic buildings at Coggeshall must have covered a large area, the extent of which can in some degree be gathered from the foundation lines of the church, and the few buildings

THE AMBULATORY.

which still remain, and among these may be noticed the principal walls of the present Abbey House, about 30 inches thick. In the kitchen, a pointed or transition Norman arch, forming part of an arcade, attracts the attention, and over it may be seen the sill of one of the clerestory windows thus leading one to suppose that we have here a portion of the Chapter House, similar in fact, to the Chapter House which figures in the plan of the Cistercian monastery of Fountains Abbey, except, perhaps, the arch is a little

H

too much to the south of the church. The wall, of which this arch is a continuation, runs from west to east. The respond has angular corners and is built of brick, but the column, which is also of brick, is round, and is surmounted by a Norman limestone capital.

Forming the southern portion of the eastern side of the cloister-quadrangle is a long vaulted apartment with chamfered brick arch and groin ribs with spandrils composed of rounded blocks of chalk. This was probably the calefactory or ambulatory, where the monks warmed themselves, and above is what was doubtless a dormitory. In the west wall of this building, as also in the north wall of the building next described, may be seen the capitals from which sprung the groin ribs of another apartment or series of chambers, the western façade of which, continued northward, would concur with the western wall of the south transept of the church, and thus the eastern side of the quadrangle would be complete.

To the south of the last mentioned buildings is a parallelogram of two stories, with an entry to the upper story from the dormitory over the calefactory, and to the ground floor from the ambulatory. It is difficult to conceive what this building was used for, but it is certainly one of interest, and the coloring, plain though it was, which decorated the walls, shows that it was of some importance. The doorway at the east end of the north wall in the upper floor, has a round arch of moulded brick, and above this, but not immediately over the centre of the arch, was a circular window, the lower part of which only now remains. In this upper chamber, at the east end, are two lancet shaped windows, and between them is a large recess, which appears to have been used for a seat. There is another recess or seat, the occupant of which commanded a view along the dormitory over the calefactory.

To the west of this building, according to the Cistercian arrangement, the refectory would stand, and, with other buildings, would form the southern side of the cloisters.

Near to the south-east corner of the building just described, and close to the bridge over the river, is what is known as the Monk House, but why so called is not known. It has an open timber roof, and around the sides below are a number of recesses, five in the east wall, a like number in the west wall, and two beside the doorway in the north wall. It would seem that these were intended for sedilia. On each side of the building are four lancet windows splaying inward.

Such of the abbey buildings as remain are composed principally of flint rubble with brick dressings. Thin tiles are used unsparingly for bonding purposes.

Beside the large Norman capital in the Abbey House, there are two smaller capitals of coeval date with that in the house. One of them is in the garden and forms part of a bordering of a flower bed, and the other is built into the east wall of the building locally known as the Monk House; the sketch shows to some extent how it is embedded in the rubble work. Purbeck marble was used for the smaller shafts and capitals.

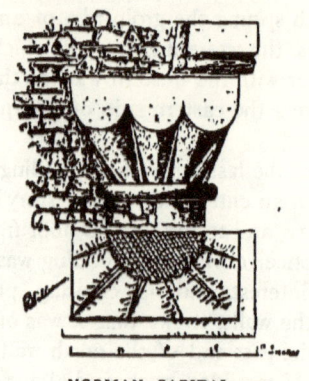

NORMAN CAPITAL.

On the north of the site of the monastery church, the contour of the ground indicates that there was a large square enclosure, but there are no signs of the foundation of a wall or other building. The Ordnance surveyors have erroneously marked this spot as the site of St. Mary's Church.

St. Nicholas Chapel.

THE woodcut represents the condition of the little Abbey Chapel of St. Nicholas, in the early part of the year 1889. It has since been partially restored by repairing the roof and other parts of the building.

Saint Nicholas, who is the patron saint of mariners and of schoolboys, was made bishop of Myra, in Lycia, a province of Asia, by Constantine the Great.   He died, A.D. 343.

Holman, writing more than a century and a half ago, and quoting from the *Villare Essexiæ*, says, that "Little Coggeshall was formerly reputed a parish, and had two churches, the one built by the abbot for himself and monks, and stood in the field called the Parke, on the left side of the abbey, and dedicated to Saint Mary the Blessed Virgin, is entirely demolished. The other was built for the inhabitants of this Hamlet and stands on the left hand of the lane leading from the king's highway to the abbey and not far from it, 'tis called the chapel of Little Coggeshall, and is now converted into a barn or hay-house and most of it is existing at this day."

Whether the church secondly referred to and illustrated above,

was the parish church of Little Coggeshall, as some have con-
tended, or was built for the inhabitants of that parish by the
monks, as stated in the *Villare Essexæ*, seems open to question.
It is more probable that it corresponds with the chapel shown on
the plan of the Monastic Establishment of Citeaux as close to the
Gate House; and, if such was the case, we may picture the welcome traveller of past ages being led thither by the Lord Ralph,
6th abbot of Coggeshall, or by one of the succeeding abbots, for
the short prayer which was accustomably said before the guest
was the recipient of the hospitality generously accorded by the
brethren; but having regard to the dedication, it may be suggested
that the chapel was built for the scholastic department of the
abbey.

The plan of the building is of a simple quadrilateral design
without aisles or transept, and measures internally from east to
west, 43 feet; and from north to south, 20 feet. It is constructed
of rubble, consisting principally of flints and fragments of early
English brick and tiles, while the quoins and dressings are of
bricks, varying from $1\frac{1}{2}$ to 2 inches in thickness, and being about
12 inches by 6 inches in length and breadth. *It is considered a
remarkable example of early English brickwork,* and especial attention is directed to the mouldings of the bricked mullions of the
east and west windows. *It is one of the earliest instances, if not the
earliest, of moulded brickwork in the kingdom.*

The walls rest upon a concrete bed and are about 3 feet thick,
and it would seem were originally coated with plaster or stucco,
both inside and out. The building is entered by a door on the

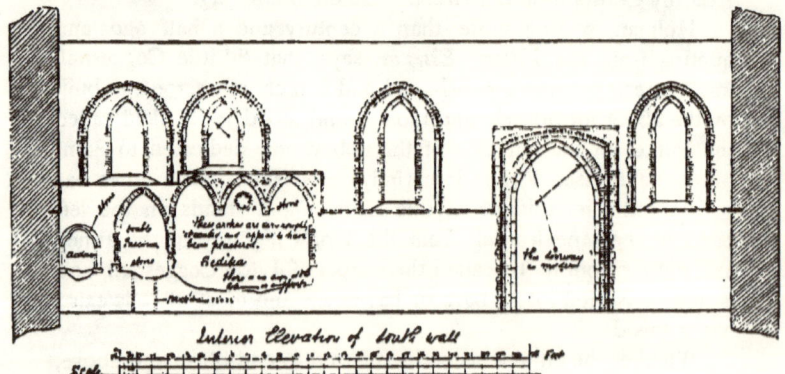

Interior Elevation of South Wall

Scale

south side near the west end.   On each side of the door is a lancet
window, with exterior dimensions 6 feet 4 inches high and 2 feet
broad, splaying inward to a height of 8 feet and a breadth of 4
feet 7 inches.   There are two other windows on the south side,
but their sills are elevated to give height to the sedilia and piscina.
In the north wall there are four lancet windows, similar to those
east and west of the doorway.   The windows in the east and west
walls are triple lancets within a containing arch ; these windows
are of remarkably graceful proportions, and the curve of the containing arch with the hood moulding over the western window
is particularly worthy of notice.

Round the interior of the chapel, just beneath the windows,
there is a string course of semi-circular faced bricks projecting
about $1\frac{1}{2}$ inches, each of which is about 12 inches long by 2 inches
in thickness.   At the east end of the south wall the string rises
and runs along the top of the sedilia, three in number, the arches
of which are composed of brick and spring from limestone supports.   To the east of and adjoining the sedilia is an arched recess,
and there were formerly the remains of two square drains pierced
through the bricks which formed its sill ; the sill is gone, but the
drains are still extant.   This recess was doubtless a double piscina.
Between it and the east wall is a niche, 23 inches wide, 2 feet 6
inches high and recessed about 13 inches, formed of limestone
and having a trefoil-shaped arch-heading.   It is still in good preservation and most probably served as a credence.   The aumbry
with its new oak sill and top, restored as far as was practicable to
its original state, is to be seen in the north wall near the east end.
A small part of the original moulded oak wall-plate, with its somewhat singular stop, remains at the east end of the north wall.
The roof is high pitched, the eastern half being raised slightly
above the other portion.

The plastering of the interior, above the string course, was
relieved by coloring of a simple character, consisting of double
chocolate one-eighth inch lines three-eights of an inch apart.
These ran round the building at horizontal intervals of five inches,
divided vertically so as to represent stone work.   The pattern may
still be seen, and there may yet be traced the emerald green which
gave colour to the string course, and there is enough of the flowing foliage pattern which filled the spaces between the lancets and
containing arch of the east window to show its early English

character. In the upper part of the central seat of the sedilia there remains part of the original cruciform nimbus of reddish colour.

Many years ago this sacred building was converted into a barn, part of the south wall being removed and a wing attached. The unsightly addition was demolished shortly after the conveyance of the building and the surrounding three roods and thirty-five perches was made to the vicar of Coggeshall, the late Rev. William James Dampier, and his successors in the vicarage. Through the energy of this good man a partial restoration was effected. The property was purchased from Mr. Jonathan Bullock, on 3rd January, 1860, for £100—the proceeds of the sale of one rood and five perches, part of the glebe land of the vicarage, sold as a site for Sir Robert Hitcham's School. This statement will remove the erroneous impression, which has prevailed with some, to the effect that the piece of ground was given to the vicar of Coggeshall for the maintenance of the fabric of the building. The land belongs to the vicar of Coggeshall as part of his glebe.

On the 19th March, 1860, the ground was fenced in; and, on the 21st April, 1863, the first stone of the restored doorway was laid by Miss Ellen Bithia Appleford, daughter of the late Mr. William Appleford, of the Abbey Mills, and possibly a descendant of Richard Abberforde, who farmed the woods of Coggeshall Manor in the 22nd year of Queen Elizabeth; and it is parenthetically suggested that this family derived its name from the fact that they resided hard by the Abbey-ford. The doorway was finished on the 11th May following, and in November of the same year the building was new thatched, and some of the quoins and dressings were about the same time restored with bricks of the original type specially moulded for the purpose.

During this partial restoration, fragments of coloured glass, pieces of the Purbeck marble shafts of the sedilia and part of the font or of the stoup were found, also the base of the font nearly opposite the door and close to the north wall, and with these remains were associated pieces of the pavement, which was of tile, coloured black, yellow, or buff and green. The bricks which form the step of the doorway appear to have been part of the jambs of the original doorway.

The Abbots of Coggeshall.

THE following brief notes concerning the Abbots are chiefly extracted from the Chronicle of Ralph de Coggeshall *(Stevenson's Edit., Master of Rolls Series, 1875)*, these excepts, translated into English, appear in inverted commas; the further details are principally from *Dugdale's Monasticon.*

(1.) WILLIAM was the first abbot. He occurs as a witness to a deed, about 1144, in the Chartulary of Colne Priory.

(2.) SIMON DE TONI was the next abbot. " 1168, Lord Simon, the second abbot, retired from Coggeshall, and returned to his monastery at Melrose."

(3.) " 1169; to whom succeeded LORD ODO, third abbot of the same place." " 1172 ; the ordination of Lord Simon, Bishop of Moray (Maraviensis), 10th Kalends of February, sometime Abbot of Coggeshall." " 1176; died, Lord Odo, of pious memory, third Abbot of Coggeshall :

(4.) To whom succeeded LORD PETER, Monk of Valle Dei, brother to Master Stephen, Chancellor of the Church of Lincoln." " 1194 : died Lord Peter, fourth Abbot of Coggeshall :

(5.) To whom succeeded LORD THOMAS, a monk of the same place." " 1207 : died Lord Thomas, fifth Abbot of Coggeshall :

(6.) To whom succeeded, LORD RALPH, a monk of the same place, who wrote this Chronicle, from the taking of the Holy Cross to the 11th year of King Henry III., the son of King John ; and took care faithfully to note down certain visions which he heard from men worthy of respect, for the edification of many."

Of Ralph de Coggeshall much has been written; Dr. Cutts translating Bale *(Script Brit. centuria, 3, cap. 88)*, says, he was "a Monk of the Cistercian Order, a man of polished erudition, as well as of temperance, and arrived at such a degree of excellence in literature as to be esteemed by far the first of the brethren of his convent. He was trained in liberal studies even from boyhood, and by means of his great industry he obtained the honor of intimacy with the most eminent men ; whence, at length being found worthy to govern others, he was preferred to the abbacy of Coggeshall, in Essex ; being the 6th abbot from its foundation. In this office he scarcely suffered one day to pass entirely free from some useful study, but would always be learning something, either from humane letters or from history, or from the Sacred Scriptures. He made an Appendix to Ralph Niger's Chronicle concerning the distinguished deeds of the Emperors and Kings of France and England, from the Capture of the Cross as is therein stated, or from the year of grace, 1113, to the eleventh year of Henry the third, the son of King John; which work he calls, 'Additions to Ralph Niger, in one book, beginning in the year of grace, 1114, King Henry.' He also wrote, 'A Chronicle of the Holy Land, in one book, beginning Quantis pressuris et calamitatibus,' 'Concerning certain Visions, in one book,' 'Certain Sermons, and many other things.'"

For further information concerning the Coggeshall chronicler, the reader is referred to *Dunkin's Edition* of his works, published in 1857, one part of which, viz.: "A Chronicle of the Holy Land" by Ralph, Abbot of Coggeshall, was translated by the Rev. E. L. Cutts.

Now with regard to this "Chronicle of the Holy Land," which so many writers have attributed to the same authorship as that of the "Chronicle of Ralph, Abbot of Coggeshall," Mr. Stevenson has pointed out * that there is no direct evidence for this assumption, either external or internal; there is a marked difference between the two in respect to style and the general treatment of the narrative, and in some instances the facts recorded in the one are inconsistent with the corresponding statement in the other. The assertion that they are to be ascribed to the same pen has probably arisen from the circumstance that they both occur in the same volume, but to whatever source it be referred it would appear to be untenable.

The *Chronicon Anglicanum* contains very few notes of local interest; it however tells us that "In the year 1216, on the day of the Circumcision of the Lord, at Coggeshall, while the third hour was said, they (*i.e.* the knights and attendants of King John) violently entered the church and led away 22 horses which were the property of the Bishop of London and his brother the Treasurer, and others."

"1218. In the same year, Lord Ralph, sixth Abbot of Coggeshall, having now for eleven years and two months administered, about the feast of Saint John the Baptist, against the will of his

---

* No. 66 M.R. Series of Chron. of Great Britain. xviii.

convent; of his own accord renounced the pastoral cure, suffering from frequent indisposition. To him at once succeeded, by the choice of the same abbot and convent, Lord Benedict de Straford, a venerable man and vigorous in acting; who formerly, for 19 years, actively presided over the same Abbey of Straford, and increased it in many ways with large rents and possessions, as well in benefices as in lands and marshes."

"In the year of the Incarnation of the Lord, 1223, died Lord Benedict, Abbot of Coggeshall; to whom succeeded Lord Geoffrey, prior of the same place."

The lists of Abbots is unfortunately very incomplete.

William Joldayn was abbot in 1341.

John Taseler from 1437 to 1449, when he was succeeded by Simon Pabenham.

John Samford resigned in 1527, when

William Love was elected to succeed him.

Henry More was abbot at the time of the surrender.

A CISTERCIAN MONK.

ᚈᚼᛖ ᚨᛒᛒᛖᚤ ᚠᚨᚱᛗ.

T HE king did not long retain possession of the Abbey, for, in the same year as the dissolution (A.D. 1538), he granted the "principal or chief site of the monastery" to Sir Thomas Seymour, brother of Sir Edward Seymour (afterwards Duke of Somerset and Lord Protector of the Kingdom), who, on 12th May, 1541, exchanged it for other property belonging to the Crown. In the same grant reference is made to the Rectory and Advowson of the Churches and Vicarages of Childerditch and Coggeshall, the Manors of Coggeshall, Childerditch, Tillingham and Kewton Hall, Lions, Tolleshunt Major, Chedingsell, Tutwyke, Bonsey alias Bouseys, Holfield Grange and Bushey Gate House.

The present farmhouse has on the porch a freestone inlaid with these initials: $_R{}^B{}_A$ and under them the date, 1581. The B is probably the initial letter of the surname of the owner or occupier, who may have been a Bacon, a Benion, or a Bettenson. Matthew Bacon had a lease in 1598, of the Mansion house previously held by Sir John Sharpe, lying within the monastery, and later on, the Benyans and Bettonsons were owners or tenants of some importance in respect of lands in this locality. The R and the A would doubtless be the initials of the christian names of the husband and wife, and possibly are those of Richard Beniyam generosus, whose wife (H)anna was buried in the parish churchyard, 16th Jany., 1603.

The Abbey Farm was afterwards possessed by Sir Mark Guyon, who died in 1690, leaving no male issue, but two daughters as his co-heiresses, one of whom, Elizabeth, married Edward Bullock, Esq., son of Edward Bullock, Esq., of Faulkborne Hall; she had one child only, who, with its mother, died within a month of its birth. Rachel, the other daughter of Sir Mark, was first married to Thomas Guyon, Esq., and afterwards to her brother-in-law, John Bullock, Esq., of Dynes Hall, Great Maplestead. They had issue John, who died, unmarried, at the age of 23 years, and was buried in the chancel of Faulkborne Church, and Rachel, who survived her father, but died in 1765, a spinster and intestate. Josiah Bullock was for a time entitled to the Essex Estates of the family, and on his decease, on 29th February, 1751, his widow Hannah, the youngest daughter of Sir Thomas Cooke, Kt., was in possession. By her he had issue two sons, Edward and John, and a daughter Elizabeth, who married Jonathan Watson, Esq., of Ringshall, Suffolk. Hannah Bullock died, 8th April, 1783, whereupon the Faulkborne, Radwinter and Coggeshall Estates passed to Jonathan Josiah Christopher Bullock, Esq., eldest son of Jonathan Watson, Esq. In the year 1810, he took the name of Bullock, by permission of King George III., and in compliance with the will of his maternal uncle, John Bullock. J. J. C. Bullock died, 22nd January, 1832, aged 82 years, having married Juliana Elizabeth, daughter of Anicetus Thomas, Esq., of Chelsea, niece and heiress of Elizabeth Bullock, wife of John Bullock. They had thirteen children, several of whom predeceased them. Jonathan Bullock died, 30th Sept., 1860, possessed of the Abbey and other estates at Coggeshall. He was succeeded by his son, the Rev. Walter Trevelyan Bullock, by whose trustees the abbey was sold in 1879. Arms of Bullock: gu., a chevron, erm., between 3 bulls' heads cabosed, arg., horned or., crest, on a torse, ar., gu., five bills or staves sa., bound with an escarf knot, tasselled gu. The family first appear in Coggeshall in 1566, in which year, on 15th October, Robert Bullock married Elizabeth Trewe.

The purchaser of the Abbey was Sidney Pattisson, Esq., who resided there for a short time. He is the eldest son of Jacob Pattisson, by marriage with Emily Elizabeth Hawkes, of Bishop Stortford. Jacob was the son of Fisher Unwin Pattisson, who married Eliza Houston. Fisher Unwin Pattisson was a son of Jacob Pattisson and Elizabeth (Unwin), who were married at Coggeshall on 24th August, 1785. Jacob was a son of Joseph and Elizabeth (*née* Wallman). Joseph was a son of Robert and Rachel (*née* Todd). Robert was a son of Jacob and Elizabeth (*née* Bidwell). Jacob was a son of Jacob, who died in 1709. The father of the last-named was William, who lived at Ulting; and William was a son of John Pattisson, who lived at Heybridge near Maldon, in the reign of Elizabeth. For some further account of this family see Benton's *Rochford Hundred*, and the memorials of the family in Witham parish church. Their arms are :—An elm tree eradicated between 3 pelicans in their nests, with their young vulning themselves. Crest :—a pelican, in her nest with her young, vulning herself, collared ringed and chained ; the chain reflexed over her back.

The Abbey Farm now belongs to the Law Union Life Insurance Company.

MANORIAL.

THE Manors of Great Coggeshall and Little Coggeshall which originally were but one Manor, known as the Manor of Coggeshall, belonged in Saxon times to Colo, a freeman. At the time of the Domesday Survey (*vide* page 88), it was possessed by Eustace, Earl of Boulogne, from whom it descended to his only daughter and heiress, Maud, who brought it in marriage to Stephen, Earl of Blois, afterwards King of England. Stephen and his queen granted the Manor to the abbot and convent of Coggeshall about 1139, and it remained one of the monastic properties until the surrender of the house in 1538. Soon after the dissolution, Henry VIII. granted it to Sir Thomas Seymour, who, in 1541, released it to the Crown in exchange for other properties. In the first year of Queen Mary's reign, the Manors of Great Coggeshall and Little Coggeshall, a grange or farm called Home Grange, a water mill and the fishery of the river, were, with other estates in the parish, granted by the Queen to Dorothy, wife of Thomas Leventhorpe, for life, if it pleased her Majesty she should so long enjoy it. The Manors were afterwards possessed by Sir Henry Bromley, by virtue of a grant made on 2nd September, 1604, and at his nomination they were conveyed on the 24th January following, to Cyprian Warner and others. In the 12th year of King James I., they were granted to Sir James Fullerton and James Maxwell, at a rent of £42 6s. 8½d.

Augustine Mayhew, Esq. was subsequently possessed of these Lordships. He married Alice, daughter of John Wells, but when he sold the manor to Nehemiah Lyde, Esq., of Hackney, on 9th May, 1693, his wife's name was Elizabeth. He then resided at Witham, and his son and heir was William Mayhew, of Pattiswick. Bufton says, "In 1693, Mr. Mayhew sold Coxall lordships to Mr. Nehemiah Lyde. May 11th—He first came for his rent, and June 5th being Whitsun Monday, kept Court, and Counsellor Cox was his steward. 1st Sept.—Old Mr. Augustine Mayhew was carried through Coxall to be buried at Passwick."

Nehemiah Lyde, by Priscilla his wife, had an only daughter Ann, his heiress, who married in 1710, Richard DuCane, Esq., of London, the only child and heir of Peter DuCane. Nehemiah Lyde died in July, 1737, but the first General Court of his son-in-law, Richard DuCane, was held on the 14th June, 1735.

Richard DuCane, by his will, dated 1743, gave his Manors and other estates at Coggeshall to his son "Peter DuQuesne alias Du Cane" and his heirs. Richard died in 1743, leaving Peter DuCane his only surviving son (his other son, Richard, having died on 4th Feby., 1743). Peter DuCane died in March, 1803, having devised the Manors to his son Peter, for life, with the remainder to his grandson Peter. Peter DuCane the younger, of Braxted Park, Essex, married in 1769, Phœbe Phillips Tredcroft, eldest daughter of Edward Tredcroft, Esq., of Horsham. Captain Charles DuCane succeeded to the Manors in 1841, and on his death in 1850, his son, the late Sir Charles DuCane, K.C.M.G. became entitled to the Lordships, and on his death on 25th Feby., 1889, his eldest son, Charles Henry Copley DuCane, Esq., succeeded and is the present Lord of these Manors.

The Court Rolls of the Manors, in the custody of the present steward, do not date earlier than 1693. If the ancient rolls could be discovered they would throw considerable light on the past history of the town. Fortunately there is preserved in the Public Record Office (Duchy of Lanc. Court Roll, Bundle 58, No. 727), an extract of a Court held upwads of 300 years ago, and from this we are enabled to form some idea of the ways in which our Elizabethan ancestors conducted their sanitary and other affairs; we shall see for instance, that a fine was imposed on such of the inhabitants as were wont to dig sand and gravel out of the highways, or to throw their refuse into the street, or to allow their ditches to become choked. Roger Jegons is ordered not to allow his hogs to pollute the church-pond; we have mention of the brook which ran from the Church-pond to Haresbridge, a state of things which continued till comparatively recent times—many of the older inhabitants well remember the stream flowing in its open course down Church Street; the sewers in the principal streets were also uncovered; and Church Lane, at the upper end, was nothing more nor less than a wide ditch with a footpath on one side of it. Those who persisted in keeping open their shops on Sunday, after the bells had rung two peals, were to be fined 1s. There were regulations also as to fishing and the keeping of dogs, ferrets, &c. The whole extract is of so interesting a nature, and is written in such quaint style, that it is here reproduced *in extenso*, save that one or two items are for decency's sake omitted.

"The extracte of the Corte there holden the Mondaye, beinge the sixte day of October, in the nyneth yeare of the reigne of or Sovreigne Lady Elizabeth, by the grace of GOD, of England, Ffraunce and Ireland, Quene, defender of the faythe, &c., as followeth —— That is to saye

Imprimis of Willam Coates for his admysson to one garden called Starres, witche he had by and after the death of Willam Coates his father, deceased. } xijd

Item of Elizabeth Wade, for hir admysson to one close wyth an ortyard, whitche she dyd recover by her wryte of Righte ayens Christopher Wade. } ijs. vjd.

Sum of this Corte — iijs. vjd.

vnde allocat : in expense Se li.

yt ys comaundyd the Baylif to warne all the inhabytans of this Lordeship that they hereafter digge no lome, claye, sand or gravell in the Quene's highe waye, upon payne to forfette for eury lode so taken—iijs. iiijd.

Also yt ys comaundyd that no maner of pson or psons shall from hence forthe caste their duste or fylthe owte of their houses into the streate, upon payne to forfet eury tyme—xijd.

Also yt ys ordered and decreyd by thole homage that no Inhitant of this towne shall let from henceforthe his tenement to anye comon fetchers of woodde or breakers of hedges, or cutters and destroyers of springes, but that sutche an owner shall wythin one qter of a yere put owt the same Tenant so offendynge, upon good proofe made in that behalfe, upon payne eury owner so offendinge shall forfette—xv., and that eury Subtenant so convicted shall forfett eury tyme—xxd.

Also yt ys comaundyd that no Inhitant from hence forthe shall let their logges or wood lye abrode in the Quene's highe waye, and the same not to be layde wythout his Evesdrop upon payne to forfet eury tyme—iijs. iiijd.

Also yt ys comaundyd the Baylif to warne the landeholders betwene Heres brydge and th'ende of John Webbe's garden to make their brookes as brode and as depe as they have bene in olde tymes, whitche be by or estymacon sixe or seaven foote, and the same to be done before michelmas next comynge, upon payne to forfet for eury Rodde not so done—xijd.

Also yt ys comaundyd to warne John Webbe to cutte and take awaye his bancke next adjoyninge vnto th'old Ryver, in bredth one yarde and in lengthe two Rodde, and to make the same as depe as it hath bene in owlde tyme and to make all the rest to the wynge of the brycke that cometh from the arche thre qters of an yearde in like maner of depthe, before the feaste of Pentecoste next ensuynge, upon payne to forfet for eury Rodde not so done— iijs. iiijd.

Also yt ys comaundyd to warne all the landeholders betwene the vpper ende of John Webbe's garden and the drawe brydge, to scower the backe Ryver and to make the same as depe and as brode as yt hath bene of olde tyme or at the lest twelfe foot wyde, before Michelmas next comynge, upon payne to forfet for eury Rodde not so donne—ijs.

Also yt ys comaunded to warne all the landeholders from Shorte brydge vnto the drawe brydge to drawe up all the hassocks and Rere rooshes before the feaste aforesayd, upon payne to for- fet for eurie rodde not so donne—iiijd.

Also yt ys comaundyd to warne the landholders of the Crowne to take vp the gate in the water lane and to wyde the sayd lane before the sayd feaste, upon payne to forfette—iijs. iiijd.

Also yt ys comaundyd that no Inhitant from henceforth permyt or suffer his or their cattayle to goe in the highe waye wythowt a folower, vpon payne to forfet for every offence so comytted—iijs. iiijd. And further that eury person from henceforthe kepe their hogges in their owne grownde and not to go comonly in the highe waye wythowt a kepar, upon payne to forfet for eury hogge—xijd.

Also yt ys comaundyd to warne Roger Jegons to take awaye his hogg coate and to sarve his hogges no more at the churche ponde in the Churche lane, vpon payne to forfet evry tyme—iijs. iiijd.

Also yt ys comaundyd to warne all the landeholders between Alets Crosse and Tylkell to scower their dytches on both the sydes of the way before the feast of Pentecoste next comynge, vpon payne to forfet for eury Rodde not done—iiijd.

Also yt ys comaundyd to warne Thomas Clerke th'elder to caste downe his bancke and to fyll vp the ditche that he hathe made in the highe waye, agenst his pale, betwene the house of Willam Sutton and Sterlinge leaz Style, before Christmas next, vpon payne to forfet—vs.

Also yt ys comaundyd to warne Thomas Tyll to open the comon dytche at his gate in Churche Streate, and to receve the fall of the water of the streate vpwarde, and Hilliary Johnson to receve the same of Thomas Tyll, and Willam Tyll to receve the same of Hillary Johnson, and Rychard True to receve the same of Willam Tyll, and Willam Saunder to receve the same of Rychard True, and Thomas Clerke th'elder to receve the same of Willam Saunder, and so the sayd comon dytche to goe throwghe owte the said Thomas Clerke's grownde tyll yt come to Sterlinge leaz dytche, as yt hathe done tyme owte of mynde, and this to be done before the feaste aforesayd, vpon payne eury one offendinge herein shall forfet—xxs.

Also yt ys comaundyd to warne Thomas Clerke th'elder to reforme his encrochment that he hath made in Starlinge leaz comon.dytche : that is to saye at the elme fyve foote, at the pere tre fyve foote, and at the comynge owte of the comon dytche nere a gardeyn sometyme in the occupacon of John Clerke, sixe foote and a halfe, and to sett his newe pale on the bancke where his oulde pale stode before, and to open and make the sayd comon dytche the lenghte of his newe pale, and so to go into Starlinge leaz comon dytche as yt was wont to doe next to the highe waye, before the feaste aforesayd, vpon payne to forfet for eury Rodde not so donne—xs.

Also yt ys comaundyd the Baylif to warne the sayd Thomas Clerke that he doe reforme his encrochement made wyth his newe pale in Sterlinge leaz dytche, from the ende of the garden of the sayd John Clerke vnto the garden nowe in the tenure of Rychard True, nyne foote, and to sett his fence where it was wont to be of oulde tyme, and further to receave all the fall of the water from George Cokerel into the same dytche, and further to make and scower the sayd dytche that the water mighte avoyde through the same as of olde tyme yt was wonte to doe, before the feaste aforesayd, vpon payne to forfet for eurye rodde not so donne—xs.

Also yt ys comaundyd to warne that no maner of persons shal have or kepe open their shope wyndowes on the Saboth daye in selling, uttering, or putting awaye any kinde of their victayles or wares after that hit hath ronge two peles, ether to morning service or evenyng, vpon payne to forfet eury tyme—xijd.

Also yt ys comaundyd that no maner of person shall take fysshe in the Ryver wyth nets, baskets, angels, or with any other kynde of engyne, vpon payne to forfet eury tyme—ijs.

Also yt ys comaundyd to warne that no maner of person kepe any greyhounds, hownds, spanells, except he maye dispend xls. by yeare on freholde, vpon payne to forfet—iijs. iiijd.

Also yt ys comaundyd that no maner of person shall kepe any hayes, ferrets, or presenets, onlesse they have game and grownde of their owne, upon payne to forfet eury tyme so offendinge—vs.

Also yt ys comaundyd to warne all the landeholders betwene Batfeld and nighe vnto Clement Sutton's gate to skouer their dytches in Churche lane, and then Willam Saunder to receve the water from the sayd dytche and to skoure his dytche, ayenst the next corte, upon payne to forfet for eury rodde not so donne—iiijd.

Also yt ys comaundyd to warne all the landholders betwene Rychard Coxcheif's howse and the churche ponde to scower the comon dytch wythin their yeards and not to permit any pryvie over the sayd dytche, vpon payne eury one so offending shall forfett—ijs.

Also yt ys comandyd to warne all the landholders betwene the churche ponde and Heres bridge to skower brookes and to amende them where nede ys, and not to cast on them any kinde of filth, vpon payne eury one so offendying shal forfette—iijs. iiijd.

The following is a specimen of a Court held nearly two centuries ago :—

Great Coggeshall, 1693.—View of Frank pledge with the first Court Baron of Nehemiah Lyde, Esquire, held for the Manor aforesaid on Tuesday in Whitsun week, being the 5th day of June, in the 5th year of the reign of William and Mary, by the grace of GOD King and Queen of England, Scotland, France and Ireland, and in the year of our Lord, 1693 ; and from thence adjourned to the 6th day of the said month of June, and held before John Cox, Esquire, Steward, there :—

| The Capital Pledges with the Homage . . . | Thomas Buxton John Cooke Isaac Dawes John Cable Robert Nicholls John Thorne Anthony Jepps John Ilger | Sworn. | . John Wilbore . John Taylor . Joseph Whitacre . Benjamin Pemberton . John Abbutt . John Cockerell . John Tunbridge | Sworn. |

who say upon their oaths that they give to the Lord for a Common Fine always on this day due by ancient custom, twelve pence.

On this day any inhabitant within this leet making default in his attendance is amerced [*i.e.* fined or put in mercy].

At this Court it is presented that all the inhabitants within this leet shall remove their trees lying in the king's way within 28 days after notice to them given by the Bailiff of the said Manor, and that in future no more trees placed in the said king's way shall remain beyond 28 days after notice thereof given by the bailiff of the said manor, under penalty of forfeiting for every load not removed for every week—1d.

- Also it is presented that the inhabitants within this leet shall remove their manure [*sterquiliana*] lying in the king's way within 6 days after notice to them given by the bailiff of the said manor, and that in future no more manure placed in the same king's way there, shall remain beyond 6 days after notice thereof given by the bailiff of the said manor, under pain of forfeiting to the lord for every offence in the premises—5s.

Also the Jury present that the water running from the ditch of William Enew now flows in the street called Stoneham Street, within this leet, to the annoyance of the people of the Lord and Lady the King and Queen, which said water ought to flow in —— [*strobe*] at Robins Bridge. Therefore it is presented that the said William Enew shall divert the water, running as aforesaid, to Robins Bridge aforesaid, under pain of forfeiting to the lord—10s.

Also they present that William Cox, Senior, James Warley, Elias Reynolds, Thomas Smith, James Gardiner, Thomas Belchamp, John Harvey and Anthony Jepps have not scoured their ditch leading from Buttfield to Stoneham Street. Therefore it is presented that they, well and sufficiently, scour their said ditch within 14 days after notice thereof, under pain of forfeiting for every rod not scoured—12d.

Also they present that Anthony Jepps, Thomas Beckwith, John Wilbore, Isaac Benthall and Martha Keble, widow, have not scoured their ditch near the yard of the said Martha Keable. Therefore it is presented that they well and sufficiently scour the said ditch within 14 days after notice thereof, under pain of forfeiting to the lord for every rod not scoured—12d.

Also it is presented that Henry Creeke shall remove and carry away earth and manure lying in his ditch near Starling Leeze within 12 days, under pain of forfeiting to the lord for every rod of ditch aforesaid—12d.

Also it is presented that Charles Guyon, Gent., Mark Guyon, —— Nash, widow, —— Hull, widow, William York, John Good-ay, —— Turner, widow, Richard Shortland, Gent., Elizabeth Guyon, widow, John Bowyer and William London, well and sufficiently, scour the Back ditch near adjoining their several yards within 10 days after notice thereof given, under pain of forfeiting for every perch not scoured, per week—11s.

Also the Jury humbly pray that the lord of the manor will deign to erect a pound for the leet aforesaid.

At this leet, Robert Cooke, John Hatton and Thomas Philbricke are elected to the office of Constable of this leet, and it is presented that they be sworn in that office before a Justice of the Peace for the county of Essex within 10 days next following the date of this Court.

And also John Cockerell, John Gooday and Isaac Dawes are elected to the office of Taster of Beer (Gustator Cerviciæ) and they are sworn well and faithfully to execute that office.

And also Thomas Picknett and Thomas Hance are elected to the office of Water Bailiffs.

And lastly, Thomas Overall and Jeremiah Huke are elected to the office of Leather Sealers.

Now of the Court Baron. At this Court it is presented by the Homage that according to the custom of the manor aforesaid, fines for whatsoever admissions to customary lands and tenements held of the manor aforesaid, either after death or upon alienation, are double the annual value of the rent payable to the lord of the manor aforesaid for the lands and tenements aforesaid, and no more for any particular admission. [This however is not the case with certain pieces of land, formerly waste of this manor ; these being subject to fines arbitrary].

Then follow the admissions which have become due by the deaths of copyhold tenants, or by reason of the sales of properties held of the manor.

Among various other matters presented at the courts, the following may be mentioned as some of the most interesting, or as tending to elucidate the past history of the town :—

1694—May 28. Thomas Cox ordered to repair his ditch in Stock Street.

Anthony Jepps ordered to open up the footpath in Crouches field, which he had obstructed.

1695—May 13. John Radley was ordered not to wash fish in the brook adjoining his mansion house in Church Street, and not to throw fish water in the brook. . Penalty, 2s. per week.

John Bales was ordered not to throw scouring suds [*aquas fullonicas*] in the king's way. Penalty, 1s. for every offence.

Nicholas Foster was ordered to amend his gutter opposite his house in Stoneham Street.

Anthony Jepps required to place a "wholve" or bridge next Hart Field.

George Larke to remove his hogs-sty [*hara*], being near the highway and a common nuisance.

1696—July 1st. Anthony Jepps to repair his ditch adjoining Crouches.

Henry Abbutt to scour his ditch in Dead Lane.

John Enew to scour his ditch adjoining Church Field.

Thomas Guyon and others, inhabitants of New Row, to repair their ditch.

John Hance presented for pouring scouring suds in the stream in Church Street.

1698—June 13th. Peter Everett ordered not to throw scouring suds in his yard so that they run in the pond called Church Pond. [This was a very common offence].

Hares Bridge being decayed, and Thomas Attwood being found liable to repair it, was presented that he was in mercy, 5s.

1699—May 29th. Several persons presented for allowing filth to flow into the Church Pond and in the stream running thereupon.

1700—May 20th. The constables ordered to repair the bridge adjoining Mans Green.

Presented that the gutters adjoining the Bird-in-Hand were not scoured.

John Barnard having erected a post and rail across "The Causy," was ordered to remove it.

1701—June 9th. John Cockerell, Matthew Fenn, Isaac Elliston, Mark Guyon and very many others required to scour the stream leading from Church Pond to Hares Bridge.

1706—May 13th. Certain of the inhabitants within the leet, presented for selling unwholesome meat.

1709—June 13th. Presented that the Back ditch, leading from the Wash or Wain of John Ludgater be scoured.

Presented that the Back ditch, from the Great River up to the Stone Bridge, and within the jurisdiction of the leet, was not scoured.

Presented that the Brick Bridge (*Pons Lateritius*), which separates Great Coggeshall from Little Coggeshall, is in great decay and defective repair; and ordered that the bridge aforesaid, within the jurisdiction of the leet, be well and sufficiently repaired before 25th July after the court.

Presented that the ditch running from Hares Bridge to the Brick Bridge adjoining and being within this leet was unscoured.

1711—May 21st. Presented that the Stream under the new market of the lord of the manor, up to "le Grate," within the leet, is not scoured.

1715—June 6th. Presented that John Fryitt, being a common baker of man's bread (*comunis pistor humani panis*) within this leet, at divers times in the month of May last, broke the assize of bread by making light bread and selling and uttering the same bread to divers persons within this leet, contrary to the form of the Statute. Fined 6s.

At this Court, a Taster *of Bread* and Ale was appointed; the previous appointments having extended to beer only.

1716—May 21st. It was ordered that William Cox, William Clarke and Mark Belsham Grimes, who at this court were appointed constables of this leet for this year following, well and sufficiently repair the stocks and cage (Cippos et carsarem calathariu) being within this leet within 40 days after notice thereof under pain of forfeiting to the lord in default thereof £5.

Robert Sutton, sen. presented for selling meel by false weight. Fine, 2s. 6d.

Several persons presented for breaking the assize of bread. Fines, 15s. in each case.

1720—June 6th. Presented that the hedge lately surrounding a place called Le Wayne Yard, of Mary Cox, widow, in Back Lane adjoining Peter's Well within this leet is in great decay, &c.

1730—May 18. Presented that the stream or Tye Mill brook, leading from Hares Bridge to the Old Ditch in the river of Great Coggeshall is unscowered, &c.

1731—June 7th. Presented that the Bridge, called the Turnpike Bridge or the Short Bridge, within this leet, is in great decay and that the surveyors [Supervisores Regie vie] ought to repair the same bridge. Order accordingly.

Presented that the water-course running from the workhouse in Stoneham Street is out of repair.

1733—May 14.* John Mount and Henry Turner are presented for not cutting the boughs hanging over the Church Pond within this leet to the annoyance of the water there, &c.

Several persons presented for not cleaning the brook leading from Church Pond to Hares Bridge, as well as for setting their necessary houses over the same brook.

Presented that the constables of this leet have constantly cleansed and scoured Church Pond and Peters' Well within the leet and the same being foul they were ordered to cleanse same.

The last View of Frank Pledge and General Court Baron of Nehemiah Lyde, Esq., was held 26 May, 1735.

The first View of Frank Pledge and first General Court Baron of Richard Du Cane, Esq., was held on the 14th June, 1736, and of Peter Du Cane, of 3rd June, 1745.

Henry Turner (Baptist teacher), presented for emptying stagnate water out of the Baptist Meeting House into Church Pond.

1747—June 8. The surveyors presented for not repairing the bridge, the wharfage and passage for the water out of the road at Mans Green, and also for not opening and repairing the Brook watercourse by the *Fishmarket.*

---

* This is the first Court the proceedings of which are entered in English.

1759—June 4th.   Constables presented for not setting up a post of correction.

1765—May 27th.   Constables presented for suffering shaving, fishing, and selling goods on the Lord's Day.

The cage and post of correction found to be out of repair.

1775—June 5th.   The Lord of the Manor presented for permitting the drain belonging to the *Old Hall*, otherwise the Shambles, to run into Shambles Lane.

The last View of Frank Pledge was held for this Manor on 24th May, 1779.   There were fifteen Capital Pledges, who on their oaths say " that they give and have always given to the Lord of the Manor at the leet day, always in certain, as well for every head of the tenants of this Manor as of the Capital Pledges and Deciners within the precincts of this leet, one penny each, amounting this year to 15 pence."   They then chose three constables, three persons as Ale Tasters and Bread Weighers, and two Water Bailiffs who were ordered to take care that the brooks and water passages were always cleansed, and that the water should not be turned out of the ancient courses, or impeded, under a penalty of 20s. for every neglect.   They also chose two Leather Sealers. They presented several persons for permitting filth to run into the Church Pond, and others for not cleaning their ditches.

Little Coggeshall.   The first view of Frank Pledge with the first Court Baron of Nehemiah Lyde, Esq., for the Manor of Little Coggeshall, was held on the 5th June, 1693.   Twelve persons were sworn as the ' Capital Pledges with the Homage.'

The principal presentments are with reference to the cleansing of ditches.   Two constables were appointed.

1730—May 18th.   The Brick Bridge which divides the parishes of Great and Little Coggeshall is presented to be in decay, and the Surveyors of the King's highway ordered to repair the same.

1734—June 3rd.   Presented that the Stocks * and Cage within this leet were out of repair, and the Constables were ordered to repair the same.

1738—May 22nd.   Presented that the Pound was out of repair.   Also that the Stock House was out of repair.

---

* These were on the top of Grange Hill, on the east side.   The field, No. 71, O. S., is called Stock Field.

1741—May 18th. Presented that Isaac Ludgater had obstructed an ancient watercourse leading from the well called Cockerells Well, adjoining to the Grange Hill, and he was commanded to remove the obstruction and open a free passage to the water running from the said well, so that the same might be conveyed within and through its usual channel, as anciently it had been, without any obstruction, into the Great River.

The last View of Frank Pledge was held on 24th May, 1779, when fifteen persons were sworn as the "Capital Pledges with the Homage;" two Constables were chosen; Edmund Wood was presented for carrying on the trade of a wheelwright in the king's highway, and for suffering his timber, &c. to lie on the highway; and it was also presented that the water running out of the ditch on the south-east corner of a field called Hare Field, into the ditch on the opposite side of the road, overflowed the road, and was a nuisance, and the Surveyors and Constables were ordered to make a drain for the water.

The following items are reproduced from Mr. Dale's *Annals.* The original document was formerly in the late Mr. Charles Smith's possession; the writer made every effort to learn from Mr. Smith what had become of the document, but could not obtain any information.

"Abstract taken out of the Court Rolles of the Mannors of Great Coggeshall and Little Coggeshall, of all such surrenders and deaths of customary tenants, wherein are expressed as well the yearely rent, paiable for their customary lands and tenements, as the fynes, which they respectively paid to the lord for their admittances to the same. 17 Rd. II. to 38 Hen. VIII. and 9 to 14 Eliz.

17 Richard II.—William Fuller surrended into the lord's hands, two parts of a tenement once called *Herings'* tenement, to the use of Richard Parker, to whom siesin is granted to hold to him and his heires, at the will of the lord, by the antient suites and customes. And he gave to the lord for a fyne, 20d. [In Church Street, occupied by Mr. D. Mount, between Swan Yard and Plummers.]

20 Richd. II.—At this court came Richard Dodding, and did take of the lord one parcel of land in litle Cherchfeild, over against his tenement, and also a footway from his garden to the lord's pond, called *Cherch pond*, to drawe water there. To holde

to him and his heires, paying yearely to the lord, 6d. Fine, per donation.

1 Hen. IV. (1399.)—The lord granted to Walter Hares a peece of land lying at the *Short bregge* nere the floudgates of *Tye Mill,* to hold from Michas. last for 100 years, paying to the lord yearly, Rent, 12d. Fine, 4d.

13 Hen. IV.—The lord granted to Robert Cardinall one messuage, with a little croft of land adjoyning, called the *Gate House.* To hold from Michas. last for 8 years, paying yearly to the *Ranger* of the Home Grange, 8s.

7 Hen. V. (1420.)—The lord granted to John Brooke and Mary his wife, a messuage, to hold from Michas. last for 10 years, paying to the *Priest of the Abbey,* yerely, Rent, 8s. Fine, 4d.

4 Hen. VI. (1426.)—The lord granted to John Cressing and Christian his wife, a messuage in Church Street, to hold from Easter next for 12 years, paying to the *Hog-heard* of the Abbey, yerely, Rent, 11s. Fine, 3d.

The lord granted to John Sawbyn, a messuage in Church Street, to hold from Midsummer next for 12 years, paying yearly to the *Singer* of the Abbey, Rent, 7s. Fine, 4d.

The lord granted to John Lawford a decaied cottage, with a pcell of a garden adjoining in Stonhey Strete, called the *Crouch House,* to hold from Easter next for 40 years, paying to the lord, yearly, Rent, 12d, Fine, 4d.

The lord granted to Walter Hares a messuage and a peece of meadow, lying next Sir William Coggeshall's meadow, called *Polerd's Mead,* and one shoppe in the market, to hold from Michas. last for 20 years, paying yearely to the lord, Rent, 29s. Fine, per donation.

2 Edwd. IV. (1462.)—Richard Bullocke died, seised in fee of one customary tent called *Moises,* holden by the rodde at the lord's will; and that Richd. is his sonne and heire, and 7 yeares old, who, by Robert Fabian and John Fabian, is admitted tenant, and paies to the lord for a fine, 20d.; and they pray to occupy the land untill his full age, and for that license they gave to the lord for a fine, 6d.

10 Edwd. IV.—The lord granted to Thomas Clerke and Christian his wife, 2 tents, lying together over against Cogshall markett, and a cottage within the market-place, called the *Castell of Gynes,* and a garden thereto annexed, Rent, 32s. Fine, 20d.

12 Edwd. IV.—The lord granted to Richard Chapman, Sen., a messuage and curtilage adjoining, as it is enclosed, called *Lavender*, lying over against the markett of Cogshall, betweene the lord's tent called the *Cocke*, on the east, and the messuage of Wm. Doreward, Esq., west, paying to the lord, yearly rent, 13s. 4d. Fine, 13d.

21 Edwd. IV.—The lord demised to John Trewe, a field called *Starlings Lese*.

21 Edwd. IV.—John Windlove died, seized in fee of a tenement called *Vernolds*, *alias Heywards*, in Cogshall magna, after whose death noe herriott falls to the lord, because hee had noe living creature; but hee surrendered it to the use of Christian his daughter.

7 Hen. VII. (1492.)—The lord, upon John Turner's surrender, admitted John Paicock to a garden and pcell of land, pcell of Nether Church Field, paying yearly, 1 *clove gilly floure*, 2 *capons*.

13 Hen. VII.—The lord granted to Thomas Cavill one piece of pasture, pcell of a field called *Ingring-downe*, betwene the lord's bankes, called Robin's brooke and Ingring-downe, paying to the lord, yearely, 9s. and 6l. pepper.

4 Hen. VIII. (1513.)—The lord granted out of his lands one peece of land or garden called pcell of *Old church*.feild, lying in Church Street, one head abutting upon Over-church-feild lane, and the other upon the garden and messuage of Agnes Clerke, wid., by the antient rent of 6d. Fine, one capon.

5 Hen. VIII.—The lord granted, out of his hands, to John Bland, a cottage and customary yard adjoining, once John Sweeting's, in *Gallow Strete*.

38 Hen. VIII.—Robert Whepsted surrendered one messuage with a garden, adjoining Cogshall market."

The Manor of Coggeshall Hall.

THE Manor of Coggeshall Hall seems to have comprehended what in *Domesday Book* is mentioned thus:—"In Coggeshala tenuit Sancta Trinitas * iii virgates terre, tempore regis Edwardi et modo similiter. Semper ii carucate. Tunc i bordarius, modo viii. Tunc iii servi, modo i. viii acres prati. i molendinum. Et valuit lx solidos in dominio, iv runcini, iii animalia. xx oves, vii porci;" which is translated:—"The Holy Trinity held in Coggeshall 3 yard lands, in the time of King Edward and now likewise. Always two teams. Then one bordar, now 8. Then 3 serfs, now one. Eight acres of pasture. One mill. And it is worth 60s. In the demesne. Four horses, three beasts, 20 sheep, seven swine."

This estate was held by the Cathedral Church of Canterbury for the sustenance of the monks.

---

* The grant to the Cathedral Church of Canterbury was in these words:—
"Ego Godwinus et Wolgith, concedente et consentiente Domino meo Rege Edwardo, donanus Ecclesiæ Christi in Dorobernia partem terre juris nostri nomine Stigestede et Coggashael in East Sexia, liberas ab omni seculari servitute, sicut Ego a presato Domino meo Rege Edwardo et a Patre ejus hactenus tenui. Si quis erit a jure ejusdem Ecclesiæ abstulerit, auferat ei Deus gloriam suam."—*Ex. M.S. in Bibl Col., Corp., Cant.* It is extant, though in a somewhat different manner, in *W. Thorne, Decem. Script, Col., 2224;* and in the *Antiq. of Canterb., p. 39, Append.,* where Wolgith is stiled "relicta Elfwine," *i.e.* widow of Elfwine, most probably some great Saxon lord, in whose right or in her own, Wolfgith had an interest in these lands. (*Morant.*)

Domesday Book also mentions that "Tedricus tenet i hidam et dimid' pro escangio de Cogeshala quod tenuit Tiselinus. Tunc ii carucate, modo nulla. Tunc tres bordarü, modo nullus. Silva iii porcis, xii acre prati. Tunc valuit xx solidos, modo x ; " or in English :—Tedric holds one hide and a half by exchange, for [or of] Coggeshall, which was held by Tiselinus. Then two teams, now none. Then 3 bordars, now none. Wood for 3 swine. 12 acres of meadow. Then it was worth 20 shillings, now ten.

It may be that the Manor of Coggeshall Hall comprised the estate of Tedricus [Tedricus Pointell], and it is worthy of note that the way leading from the Grange Hill to the Hamlet is known as " Pointell's Street," and Mr. Barnard's Mill is called " Pointells Mill."

The Manor of Coggeshall Hall was held in the 13th century by a family surnamed De Coggeshall, and possibly much earlier, for there was a Sir Thomas de Coggeshall living in the reign of King Stephen, and this Sir Thomas held large estates in the county of Essex.

Sir Ralph de Coggeshall died in the 33rd year of King Edw. I., possessed of Coggeshall Hall, which he held partly of John Filoll and partly of the Abbots of Coggeshall and Westminster and of William atte Napleton.

John de Coggeshall, the son and heir of Sir Ralph, died in the 13th year of King Edw. II., seized of a capital messuage, a water mill, 8 and a half acres of wood, 203 acres of arable land, 6 acres of meadow, 3 acres of pasture, and 6s. 8d. rent; which property he held of John Filloll, by the service of half a knight's fee and the yearly rent of 64s. 4d. He also held of the Abbot of Westminster, by the service of 16s. per annum, 33 acres of arable, 1 acre of meadow, 4 acres of pasture, a grinding house with a barrel or wheel, a pond, and 2s. 7d. rent. And of the Abbot of Coggeshall, by knight's service, 44 acres of arable with 3s. rent. And of the same abbot in socage, 2 granges, 2 chambers, a garden and 5 acres of arable, by the service of 17s. 2d. per annum.

Sir John de Coggeshall, son of the before-mentioned John, held this property at the time of his decease in 1361, and he was succeeded by his son and heir,

Sir Henry de Coggeshall, who died in 1375; from him the estate devolved upon

Sir William de Coggeshall, who, dying at Codham Hall,

Wethersfield, in the early part of the reign of King Henry VI., left four daughters his co-heiresses, viz. : Blanch, who married John Doreward ; Eleanor or Alice, who married Sir John Tyrrell ; Margaret, who married William Bateman, Esq., and afterwards John Roppeley, Esq. ; and Maud, who married Robert Dacre, Esq., and afterwards John St. George.

John Doreward, Esq., by his marriage with Blanch Coggeshall, became possessed of Coggeshall Hall, and on his death, about 1426, his eldest son,

John Doreward became the owner, and so remained till his death in 1476, when it descended to his son,

John Doreward, then aged 21 years. He held the Manor of Coggeshall Hall, with two water mills called Pointell Mell and Estford * Mell, also 200 acres of arable, 100 acres of meadow, and 10 acres of wood in Coggeshall, Markeshall, Colne, Feering, Kelvedon, Blackwater, Inworth, Stisted and Fordham-forth ; and 32 messuages, with the appurtenances, in Coggeshall. John Doreward died in 1495, having been married to Margaret Lyhert, by whom however he had no issue, and on her death the estate passed to his neices, daughters of his sister Elizabeth, viz. : Margaret, the wife of Nicholas Bewpre, aged 19. Elizabeth, the wife of Henry Thursbie, Esq., aged 18 ; and Christian, wife of John de Vere, aged 14.

Ralph Chamberlayn and Edward Chamberlayn, the trustees of the property, on the 27th Ayril, 1513, sold the reversion, after the death of Margaret Doreward, (afterwards the wife of Sir James Hobert, Knt.,) for £172, to

Sir Robert Southwell, of Filiols Hall or Felix Hall in Kelvedon, who died 30th March, 1515, leaving as his heir his nephew,

Richard Southwell, (son of his brother Francis), then aged 10 years ; but as Sir Robert died without male issue, this estate and Filiols Hall escheated to the Crown.

Henry VIII., on the 20th April, 1539, granted the same properties to Richard Long, Esq., but as his son, Henry Long, died without issue, they passed to his four sisters, of whom the eldest, Elizabeth, brought them in marriage to her husband,

Sir William Russell, by whom, on 18th May, 1584, they were sold to

---

* Easterford, the old name of Kelvedon.

Henry, Earl of Kent; George, Earl of Cumberland; and Robert, Earl of Sussex, as trustees for Sir Thomas Cecill, fifth and youngest son of Thomas, Earl of Exeter. Sir Thomas married Ann, daughter of Sir Robert Lee, Alderman of London, by whom he had Benjamin, Charles, Dorothy and Anne. Dorothy, the eldest and last surviving daughter, brought the estate in marriage to Thomas Cudmore, Esq. (son of John Cudmore, Esq., of Kelvedon, Barrister-at-law). Their son, Thomas, married Anne, daughter of John Anger, Esq., of Boxted, and had by her,

John Cudmore, Esq., who died, 8th December, 1630, holding this Manor of the king, in capite by knight's service, at which time it was worth £6 13s. 4d. John, his eldest son and heir, dying without issue, was succeeded by his next brother,

Thomas Cudmore, Esq., who died, 25th July, 1637. Thomas, a posthumous son, born 3rd January following, inherited next. By his will he devised this Manor to one Latham, subject to some power vested in his two daughters, who jointly with Latham, sold this estate to

— Blackmore, Esq., of Lincolns Inn, and he in turn sold it to

Hugh Raymond, Esq., a Director of the South Sea Coy., from whom it passed to

Jones Raymond, Esq., who owned it about 1768.

The Hall and demesne lands have for many years been part of the estate of the Western family, whose seat is at Felix Hall, Kelvedon. Their arms are :—Sable, a chevron between 2 crescents in chief and a trefoil slipped in base. Crest—a demi lion, or., in its dexter paw a trefoil slipped vert. Motto—*Nec temere nec timide.* The present representative of the family is Sir Thomas Charles Callis Western, 3rd Baronet; he succeeded on the death of his father, Sir Thomas Sutton Western, in 1877. The present baronet married, in 1883, Elizabeth Ellen, eldest daughter of the late T. Newton, Esq.

The lordship of the Manor of Coggeshall, otherwise Coggeshall Hall, consisting of the seignory, was severed from the demesne lands during the latter part of last century or the beginning of the present. About 1775, the Manor belonged to Daniel Mathew, Esq., and on his death a few years later, it was sold by order of the Court of Chancery, by, among others, Edward Mathew, Esq., and the Right Honourable Lady Jane Mathew, his wife, Mary Mathew, widow, Daniel Byam Mathew, Esq., George

Mathew, Esq., Mary Mathew, spinster, Louisa Mathew, spinster, Samuel Gambier, Esq. and Jane his wife, late Jane Mathew, spinster, and Brownlow Mathew, Esq.; the purchaser being Samuel Tyssen, Esq., who, in 1786, sold it to Abram Newman, Esq.

Newman made his will in 1796, and gave the Manor to his daughter Jane, the wife of William Thoyts, whose trustees sold it in 1842, to James Cuddon, Esq. His sons, Francis Thomas Cuddon and James Cuddon, Esqrs., succeeded to it on the death of their father. It was sold by them to the Rev. Walter Trevelyan Bullock, in whose family it remained until 1879, when it was sold to C. J. Daintree, Esq., of Petworth, Sussex, the present lord.

The following is an epitome of an extract of the Records of the Courts held for the Manor in the time of King Henry VIII. The extract [a copy in the writer's possession], is on parchment, and is bound with some records relating to the Manor of Felix Hall, and is now in the Public Record Office, Bundle 58, No. 726 Duchy of Lancaster Court Rolls.

Court held on Wednesday in Whitsun week, 17 Henry VIII. The jury were John Copscheff, Richard Peverell, in right of his wife, Robert Goldwire, John Clerk, Robert Dawes, John Ayleward, Christopher Pyper, John Borle, William Bery [John Porter struck through and marked dead], John Waleis, Andrew Turvy, Thomas Clerk, Robert Rande.

The bailiff is ordered to distrain John Fabian, of Bekenham, so that he may be at the court to show in what right he holds one tenement in Poyntell Street, held of the Lord by the rent of ——, and in what manner he holds two crofts there, held by the rent of 4s. per annum, after the death of John Fabian, of London, his father, so that he may satisfy the relief fealty, and other services.

The bailiff is also ordered to distrain the lands, tenements, and tenters in Poyntell Street, called Gulles, late of Sir John Sharp Knight, deceased, and before that of Christopher Sharp, his father held of the Lord by the rent of £1 8s. 1od. per annum.

The death was presented of John Porter, who held a field divided by a fence, and called Longlond, containing by estimation 22 acres and 3 roods adjoining land called Shadwell, and it was stated that John Porter was his son and heir, and he being a minor, of the age of 13 years or thereabouts, was admitted by his mother, Margaret Purcas, the wife of John Purcas.

Robert Goldewer died before this court, possessed of a tenement near Hare's Bridge [Breg], held of the Lord by the rent of 4s. per annum, also a piece of pasture in Braxted Mede by the rent of 2s. per annum.

Thomas Waleys, who had also died before this court, held one tenement called Geno . . . s, held by the rent of 2s. and also certain land called *Bancroft*, by the rent of 6d.

The bailiff was commanded to distrain John Paycock upon a garden in Galoiostrete (Gallows or East Street), late belonging to John Chapman Senior, held of the lord by the rent of 8d. per annum ; and also upon a tenement and garden late in the tenure of John Paycock, cousin of his father, lying next the orchard of William Garrard, held by the rent of 12d. so that the services due to the lord of the manor might be duly performed.

Court held 14 Henry VIII.

The bailiff was ordered to warn the Abbot of Coggeshall to show in what manner he held all his lands and tenements in Great and Little Coggeshall, and to be at the next court to produce his documents of title.

Court held 17 Henry VIII.

There is a reference to a mansion in Stoneham Street, which appears to have belonged to William Glover, of Thaxted, and Isabel his wife, late the wife of Richard Leman. They surrendered the property to Robert Lamberd.

Thomas Paycock, aged 12, was the son and heir of Robert Paycock, deceased, who died possessed of *Maykynes*, then late belonging to John Paycock, his cousin, adjoining the inn called *The Dragon*, on the one part and a tenement, then of Richard Fellex, formerly of Wm. Sponer, called *Mabsons*, on the other part.

The rental of the copyhold and freehold tenants of the Manor, dated in 1789, contains much valuable information and is considered well worthy of reproduction in these pages, and from it it will be seen that the Manor was of considerable extent, and comprised the seignory of lands in Great Coggeshall, Little Coggeshall, Bradwell, Markshall, Feering, Kelvedon and Inworth. The copyhold tenure of nearly all the properties in the Manor has been extinguished by enfranchisement, and the value of the Manor has consequently been reduced to a minimum.

The Manor of COGGESHALL, other- \ wise COGGESHALL HALL.} Rental of the Copyhold and Freehold Estates held of the said Manor.

NO.	ANNUAL RENTS. £ s. d.	OWNERS OF THE ESTATE AT MICHAS., 1789.	OCCUPIERS THEREOF AT MICHAS., 1789.	DESCRIPTION OF THE COPYHOLD PREMISES.
1	0 2 2	Henry Blackbone	Himself and others	Two cottages and one close of arable land containing two acres, lying at Blest End, in Bradwell, next Coggeshall, adjoining No. 3.
2	0 0 4	Andrew Blackbone		A cottage next Souths Lane, at Blest End, in Bradwell, next Coggeshall, adjoining to No. 3.
3	0 1 6	Richard White	Robert Chaulkey	A messuage or tenement with a barn, stable, and orchard, at Blest End, in Bradwell, next Coggeshall, adjoining No. 1.
4	0 2 10	Do.	Do.	Two closes of arable land containing four acres, belonging and adjoining to No. 3.
5	0 3 4	Henry Skingley	Himself	Gullmore meadow containing three acres, adjoining to lands called *Cross path field*, belonging to Coxall Hall farm, towards the east in Little Coggeshall.
6	0 11 6	Do.	Do.	Three crofts of arable land formerly called *Gulls Crofts* now *Springfields*, and Six Acre Piece, in Little Coggeshall, adjoining to Gullmore meadow towards the south, and Pointoll river towards the east, containing together nine acres.
7	0 13 4	Do.	Do.	A cottage, barn, and twenty-two acres of arable land, lying at Cuthedge, in Little Coggeshall, called *Cutlers Crofts*.
8	0 5 0	Do.	Do.	A croft of arable land called *Rands*, containing four acres, in Little Coggeshall, adjoining to the road leading to Kelvedon towards the east, and to the road leading to Cuthedge towards the north, and to lands belonging to Scrips farm towards the west and south.
9	0 11 6	Do.	Do. and others	A cottage made into two tenements, in Pointwell Mill Lane, and a parcel of arable land adjoining thereto, formerly called *Samsonsfield* now *Tainter Plott* and a croft of arable land adjoining thereto, next the river, containing together nine acres.

No.						Description
10	0	2	0	Do.	Do.	A croft of arable land called *Norfolks*, adjoining to Cutlers Crofts, No. 7, containing two acres.
11	0	0	6	Do.	Do.	A garden plot, lying before the messuage called *New House*, No. 43, containing about ten rods of ground.
12	0	2	6	Emerson Cornwell	Richard Appleton	A messuage situate in Great Coggeshall, in a place called the *Gravell*, adjoining to No. 36, on the part of west.
13	0	9	10	James Corder	Habakkuk Layman	Twelve acres of arable land, formerly part of Bancrofts farm, in Kelvedon, adjoining to No. 29.
14	0	2	1	Sarah Choate, Wo.	John Birkin	A tenement called *Simons*, in Stoneham Street, Great Coggeshall, adjoining to No. 27.
15	0	5	0	Peter Du Cane, Jun., Esq.	Andrew Blackbone	A messuage, barn, and four closes of arable land, in Little Coggeshall, formerly called *Sherleys* now called *Burnt House*, containing fifteen acres.
16	0	1	7	Robert Evens	Mary Evens, Wo.	A pantry, yard, and entry, laid to and used with the messuage of the sd. Robert Evans, in Market End, in Gt. Coggeshall, formerly part of the premises No. 24.
17	0	2	0	Osgood Hanbury Esq.	Samuel Harrison	Five acres of land called *Brookmans* otherwise *Bakers*, situate at Stock Street, in Great Coggeshall.
18	0	6	0	Filmer Honeywood, Esq.	John Tottman	A farm called *Marigolds*, at Marks Hall, containing — acres.
19	0	2	0	Do.	Gooday Pudney	A croft of land called *Shermans*, containing — acres, in Feering, part of the farm called *Herrings*.
20	0	2	3	Fisher Unwin	Sarah Harrison, Wo.	A messuage and premises called the *White Hart*, in Great Coggeshall.
21	0	10	4	Do.	Thomas Ellisdon and others	A messuage adjoining to the White Hart called the *Trueblue.*
22	0	2	3	Do.	Thomas Heward	A messuage adjoining to the Trueblue formerly called the *Green Dragon.*
23	0	4	6	Do.	Himself	A messuage and divers outhouses and buildings, called the *Cellar*, adjoining to the Green Dragon, now a brew office and storehouses.

OWNERS OF THE ESTATES AT MICHAS., 1789.	OCCUPIERS THEREOF AT MICHAS., 1789.	DESCRIPTION OF THE COPYHOLD PREMISES.
John Harrington	John Harrington, Jun.	A messuage, barn, stable, and seven closes of arable and pasture land, called *Mockbeggars*, with a chaceway lying in Feering, and containing twenty-eight acres.
Do.	Do.	A barn and four closes of arable and woodland, called *Greensteds*, adjoining to Mockbeggars, lying in Feering, and containing twenty-eight acres.
William Townsend	Thomas Bennet	A small piece of ground used for a garden, belonging to a freehold messuage, situate in Gt. Coggeshall, opposite the *White Hart*.
Thomas Hutley	Himself	A cottage called *Goldcuers*, situate at Hares Bridge, in Gt. Coggeshall.
James Whitaker	Himself and others	A messuage now divided into several tenements, called *Durdens*, in East Street, Gt. Coggeshall.
Thomas Argent Powell	Joseph Clerk and J. Sayer	Two tenements in Stoncham Street, in Great Coggeshall, adjoining to No. 14.
William Raven	Joseph Docwra	Lands in Inworth, called *Longlands*, *Messingfield*, and *Oynes Mead*, containing twenty-six acres, with a potash office thereon.
John Russell, Esq.	Thomas Lake	Lands called *Dobernells* and *Bancrofts*, with a barn thereon, belonging to the farm called the *Watering farm*, in Kelvedon, containing — acres, and adjoining to No. 13.
Abraham Totman	Stephen Leaper	A toft and garden at Hares Bridge, in Gt. Coggeshall, adjoining to No. 27.
Thomas Unwin	Thos. Carrington and another	A messuage called *Wilcocks* or the *Cornerhouse* (part thereof the Redlion Alehouse), at Market End, Gt. Coggeshall.
Thomas Whitaker	Himself	A messuage called the *Dyehouse*, in East Street, in Gt. Coggeshall (part thereof was formerly pulled down to make a gateway to his dwellinghouse), and adjoining to No. 28.
William Frost and his wife	Mark Guyon	Lands called the *Mount lands*, in Gt. Coggeshall, whereon a dovehouse lately stood, containing eight acres, more or less.

Description of the Freehold Premises.

No.	£	s.	d.	Owner	Occupier	Description
36	0	5	6	Matthias Gardner	Himself	A messuage and yard, situate in the Gravel, in Gt. Coggeshall, adjoining to No. 12.
37	0	3	8	John Webb	William Thorby	A messuage now divided into several tenements, called *Shogels*, in East Street, in Gt. Coggeshall.
38	0	15	0	John Bullock, Esq.	Daniel Barnard	A mill called *Pointell Mill*, in Little Coggeshall, with a parcel of meadow ground.
39	0	0	5	Mary Brewer, Wo.	Herself	Two tenements adjoining to Pointell Mill, in Little Coggeshall.
40	0	1	3	Henry Skingley	Himself	Two tenements called *Gofts*, in Pointell Street, in do., adjoining to No. 43.
41	0	2	0	Samuel Payne	Himself	The *Swan* Inn and Premises, in Kelvedon.
42	0	2	0	Do.	Do.	A tenement and yard laid to the Swan Inn.
43	0	15	6	Henry Skingley	Himself	A messuage called *Newhouse*, in Pointell Street, with a barn, stable, orchard, and three crofts of arable and pasture land, containing twelve acres.
44	0	5	4	Do.		A messuage divided into two tenements, with a garden and orchard, called *Mills*, lying opposite Pointells Mill, and adjoining to No 9.
45	0	2	0	Robert Appleby	Himself	A messuage called *Grangers*, in East Street, in Gt. Coggeshall, adjoining to No. 66.
46	0	1	0	William Gladwin	Henry Skingley	A messuage and premises, called the *Green Man*, in Church Street, in Gt. Coggeshall, formerly *Wybers*.
47	0	0	6	Mark Guyon	John Hunt	A messuage called the *Swan and* —, in East Street, Gt. Coggeshall, adjoining to No. 57.
48	0	2	0	Anthony Jepp	Himself	A messuage called *Mabsons*, in Market End, Great Coggeshall, adjoining to No. 20, sold to Unwin.
49	0	6	8	Osgood Hanbury, Esq.	Saml. Harrison	A messuage and six closes of land, at Stock Street, in Gt. Coggeshall, called *Widowsons*.
50	0	5	6	The Trustees of the Essex Turnpikes		A tenement formerly called the *Unicorn*, in Kelvedon, pulled down to widen the road.

NO.	ANNUAL RENTS. £ s. d.	OWNERS OF THE ESTATES AT MICHAS., 1789.	OCCUPIERS THEREOF AT MICHAS., 1789.	DESCRIPTION OF THE FREEHOLD PREMISES.
51	0 1 10	John Smith	Himself	A messuage called *Eneæus*, in East Street, in Gt. Coggeshall, adjoining to No. 37.
52	0 0 11	Do.	Do. and others	Two tenements, adjoining to No. 51.
53	0 0 5½	Do.	Wm. Thompson	One tenement, adjoining to No. 52, formerly of Thomas Clarke.
54	0 0 5½	Do.	Do.	One other tenement, adjoining to No. 53, formerly of Robert Clarke.
55	0 0 8	Richard King	Himself and others	A messuage and malt office, in Kelvedon, called *Pitmans*.
56	0 4 0	William Wallis	Andrew Blackbone	A messuage and three crofts of lands, called *Haywards*, near Cuthedge, in Little Coggeshall, containing fourteen acres.
57	0 1 0	Daniel King	James Paisey	A messuage called *Barrows*, in East Street, in Gt. Coggeshall, adjoining to No. 47.
58	0 5 0	Henry Lambe	Martha Revett. Wo.	A messuage and premises, called the *Star*, in Kelvedon.
59	0 0 6	Sarah Livermore	John Clift	A moiety of a messuage, in East Street, in Great Coggeshall, now divided.
60	0 0 6	Mary Day and Wm. Sansum	William Sansum	A moiety of same premises.
61	0 1 0	John Howlett	Himself	A tenement in Pointell Mill Lane, in Little Coggeshall, called *Cannus Hall*, adjoining to No. 39.
62	0 2 0	William Raven	Joseph Docwra	A barn and lands, in Inworth, late *Ardlics*, at Oynes Brook, adjoining to No. 30.
63	0 1 6	Jeremiah Raven	Thomas Lake	A tenement called *Woods*, in Kelvedon:
64	0 6 8	John Russell, Esq.		A messuage and lands called *Tanners*, on the Watering farm, in Kelvedon.
65	0 2 6	Henry Skingley	Himself	Lands called *Peaslands*, in Gt. Coggeshall, whereon a barn lately stood, near the road leading to Earls Colne.

No.	Owner	Occupier	Description	£	s.	d.
66	Ann Sandford, Spr.	Herself	A messuage, in East Street, in Gt. Coggeshall, next the *Crown* Alehouse.	0	2	0
67	John Playel	Samuel Musket	A moiety of a tenement called *Gofts*, in Pointell Street, adjoining No. 40.	0	0	4
68	Samuel Sullings	Himself	A moiety of same premises which are now divided.	0	0	8
69	Thomas Stammers	Himself	A barn and croft of land called *Buttal Land*, in —	0	2	0
70	Abraham Totman	Stephen Leaper	A tenement, near Hares Bridge, in Gt. Coggeshall, adjoining to No. 32.	0	4	0
71	John Scott, Esq.	Himself	A barn and lands, called *Cranbourn Moors*, at the Worlds-end, in Inworth.	0	3	0
72	Fisher Unwin	James Bickmore	A messuage and malt office, and orchard, next the *Star*, in Kelvedon, No. 58.	0	8	8
73	Saml. Walker		Brooke Meadow, Homefield, Barnold Croft, in —	0	2	6
74	Thos. B. Bramstone, Esq. and others, Trustees for a Lectureship, at Watford	Thomas Knight	A water mill called *Easter Mill*, and seven pieces of land and meadow, in Kelvedon and Inworth.	0	8	0
75	Henry Shetelworth		A messuage, in Gull Lane, in Little Coggeshall, called *Old Hall*, opposite No. —	0	5	0
76	Do.		A messuage, adjoining and laid to No. 75, called *Copthall*.	0	1	0
77	Robert Levitt	Andrew Blackbone	Three crofts of land called — *field* and *Feering Crofts*, in Little Coggeshall and Feering, near Blest End.	0	4	0
				18	2	8

A map of this Manor, dated 1758, was in the possession of the late Mr. Charles Smith. The writer has been permitted to make a copy of this valuable Survey. Maps of the Manors of Great Coggeshall and Little Coggeshall were made about the same time that the Coggeshall Hall Manorial Survey was taken, but it is not known in whose custody they now are.

THE CONGREGATIONAL CHAPEL.

The Independents.

THE Independents are a religious denomination whose distinctive ecclesiastical principle is that the individual congregation is a society strictly voluntary and self-governing. Among the nonconforming bodies in this town the Independents, or Congregationalists, have for upwards of two centuries held the leading position.

The Acts of King Charles II. by their severity did much to increase the spirit of nonconformity, the seeds of which may be said to have been sown in the reign of Queen Elizabeth by the puritans—a religious body of persons who, severing themselves from the Catholic church, Roman and Anglican, desired to be conformed in doctrine and polity to those churches of the Continent that were by them considered to be pre-eminently reformed.

The first Independent of any prominence was one Robert Brown, son of Anthony Brown, of Tolthorp, in Rutlandshire. He was born in 1550, educated at Cambridge, and afterwards followed the profession of a schoolmaster in Southwark. His denunciation of the Established Church was of a most virulent character, and for his conduct in this respect he was excommunicated by the Bishop of Peterborough. The solemnity of the censure effected his reformation, and about 1590 he was rector of a parish in Northamptonshire. Here, however, his passionate disposition lead him into trouble with the parish constable over a question of rates, resulting ultimately in blows, for which offence, combined with his insolence to the magistrates before whom he was charged, he was committed to gaol, where he died, in 1630, at the advanced age of 80 years; a great part of his life having been spent in confinement in no fewer than 32 prisons.

Robert Brown has been thus shortly alluded to as the parish registers show that he had some followers here ; for instance, we find under baptisms, " 1615, Aug. 13, Elizabeth, daughter of Christopher Pennock, a Brownist excommunicate contemptuous "; " 1615, Nov. 5, Mary, daughter of Moses Ram, an obstinate Brownist "; " 1615, Dec. 24, Martha, daughter of Daniel Pennock, a Brownist."

The first houses at Coggeshall to which licenses were granted under the Declaration of Indulgence, issued by King Charles II. in 1672, were those of John Croe, Thomas Lowry, Matthew Ellistone and William Grove; the licensed teachers being John Sammes, Thomas Lowry, Matthew Ellistone, William Grove and Thomas Millaway ; the last of whom was licensed to be a general congregational teacher.

The first meeting house of a public character appears to have been a converted barn in East Street, mentioned in the records of the Independents. In this document mention is made of Mr. Sammes having been ejected from his position in the parish church, and, as his followers " could not meet where they formerly did, they hired a barn in East Street, which they converted into a Meeting House."

In the early years of last century the Independents, who included among their number some of the wealthiest inhabitants of the place, having outgrown their humble edifice in East Street, raised a fund and purchased from Henry Ennew and Elizabeth his wife, for £77 10s. two messuages built under one roof with the gardens, &c., called " Old Ales," situate in Stoneham Street. The property was conveyed to Isaac Buxton, of Great Coggeshall, clothier, and Thomas Nicholls, yeoman, and William Brown, gentleman, of Little Coggeshall, on the 20th April, 1710. The conveyance contains several genealogical items relating to the Ennew family. By another deed of the same date the fee farm rent of £1 11s. 8d., payable to Morden College, which was charged on this and other property, was to be thenceforth payable out of a close of land containing about two acres, also parcel or reputed parcel of the property known as "Old Ales." The cottages were pulled down, and on the site there was erected the present chapel. The building proceeded with such expedition that on the 31st August, 1710, the chapel was registered in the Bishop of London's Registry "as a meeting house for religious worship of Protestant Dissenters from the Church of England, commonly called Independents."

The Deed of Settlement, declaring the trusts of the property, is dated the 9th of March, 1715, and is made between Isaac Buxton, of Great Coggeshall, clothier; Thomas Nichols, of Great Coggeshall, yeoman, and William Brown, of Great Coggeshall, gentleman, of the one part; and Nehemiah Lyde, of Hackney, Esq., Richard Ducane, of the City of London, Esq., Edward Bentley, of Great Coggeshall, clerk, John Taylor, Senior, of Great Coggeshall, glazier, John Barnard, Sen., of the same place, draper, John Cooper, of Kelvedon, gentleman, William Leppingwell, of the same place, gentleman, Thomas Potter, Sen., of Messing, gentleman, Moses Richardson, of Pattiswick, gentleman, Richard Brewer, of Great Coggeshall, yeoman, William Barrick, of Feering, yeoman, and Jeremiah Raven, of the same place, yeoman, of the other part. The Trust Deed declares that the trustees shall hold the property in trust, to permit the building or meeting-house to be used as a meeting-house or meeting-place for the worship of Almighty GOD by the people of that congregation or society for the time being, of which Edward Bentley was then pastor or minister, and whereof his successor and successors for the time being shall be pastor or pastors, and for such other persons as should attend the ministry there. There is power for the trustees, or the major part of them, to make orders and agreements for deciding controversies arising between members of the congregation concerning the pews. When the number of trustees should be reduced to five the continuing trustees were to appoint new trustees.

In 1716, the congregation consisted of 700 hearers, of whom 43 were voters for the county, and 19 came under the denomination of gentlemen, as appears by a return made by Lord Barrington.

The trustees, appointed in 1727, were John Brooks (Feering), Thomas Buxton, John Buxton, Joseph Thetford, George Abbot, John Savill (Feering), Edward Sach, Abraham Cook, Robert Salmon, George Brett, Thomas Porter (Inworth), Isaac Buxton, Jun., (Feering) and John Willsher (Marks Tey).

On the 16th of October, 1765, the only surviving trustees, viz. Thomas Buxton, George Abbott, John Savill, George Brett, and Isaac Buxton, the younger, appointed as the new trustees, Robert Salmon, Sen., Thomas Unwin, Sen., William Unwin, Sen., Thomas Unwin, Jun., William Unwin, Jun., William Sandford, Edward Powell, John Abbott, Jonathan Peacock, Edward Sach, Thomas Babbs, Sen., William Newton, Sen., Thomas Lay, Edward Walford, Ephraim Willsher, Daniel Halls, and George Jay, Jun. This deed contains special provision for setting apart pews to members of the congregation.

On the 13th of May, 1777, John Godfrey, William Babbs, Habbakuk Layman, Fisher Unwin, Jordan Unwin, Stephen Unwin, Edward Sach, John Wright, Henry Shetelworth, Sen., John Raven, Thomas Babbs, Thomas Powell, Henry Shetelworth, Jun., George Willsher, Thomas Willsher, John Everett, Haddon Rudkin and Edward Evans were appointed new trustees of the meeting-house property.

On the 24th of May, 1794, the trustees purchased for £21 a piece of ground, whereon formerly stood a cottage, lying between the meeting-house and Church lane.

The next appointment of new trustees is dated the 24th of September, 1802, and by this deed the trust property became vested in John Archer, Jacob Pattison, John Godfrey, Samuel Sach, Thomas Andrew, Sen., Thomas Andrew, Jun., Anthony Blackbone, John Davey, James Francis, John Gurton, Peter Good, Stephen Unwin, Thomas Unwin, Jun., Thomas Johnson, John Wright, Jordan Unwin, Thomas Willsher, Jun., Thomas Brown and William Potter.

On 30th August, 1845, Fisher Unwin Pattison, Jordan Unwin, Stephen Unwin, Sen., Samuel Sach, Anthony Blackbone, Stephen Unwin, Jun., Thomas Chalk Swinborne, Jacob Unwin, Harold

Giles, Fisher Unwin, William Beard, George Beard, Jun., Charles Moore, Sen., Henry Moore, Thomas Kettle, Alfred Denny, Joseph Denny, William Lemon Oliver, Joseph Sach, Matthias Gardner and John Appleford Clemance were appointed trustees.

The last appointment of trustees is dated the 17th August, 1884, when twenty-four of the leading members of the congregation were elected.

In 1834, the Chapel was considerably enlarged at a cost of about £1,000, and it was further improved in 1865, by throwing out an apse behind the pulpit for the organ and choir. In 1882, the interior of the building was entirely reconstructed, at a cost of £1,500.

The present manse in East Street was purchased and enlarged by the congregation, and conveyed in trust for their minister, in 1870.

The following is a list of the ministers :—

LOWREY, Thomas, has already been noticed on page 62. He was ejected from the Church of England. He purchased the property now known as the Woolpack Inn, in Church Street, in 1665 ; made his will, 12 March, 1680, and gave his residence and £900 to his son, Jeremy Lawrey (his name is variously spelt, but in his will he adopts this form) ; gave his daughter, Rebecca, the wife of Samuel Crossman, among other things a silver tankard, and one silver wine cup ; mentions his grandchildren (then infants), Samuel Crossman and Thomas Crossman, children of his daughter, Rebecca ; appointed his son, Jeremy, to be the guardian of his son, Richard, during the latter's minority ; gave £5 for division among certain nonconformist ministers, viz. Robert Gouge, of Great Coggeshall, 20s., William Lyle, of Witham, 20s., Mr. Legg, of Ipswich, 10s., Richard Rand, of Marks Tey, 10s., Mrs. Stulham, of Terling, 10s., Mr. Chadley, near Yeldham, 10s., Mr. Crow, near Hundon or Clare, 10s., Mr. Clarke, of Raine, 10s ; gave £5 to the poor of the society or church with whom he was in fellowship ; and the residue of his estate he gave to his three children, Jeremy, Richard and Rebecca ; appointed his friend, Isaac Hubbard, of Great Coggeshall, grocer, supervisor of his will. The will was proved by his son, Jeremy, on 2nd August, 1681. Jeremy Lowrey, the son, sometime a citizen and apothecary of London, was dead in 1708, when his son, Jeremiah, also a citizen and apothecary of London, sold the residence, which had then lately been converted into an inn called ' The Woolpack,' to George Long. Thomas Lowrey's funeral sermon was preached by Robert Gouge. A John Lowrey [query of this family] was M.P. in the time of the Long Parliament, and sat with Cromwell not long after the general election. He was appointed one of the King's judges, but did not act ; was living in 1659 [*vide East Anglian Notes and Queries*, N.S. vol I., p. 78.]

SAMES, John (ante p. 62), was probably of the family of Sames or Sammes, of the Totham, Tolleshunt and Goldhanger district (*see Morant*, vol. I, pp. 386-392). Is said to have resided for a time in New England ; vicar of Kelvedon, 1647 ; vicar of Coggeshall, 1654, from which vicarage he was ejected at the time of the Restoration ; died at Coggeshall, and was buried in the churchyard on 16th December, 1672. His funeral sermon was preached by Mr. Lowrey, who spoke of his deceased friend as the jewel of the town," "the salt as it were of the town," and "the light of the town ;" and, from this discourse, he appears to have been a tender-hearted, patient, conscientious and godly man.

ELLISTONE, Matthew, GROVE, William, and MILLAWAY, Thomas, were also nonconformist ministers here about this time. Matthew Ellistone was buried at Marks Hall, on 3rd May, 1693.

GOUGE, Robert, who was a congregational minister here from 1674 till his death in 1705, appears to have been a man of some property, as he was the owner of a farm in Stock Street, occupied by one Robert Cornell ; he also had three houses in Stoneham Street, in one of which he resided. When he made his will on 14th April, 1703, he described himself as Robert Gouge the elder, of Great Coggeshall, Clerk ; his wife's name was Katherine ; he had a son, Robert, and a granddaughter, Sarah Gouge. He was buried at Coggeshall, on 16th October, 1705. He was a native of Chelmsford ; educated at Christ College, Cambridge ; sometime a schoolmaster at Maldon ; in 1658 was a congregational minister at Ipswich. Bufton has a few notes about some members of this family :—"1680, April 27, Mr. Thomas Gouge was married to a rich gentlewoman of

Chelmsford; 1689, Oct. 31, Mr. Thomas Gouge brought
home his second wife from London; 1689, May 19, Mr.
Samuel Gouge, a lawyer, was buried."

BENTLEY, Edward, succeeded Gouge in 1706, and continued
pastor until his death on the 9th June, 1740. He was
buried at the foot of the pulpit stairs in the Chapel. His
successor was—

FARMER, John, from whom the pastorate devolved upon—

HUMPHREY, Nicholas, who after two years duty resigned, and
was followed, in 1751, by—

PEYTO, Henry, who died at the age of 74 years, on 7th
November, 1776.

ANDREWS, Mordecai, was the next minister. He resigned in
1797, and was succeeded by—

FIELDING, Jeremiah, who, however, failed to work in harmony
with a large portion of his congregation, which resulted
in some of the principal members forming a separate meeting in East Street, where they continued to assemble until
Fielding's retirement in 1818. On the 12th January, in
which year—

WELLS, Algernon, was appointed pastor. By his kindly disposition and strict devotion to duty he reunited the severed
congregation, and ably ministered to his flock until his
resignation in 1837.

KAY, John, was the next minister, and served that office for
fifteen years, namely, till his death on the 14th of October,
1854. His successor was—

DALE, Bryan, of Western College, Plymouth, and London
University. He was ordained on the 18th October, 1855,
and continued here till 1863. He is well known as the
author of the "*Annals of Coggeshall*," a work of considerable
research and varied interest. The history of nonconformity
occupies a large portion of the volume, and the detailed
biography of most of the Independent ministers is there set
forth. He is now Secretary of the Yorkshire Congregational
Union. The present minister is—

PHILPS, Alfred Downing. He entered Hackney College in
1860. During his college course he gained the first Holmes
Jubilee Prize. He was ordained pastor at Coggeshall, 20th
September, 1864, and among those present at his ordination

were the Rev. Samuel McAll, President of Hackney College (afterwards his father-in-law), and the Rev. S. W. McAll, M.A., of Finchley.

The Society of Friends
Commonly called Quakers.

THE members of this society who, Fox says, were first called Quakers by Justice Bennet, of Derby, because "I (Fox) bid them tremble at the word of the Lord, and that was in the year 1650." They had some followers here as early as 1655, who are thus mentioned by the founder of the society, (born 1624, died 1690), in his journal:—"After the meeting at Reading I passed up to London, where I stayed awhile and had large meetings, and then went into Essex and came to Cogshall, and there was a meeting of about 2,000 people, as it was judged, which lasted several hours; and a glorious meeting it was, for the Word of Life was freely declared, and people were turned to the Lord JESUS CHRIST." And, writing again in 1661, he says, "having now stayed in London some time I felt drawings to meet friends in Essex, so I went down to Colchester where I had very large meetings, and from thence to Coggeshall, not far from which there was a priest convinced, and I had a meeting at his house."

Among the early quakers was one James Parnell, who acquired notoriety in the year 1655. This enthusiast in the cause of religious liberty, during a service held in the parish church, on the 4th of July, and at which a collection was made for the poor and persecuted protestants of Piedmont, occasioned a disturbance, which resulted in his being taken before the local magistrates and ultimately committed to prison. He was subsequently imprisoned in the castle at Colchester, where he died in the month of April, 1656. The following account of his sufferings is extracted from a lecture by William Beck :—

"This youth (barely twenty when he died) was actually brought up to trial with chains upon him like a felon; and had to take his stand among murderers, and the city (Colchester) authorities left him when sentenced to live as he could in a hole

in the castle wall. To this he had to clamber by a piece of rope
that hung above the ladders, so difficult of access that he injured
his health, by refraining to come down for his meals ; and one day
as he clutched at the rope, that hung dangling above the top
round of the ladder, his victuals in one hand and the rope end in
the other, his enfeebled grasp loosened and he fell down on the
rough stones below and lay there as if dead.   He revived, but
not to receive any better treatment from his gaoler ; his friends
were denied access, all comforts they brought never reached him,
the hard-hearted gaoler seemed determined to have his life—and
in a few days more the end was reached.   Unable now to ascend
the ladder, they had him laid in a hole near the ground, so
small it was called "the oven" ; and, on one occasion, when
cramped and weary, he had crawled for a little fresh air to the
yard, his cruel keeper locked him out all night, though it was
cold, snowy weather.   It was the last suffering his life could with-
stand, and James Parnell was no more ; but the people, who saw
him die, heard his song as of victory even in that hour of death ;
and the men of Essex thought all the more of the quakers and
the truth of their views through the calm, patient sufferings of
that gallant-hearted, spiritually-minded youth."

On the 21st April, 1673, Nathaniel Sparrow, of Stisted,
tanner ; Richard Pemberton, of Great Coggeshall, clothier ;
Robert Adams, of Little Coggeshall, miller ; Robert Ludgater,
Jun., of Great Coggeshall, fellmonger ; William Sewell, of Great
Coggeshall, maltster ;   Robert Harvey, of Little Coggeshall,
gardener ; John Roddley, of Great Coggeshall, woolcomber ;
John Clark, of the same place, yeoman ; and John Garrett, of
the same place, tailor ; who were probably the leading members
of the Society of Friends which met at Coggeshall, purchased
from John Raven, of Feering, yeoman ; Daniel King, of Castle
Hedingham, woolcomber ; a house in Stoneham Street, containing 25 ft. by the rule in length and 24 ft. by the rule in breadth,
with an entryway thereto.

On 1st March, 1706, Robert Ludgater, Robert Harvey and
John Garratt, the only surviving trustees, conveyed the property
to William Cooke, baker, Matthew Dollow, clothier, Robert
Evans, maltster, John Perry, grocer, John Stacey, woolcomber,
William Stacey, woolcomber, William Mast, tailor, John Evans,
maltster, Robert Purcess, tailor, all of Great Coggeshall ; and

Isaac Ludgater, of Little Coggeshall, fellmonger, but no trusts were declared.

New trustees were again appointed by deed dated 1747, wherein are the names of Ludgater, Greenwood, Bott, Hart, Evans, Woodward, Corder, Bell, Docwra and Candler.

On 5th March, 1792, Robert Evans, as the surviving trustee, conveyed the house and premises, with certain additions which had recently been made, to Osgood Hanbury, of Lombard Street, banker, and others, bearing the surnames of Bott, Brightwen, Docwra, Raven, Hills, King, Dell, Greenwood, and Kirkham, upon trust to permit the same to be used for a meeting house for the people called Quakers for their worship of GOD.

Bufton tells us, that "in April, 1693, the Quakers made a new burying-place in Crouches," this they did by acquiring a lease, for 480 years, from Joseph Drywood and others, of a piece of land, part of Ayworth's or Crouch's, abutting upon an orchard belonging to a messuage called 'Sewal's' or the 'Chapel,' and upon a pond there. The ground was to be used as a burying-place for the people called Quakers who should die in or near Coggeshall.

Osgood Hanbury (the great-great-grandfather of Mr. Osgood Beauchamp Hanbury) having heard that the burial-ground belonging to the Friends was nearly filled up, in 1783, voluntarily offered the Society a portion of his land adjoining their property, at the same time declaring that he had no intention of being reinstated in membership.

The first-named, who died at the age of 51 years, was buried in this piece of ground, on the 20th January, 1784. His son Osgood, who died, 18th February, 1852, aged 86, was also buried there, and since his decease two more of the same name, grandson and great-grandson, have passed away, but they were both buried in the churchyard at Pattiswick.

Mr. Osgood Beauchamp Hanbury, aged 22 years, married on the 17th, died on the 25th, and was buried on the 30th of the month of October, 1889. He married Flora Tower, of Takeley, and was buried at Pattiswick.

In 1856, a new burial-ground was made at Tilkey and the old one has not since been used.

The Society is also possessed of a row of cottages on the north side of Crouches Alley, purchased from the parish authorities when the old workhouse was abolished. Some cottages in

L

Little Coggeshall, adjoining the bridge over the old river or back ditch also belong to the Friends.

The present Meeting House was erected in 1878, at a cost of about £800.

It is not generally known that the marriages of the paternal as well as the maternal grandparents of William Edward Forster took place at Coggeshall. This notable politician will ever be remembered by his pre-eminent connection with the Elementary Education Act, 1870, an association which led to his being nicknamed 'Education Forster.' So remarkable a man was Mr. Forster that, on the day following his death, which happened on the 5th April, 1886, *The Times* devoted no fewer than six columns of its space to his obituary. William Edward Forster was born at Bradpole, Dorset, 11th July, 1818; his grandfather was William Forster, of Tottenham, who married at Coggeshall monthly meeting, in September, 1781, Elizabeth Hayward, of Kelvedon. Of this marriage there were eleven children, of whom was William Forster, of Tottenham, land agent, born 1784; he married in 1816, Anna Buxton, daughter of Thomas Fowell Buxton, Esq., of Earls Colne, whose wife was Anna, the daughter of Osgood Hanbury, Esq., and whose marriage took place at Coggeshall in 1782. Here are some extracts from the Society's minutes relating to the marriage of the paternal grandparents of this statesman :—

"1781, 8 Mo. 6—Monthly meeting at Halstead. Wm. Forster, of Tottenham, and Eliz. Hayward, of Kelvedon, declared their intentions of taking each other in marriage if the Lord permits. He produced a satisfactory certificate from Tottenham mo. meeting, also of his mother's consent. Her parents being present, we appointed Jos. Docwra to give notice of such intended marriage at Kelvedon meeting on a first day.

1781, 9 Mo. 3—Monthly meeting held at Coggeshall, William Forster and Elizabeth Hayward now declared the continuance of their intention of taking each other in marriage if the Lord permits, this meeting leaves them to consummate their marriage according to ye good order of friends.

1781, 10 Mo. 1—Mo. meeting held at Kelvedon. The friend appointed to attend the marriage of Wm. Forster and Eliz. Hayward, reports the same was conducted orderly. Ye certificate is in ye hands of Jos. Docwra, who is desired to deliver it to J. Bott to be recorded."

And from the same source is extracted a reference to the marriage of his maternal grandparents :—

"1782, 3 month 4th—Coggeshall monthly meeting. Friends of Coggeshall meeting report that Anna Hanbury, a member of Devonshire House mo. meeting, was lately married at Coggeshall, by a priest, to T. Buxton, a person not of our 'society;' we appoint Jos. Docwra to enquire whether she now resides within the compass of this meeting, and if so to visit her thereupon, and in case she is removed to communicate the circumstances to some suitable members of the mo. meeting wherein she resides, in order that she may be duly visited, requesting such friend would report to us the effect of such visit, in order that she may be dealt with agreeably to the rules of the society."

The following refers to a member of the Buxton family :—

"The general deportment of Anna Buxton, a member of this meeting, having for several years past manifested a disregarded to divers testimonies, which we as a religious society believe it incumbent on us to support, particularly in the attending of places of diversion and other vain amusements, on which account much private labour hath been extended, which proving ineffectual, she has been divers times visited by appointments of men and women Friends in order to endeavour to convince her of the inconsistency of her conduct and thereby induce more circumspection in future, which labour hitherto does not appear to have answered the desired end having in the last opportunity acknowledged that her conduct was in some respect irreconcilable with the principles which we profess without a prospect of its being otherwise at present; and having entered into an engagement for marriage with a person not of our society, which she is not at all disposed to relinquish, this meeting apprehends an individual thus circumstanced as calling for the exercise of the rules of our society to the full extent, and accordingly hereby declares the said Anna Buxton is no longer considered a member thereof. Yet seeing that it is the nature of our discipline to embrace the offers of those, who having subjected themselves to its operation in separating them from the body, when from a right sense of the loss they have thereby sustained they are engaged to apply for re-instatement, should Anna Buxton hereafter evince a disposition of this sort accompanied with conduct correspon-

dent therewith, her restoration to membership would be acceptable
to us.

Signed in and on behalf of Cogges-⎫
hall monthly meeting, held at ⎬ WM. DOUBLEDAY, Clk."
Halstead, 5th of 5th mo., 1806. ⎭

The Baptists.

IT will have been noticed (p. 119) that there was a Baptist
Meeting House in this town nearly 150 years ago, and
further, that it was in close proximity to Church pond, and that
Henry Turner was the minister, or baptist teacher, as he is called
in the court rolls of the manor of Great Coggeshall.

From Josiah Thompson's MSS. in Dr. Williams' Library,
'*Dissenting Interest in England and Wales, 1715 to 1773*,' are
extracted these notes under date 1772 : "—

"Crouch Green. There is a little congregation of general
baptists, which together with Coggeshall is supposed to be as
ancient as any of the dissenting congregations in the county."

"Coggeshall. There is a meeting house with a baptistery in
it. Their numbers are but small and ye people poor."

Some additional information is gleaned from the books of the
Eld Lane Chapel at Colchester :—

"In January, 1782, Samuel Britton and Richard Rand, late
members of the Independent Church at Coggeshall, under the
pastoral care of Mr. Richard Andrews, and Gooday Pudney, a
hearer of Mr. Duddle, the church minister at the same town, and
till now a communicant with him, gave a circumstantial and
convincing relation of their experiences and very satisfactory
reasons for embracing believer's baptism, and of their wish to
join with us, making this provision, that they should choose to
be dismissed from us if in any future period a Baptist Church
should be established at Coggeshall. They were all three
baptised a week before at Mr. Pudney's house, by Mr. Hitchcock.
Testimony was borne to their character and they were received
into the fellowship of Eld Lane Church."

"June 26th, 1791. Notice was given that a new Meeting
House was to be opened, and Mr. Hutchins ordained to Coggeshall the first week in July."

In *Rippon's Register*, Vol. I, p. 519, is contained an account of the services held at Mr. John Hutchings ordination at Coggeshall, on 7th July, 1791. The service was opened by Mr. Richard Hutchings, the father of the future minister.

On 20th September, 1796, the Essex Baptist Association was formed, Mr. John Hutchings being in the chair; it was resolved that until the general meeting in May, 1797, the place for transacting the business of the Association should be at Coggeshall.

On the last Tuesday and Wednesday in May, 1797, the first annual meeting of the Essex Association was held at Coggeshall (put up at Swan Inn). The rules of the Association were attended to; Mr. Stevens spoke on the design of the Association, and addressed Mr. Pilkington who had been appointed an itinerant preacher. The meeting on Wednesday was held in the Independent Meeting House.

For many years the baptists met at a house adjoining Hares bridge.

On the 28th April, 1825, a piece of land on the north side of Church Street was purchased by Thomas Rowland, John Collis, Thomas Wheeler, James Potter, and Jephthah Threadkell, from Charles Smith for £180, and thereon was erected a suitable building, which has since been used as the Meeting House of the society.

The Wesleyan Methodists.

COGGESHALL was formerly in the Colchester circuit of this society or connection, but a few years ago was transferred to the Chelmsford circuit. The first mention of the Wesleyans at Coggeshall is in 1811. For some time they assembled for worship at a house in Stoneham Street, since converted into an Inn called the 'Foresters.' Afterwards they had a chapel in East Street.

On the 25th January, 1883, the new Wesleyan Methodist Chapel on the west side of Stoneham Street was opened, the first sermon being preached by the Rev. Ebenezer E. Jenkins. For this building, which is of white brick, a sum of £1,200 was collected. It is constructed to seat about 250 persons.

Sir Robert Hitcham's School.

THIS School was founded in 1636, by Sir Robert Hitcham, who was born in the 14th year of the reign of Queen Elizabeth (A.D. 1572), at Levington, in Suffolk, where his father and grandfather carried on the business of cutting heather and carrying it about for sale as material for the manufacture of brooms and brushes.

The family of Hitcham derived its name from the village of Hecham or Hitcham, near Bildeston, in Suffolk; and there is mention, in records dated 1355, of a Ralph, son of John de Hecham, who recovered certain lands in Hecham from a Robert de Hecham, but whether Sir Robert Hitcham of the 16th century was of this family or not is not known. An old manuscript "History of Suffolk families," written upwards of two centuries ago by Robert Ryce, of Preston, in the neighbourhood of Hitcham, says that Sir Robert "was not born to £200 per annum, and rose to an estate of about £1,500 per annum;" but a marginal note of great antiquity but written in another hand, referring to the £200, says, "Nor to £20, nor to £2." (*Vide Green's History of Framlingham*).

Be his birth what it may, Sir Robert was undoubtedly a good man, of a somewhat passionate disposition, clear in intellect and an admirable speaker. He commenced his education at the Free School at Ipswich, afterwards removing to Pembroke Hall, Cambridge, where he entered as a student. He next entered himself at Gray's Inn for the purpose of pursuing the study of the law, in which profession he was evidently destined to attain a high position. In 1596, he was elected member for the borough of West Looe. In 1603, he was appointed Attorney-General to Queen Anne of Denmark, the consort of King James I. of England. A year later, he was appointed Lent reader at Gray's Inn. King James appointed him his senior Serjeant-at-Law on the 4th of January, 1616, at the same time conferring upon him the honour of knighthood. On several occasions he acted as a judge of Assize, and in the 22nd year of King James I. was Recorder of Hadleigh. In 1623, he was elected member for Orford, near Woodbridge, for which borough he was again returned at the two subsequent elections. He represented that place as member of parliament until 1628. Sometime during the reign of King Charles I. he purchased a house in the parish of S. Matthew's, Ipswich, known as *Seckford House* or the *Great House*.

About the year 1635, Sir Robert purchased of the Duke of Suffolk, for £14,000, Framlingham Castle and the Manors of Framlingham and Saxted, in Suffolk, and held the first court for his Manor of Framlingham in the 11th year of King Charles I. The title to his estate was so complicated that it is said, had he not been possessed of a strong brain and a powerful purse, he could not have cleared it; which he was so sensible of, that in thankfulness to God for his wonderful success, he settled it upon Pembroke Hall, in Cambridge, for various charitable uses; among other objects of his bounty were the poor of Coggeshall, a knowledge of whose destitution he obtained though the wealthy family of the Guyons of this town, with whom he was familiarly acquainted.

The arms of Sir Robert Hitcham were :— Gules, on a chief or, three torteaux ; Crest a buck salient ppr, attired or, among leaves, and the trunk of a tree also ppr.

Sir Robert died the 15th of August, 1636, and was buried in the south aisle of Framlingham Church in a magnificent tomb, consisting of a table of black marble sustained on the shoulders of four angels of white marble, their hair and wings gilded, each having one knee to the ground. Under the table is an urn after the Roman fashion enriched with a mantling and two cherubim. At the west end is this inscription in gold letters upon black marble :—

SIR ROBERT HITCHAM'S TOMB.

" *Reader*
" *In expectation of the coming of our Lord Jesus, here*
lyeth ye body of Sr. Robert Hitcham, Kt., born at Leving-
ton, in ye County of Suff., Schollar in the Free School
at Ipswiche, and sometime of Pembroke Hall in Cambridge ;
and after of Grayes Inne ; Attorney to Queen Anne
in ye first yeare of King James, then Knighted ; and

*afterward made ye King's Senior Serjeant at Law, and
often Judge of Assize: aged 64 years. Dyed
the 15th day of August. Anno
1636.*

"*The children not yet borne with gladness shall
Thy pious actions into memory call;
And thou shalt live as long as there shall bee
Either poore or any use of Charitie.*"

At the east end of the tomb are the arms of Sir Robert.

The following is a copy of his will, which is of so interesting a nature that no apology is needed for its insertion *in extenso* :—

"In the NAME of the Glorious and Incomprehensible TRINITY. I Sir ROBERT HITCHAM of Ipswich, in the County of Suffolk, Knight, the King's Majesties Serjeant at Law, this present Monday, being the 8th of August, 1636, in the 12th Year of King Charles, Do make this my last Will and Testament in Writing as followeth. First, I will, after my death, that all my debts be first paid, and the profits of all my lands and hereditaments be committed only to that use, my debts being only £3,000, the remnant of my purchase of my Lord of Suffolk; other debts, I do not know that I owe £20; saving £500. which is in my hands in trust for my sister. Item, I will, for the payment of my debts and legacies, that my Lease of the Manors of Walton and Felixtow, and my Houses in Ipswich, all my jewels, household stuff, and plate, there and elsewhere, and all other my goods and chattels whatsoever, be sold for the payment of my debts and legacies, by my Executors hereafter named, and the survivor of them. My Manor of Burvall's, in Levington, the Impropriation mill, fish-ponds, park, and other roialties whatsoever, and all my lands and tenements whatsoever there, or in any Towns thereabouts, or thereunto used, now leaton to Mayhew, (except the Farm called Watkins, and that therewith leaton, as it is now ye lease) I give unto my nephew Robert Butts, and his heirs, upon condition, and to the intent and purpose, that he pay unto my sister, £1000. that is to say, £500. a year yearly after my decease; and for my Farm, Watkins, I give the same unto my sister and her heirs, the one presently after my decease, to release and convey their right in either of the other part to the other, and their heirs, and if either of them fail so to do, then this my devise to him so failing, to be void; and then I devise the same unto the other, and his or their heirs.

"For my Castle and Manors of Framlingham and Saxted, and all other the Lands, Tenements, and Hereditaments, which I and my Feoffees, purchased of my Lord of Suffolk and his Feoffees, I will, that my Feoffees and their Heirs, and the survivors of them, after my debts paid, Do presently stand seised as in Trust, to the Use of the Master and Fellows of Pembroke-Hall, in Cambridge, and their Successors, according to their incorporation, and that upon Request, to be made by them, my Feoffees, and their Heirs, and the survivors of them do make good and perfect assurance unto them accordingly. Of which said Castle, Manors, and Premises, my meaning is, and I will, that the said College shall only have to the Use of them, and their Successors for themselves, only the Castle, Royalties, and Rents of Tenure, with the Mere, and all other Fish-ponds, the advowson of the Church, the Hundred of Loes, and the Fairs and Markets there; but no part of the other Lands or Hereditaments : and this my Legacy, I will, shall be employed for the Good of the College, as my Gift alone by itself, and not to be employed to the Increase of their Fellowships, or Buildings, or of any other Thing, belonging to their House. And all the Demeans of Lands, of the said Manors, and all other the Hereditaments, and Lands purchased of my Lord of Suffolk, and his Feoffees besides, and whatsoever parcel thereof, or belonging thereunto, I do give unto them, only in Trust, to be committed by them, to the Uses and Intents following, and they to have no manner of other Benefit thereby. Item, I will, that presently after my decease, all the Castle, (saving the stone-Building) be pulled down, and the materials thereof coming, to be converted as followeth : First, I will, that the said College do presently after my death, erect and build at Framlingham, One House to set the Poor on work, the Poor and most needy and impotent of Framlingham (*and*) Debenham, (*in Suffolk*) and Coxall, (*Coggeshall*) in Essex first, and after them, of other Towns, if they see cause ; and to provide a substantial Stock to set them on work, and to allow to such needy Persons of them, so much as they shall further think fit : and likewise I will, that they do build One or Two Almshouses, consisting of Twelve Persons, (viz.) Six a piece, for Twelve of the poorest and decrepid People there ; which I will, shall have Two Shillings a

Week, during their lives, and also Forty Shillings a Year for a Gown and Firing every Year, the said Two Shillings to be paid weekly, and the other yearly. Item, I will, that a School-House be built there at Framlingham, and a Master appointed, whom I will, shall have Forty Pounds by the Year, during his life, to teach Thirty, or Forty, or more of the poorest and neediest *Children of the said Towns of Framlingham, Debenham, and Coxall,* to write, read, and cast accounts, as the said College shall think fit; then to give them, Ten Pounds a piece, to bind them forth Apprentices, at the discretion of the Four Senior Fellows of the said College: and the said School-master not to take any other, upon Penalty of loosing his Place and Stipend. Item, I will, that there be presently built after my decease, One Alms-house at Levington, for six Female Persons, of the poorest and impotent of Levington and Nacton, the same to be built upon my Tenement near the Street there, and they to have the like allowance in all Things, as the poor of Framlingham are appointed to have: to begin First, with the poor of Levington, and so successively. Item, I will, that there shall be for ever One that shall read Prayers in the Church of Framlingham daily, at the Hours of Eight in the Forenoon, and at Four in the Afternoon, unto whom I give Twenty Pounds by the Year; and to the Sexton, Five Pounds yearly: and such of the Poor People aforesaid, and the School-master, or Scholars there, as shall make Default in coming to hear Prayers there, I will, that their Allowance shall be proportionally abated for the same neglect, (except their excuse be allowed by the Minister of the Parish of Framlingham, for the time being). And whatsoever shall or may further come of this which I have formerly given and devised in Trust to the said College, I will, that they convert the same to the like Use or Uses, to continue as before for ever.

"First, I give unto my honourable friend the Lord Keeper, £100 and to his Lady, £50 and to my Lord Privy-Seal, £50, to be bestowed by my executors in such pieces of plate, as they shall think fit. Item, I do give to every of the children of my Brother Butts, that he had by my sister, which shall be unmarried at the time of my decease, £200 a piece, and to them which shall be married, £100 a piece; and to my sister, £100 to her former £500 and whatsoever I have heretofore by this my Will given unto her, to be by her put out into some trusty friends hands, and her husband to have no medling with the same ; and her children married and unmarried, to have like legacies my brother Butts his children by my sister have.   Item, I do give unto Samuel Ward, of Ipswich, £20 and £20 to the son of him of whom I bought my house and lands at Tannington, he being a cripple.   Item, I give all my servants that have served me above a year, £10 a piece, and a mourning cloak or gown ; and to my other servants, £5 a piece, and a mourning gown or cloak. Item, I will, that Gyant, my gardener shall dwell where he now dwelleth, and keep my house until it be sold, and have for the same keeping, £8 by the year, and the profits of all the gardens and orchards ; and I wish and desire that he may so have it afterwards during his life, with a reasonable allowance for his diet ; and if he shall not have his dwelling, and gardens, and orchards, with his allowance during his life-time, then, I will, he shall have the other tenement next thereto during his life, freely to dwell in.   Item, I will, that all my servants shall have reasonable allowance for their diet for one month next after my decease.   Item, I do give unto the Poor of Levington, £50, and to the poor of Nacton, £50 as a Stock, to be put out for them for ever ; and to the Poor of Framlingham, £50, and to the Parish where I now live, £20, to be distributed amongst them : and whatever I have else, I will, shall be bestowed in such like Charitable Uses as· before.   And whatsoever I have given, the same to continue for ever.   And of this my last Will and Testament, I do make Matthew Wren now Bishop of Norwich, my Supervisor ; and Richard Keeble, and Robert Butts, my Executors, giving them my Supervisor, and Executors, £50 a piece.   And if the said College shall wilfully refuse to perform this my Will : Then, I will, that this my Devise unto them shall be void ; and I do devise the same unto Emanuel College, in Cambridge, in the same manner and form, as it is formerly devised unto Pembroke-Hall, and to the same Uses, Intents, Trusts, and Purposes.   And so I commit my soul into the hands of the said Holy and Blessed Trinity, believing to be only saved by the death and passion of JESUS CHRIST, and my sins to be washed away by His blood ; and my body to be privately buried in the Church of Framlingham, in one of my Isles there, only with a fair Stone, and such like over it ; the same to be buried ten feet in the ground, and the same not to be stirred, or hurt.

And I give to my servant John Wright, £10 more, if he be my servant at my death. And to my Feoffees £20 a piece, and a mourning cloak or gown."

By deed under the common seal of Pembroke College, dated 14th August, 1666, after reciting Sir Robert Hitcham's will, and that the poor of Coggeshall could have no benefit by what was therein devised to them, and was then done at Framlingham, and to the intent that the poor of Coggeshall might partake of the charity intended for them by Sir Robert Hitcham, Robert Maple-toft, Doctor of Divinity, Master or Keeper of the said College and the fellows of the same, thereby covenanted with the inhabitants of Coxall, *alias* Coggeshall, to pay out of the rents of the demesne lands to trustees by them to be appointed for the poor of the town of Coxall, £150 yearly, at the 'Corn Cross' in Framlingham, upon the first Tuesday in September and the first Tuesday in March, to be employed for providing a work-house and a substantial stock to set the poor and most neediest at work, and to allow such poor persons such relief as the trustees should think fit, and also to provide a School House and to allow the schoolmaster £20 yearly, to teach twenty or thirty of the poorest children of Coxall to read, write, and cast accounts, and then to allow them such sums of money to 'bind them apprentices as the said trustees should think fit, not exceeding £10. The college reserved to themselves the right to appoint the schoolmaster and to audit and settle the accounts. The college accordingly paid £150 per annum to the inhabitants of Coggeshall till the year 1722, when the lands being of insufficient value to pay £150 per annum to Coggeshall, the towns of Coggeshall and Debenham, with the consent of the college, agreed to a partition of the charity lands, which was effected by an indenture dated the 18th of September, 1722, and made between Robert Townsend, of Coggeshall, gentleman, on the part of the inhabitants of Coggeshall, and John Turner, of Debenham, apothecary, on the part of the inhabitants of Debenham ; the allotment to Coggeshall consisting of lands at Saxstead, Suffolk, known as *Old Frithwood, Bradley Wood,* and *Newhall Wood.* This agreement was afterwards by deed, dated 29th September, 1722, confirmed by William Townsend, Isaac Potter, Isaac Buxton, William Fuller, Thomas Burr, John Armond, John Sparhawke, John Gladwin, Samuel Carter the elder,

John Taylor, John Mount, Matthew Guyon, and Ambrose Hayward, chief inhabitants of Coggeshall.

On 29th September, 1779, the college appointed the Rev. Henry Du Cane, clerk, William Carter, Richard White, William Moss, Jeremiah Dixon, John Deeks, John Totman, Isaac Whitaker the elder, William Walford, Thomas South, John Guyon, John Cardinal, Henry Skingley, John Durrant, Thomas Whitaker, John Olive, Thomas Rolfe, John Stafford, Robert Chaulkley, and Richard Cable, trustees for managing and disposing of the charity.

The government of this charity is now regulated by a scheme of the Charity Commissioners, which was approved by Her Majesty in Council, on the 29th June, 1878, and provides that the endowment for Coggeshall shall consist of the present School-buildings and master's house, and five-sixteenths of the net residue of the Income of Sir Robert Hitcham's Charity, to be paid yearly by the master and fellows of Pembroke College, Cambridge.

The governing body consists of nine governors, five of whom are appointed by the college, three by the vestry of Great Coggeshall, and one by the vestry of Little Coggeshall.

The present governors are the Rev. H. M. Patch, chairman, the Rev. A. D. Philps, vice-chairman, Dr. E. A. Applebe, Messrs. G. F. Beaumont, Robert Curzon, F. H. Gardner, Rev. H. F. Rackham, Messrs. Thomas Simpson, and F. W. Pfander-Swinborne; and the head master is Mr. Edw. Edgar. The tuition fee, including books, is £4 per annum, but if two or more boys are sent from the same family the fee for each boy is £3. £30 is annually awarded in scholarships which entitle the holders to a free education. Other scholarships are tenable at this school, as to which see the account of Paycock's Charity. £30 per annum is also applicable to the maintenance of Exhibitions, tenable at some place of higher education to be selected by the governors.

Provision is also made by the scheme for the education of girls, but no school has yet been established.

Under another scheme Pembroke College has a right, in preference to all other persons, of free nomination for admission to the Albert Middle Class College, at Framlingham, of one boy from the parish of Coggeshall, either as a day scholar free of all charge, or as a boarder free of charge for education, but chargeable with a reasonable sum per annum for board and maintenance, such boy to be nominated on the ground of merit, to be determined by free and open competition among those qualified for the nomination, according to such regulations as the college may make from time to time (*Scheme No. 112*).

The funds of the charity have been augmented by grants from Paycock's and Swallow's Charities (as to which see pp. 164 and 169, also *Schemes No. 827 and 828*).

The present school and the master's residence were built in 1858, on a piece of the glebe land purchased for the purpose for £100, which sum was received by the vicar and laid out by him in the purchase from Mr. Bullock of Saint Nicholas Chapel, and one acre of ground adjoining. The school was opened on the 24th June, 1859.

Mr. Henry Emery, who died on the 4th November, 1844, in the 78th year of his age, was master of the school for 49 years, and during his time the scholars assembled for instruction in a large room in Stoneham Street, part of Crane's Charity.

Mr. Thomas Hyde was the first master who taught in the present building, he was succeeded, in 1863, by the Rev. George Horrocks, who resigned the mastership on 24th June, 1864. One or two temporary appointments followed, and ultimately the present head master, Mr. Edward Edgar, was elected on the 9th January, 1865.

Thomas Paycocke's Charity.

THOMAS PAYCOCKE, was a wealthy clothier or cloth manufacturer, residing in Great Coggeshall, in the middle of the sixteenth century. His residence, situate immediately opposite the vicarage grounds in West Street, is one of the most interesting houses in the town, being rendered attractive by its ancient gateway of carved oak, at the top of the jambs of which are two carved figures on brackets; the gates are of the linen pattern. At the base of the upper floor, which projects about 18 in., is an oak frieze running the whole length of the building, and richly carved in relief, of a continuous floral design of quaint character with recumbent figures. On this frieze can also be seen Paycocke's Merchants' Mark, between the initials T.P. The ceiling of the ground floor is also of oak beautifully carved, and is probably unequalled by any in this part of the country.

Thomas Paycock made his will, on 20th December, 1580, and was buried on the 28th of the same month, in the north chancel aisle of Coggeshall Church (see *Memorial Inscriptions*, p. 41). By his will he ordained that his executors should purchase so much free lands and tenements, as with the sum of £200 they could procure, the yearly profits thereof to be bestowed amongst the poor people of Much and Little Coggeshall for ever; and that his executors should convey the premises so purchased to ten of the headboroughs of Coggeshall or more and their heirs upon the said trusts. And he willed that the rents and profits of the lands and tenements when purchased should be given amongst the poor dwelling in Much and Little Coggeshall, by the consent of the collectors of the poor and the churchwardens, in manner following, viz. :—one-half of the said rents should be expended in *wood* to be distributed indifferently to the poor of the same parishes always betwixt Easter and 1st August, and the other half should be expended one month before Lent in the purchase of *white and red herrings* to be distributed equally among the said poor always in the beginning of Lent.

The sum of £156 13s. 4d., part of the £200, was laid out by Richard Benyon, one of the executors, in the purchase of lands, at Halstead, Essex, known as "Sparkes Croft," containing twelve

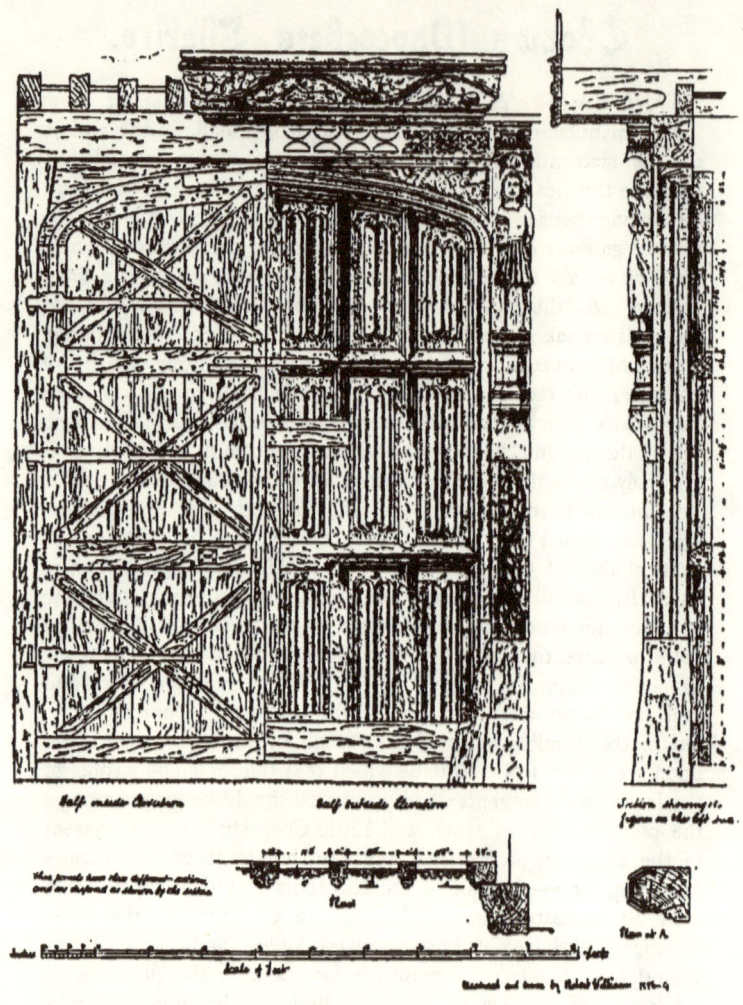

ANCIENT GATEWAY.

acres; "Gyles Croft," containing six acres; "Tanners Croft," containing three acres; and "Gerrards Meadow," containing three acres; and the same were conveyed to Mr. Benyon, by an indenture of bargain and sale, dated 20th June, 24 Elizabeth (1582).

By deed, dated the 17th March, 26 Elizabeth (1584), Richard Benyon conveyed the above-mentioned property to William Fuller, Robert Litherland, Cyprian Warner, Thomas Dammett, Thomas Till, Robert Aylett, Henry Purcas, Robert Brittle, George Lawrence, Thomas Hopper, Peter Ryse, and Edward Warner, inhabitants of Coggeshall, upon the trusts of the before-mentioned will. From time to time new trustees were by deed duly appointed, and the trust property conveyed to them, the last of such deeds being dated the 26th December, 1851, by which the following persons were constituted trustees:—The Rev. William James Dampier, Messrs. Osgood Hanbury, Fisher Unwin Pattison, Richard Meredith White, William Swinborne, Harold Giles, Charles Moore, William Gentry Dennis, Matthias Gardner, Joseph Sach, Henry Whitmore, Richard Meredith Kirkham, William Appleford, and William Doubleday; of whom, in June, 1887, two only survived, namely Mr. Dennis and Mr. Gardner.

By an Order of the Charity Commissioners, sealed on the 15th June, 1887, the following persons were appointed trustees for the administration of the Charity, viz:—The Rev. Hubert Mornington Patch, vicar of Coggeshall, the Rev. Alfred Downing Philps, Congregational Minister, Joseph Smith Surridge, Junior, (since dead), George Frederick Beaumont, John Shuttleworth, Thomas Simpson, Frederic Henry Gardner, James Simmons, William King, and Edward Doubleday, all of Coggeshall, in addition to and jointly with William Gentry Dennis and Matthias Gardner, the continuing trustees.

By the decree of Sir John Sammes and others (Commissioners of Charitable Uses), dated the 20th May, 1613, it appears that the balance of the sum of £200, which remained after the purchase of the lands at Halstead, viz:—£43 6s. 8d., at the date of the decree had by some means been augmented to four score and thirteen pounds (£93) or thereabouts, which was then "employed in a beneficial course and yieldeth an annual profit, which hath also been employed to the use of the poor people aforesaid;" and it was then intended to lay out such balance in the purchase of land; but, from the report of the Charity Commissioners, in

1837, it does not appear that the intention was ever carried out, and the Commissioners were unable to obtain any information upon the matter.

In 1837, "Sparkes Croft," in two fields, containing twelve acres, and adjoining the Sudbury Road, in Halstead, was in the occupation of Jonathan Nash, on lease expiring Michaelmas, 1844, at £25 per annum. "Gyles Croft," containing about five (query six) acres of pasture, situate close to Halstead, was in the occupation of William T. L. W. Pole, as a yearly tenant, at £15 per annum. "Tanners Croft" and "Gerrard Meadow," situate near the Silk Mills, in Halstead, and containing about six acres of garden ground, were in the occupation of John Cook, as yearly tenant, at £18 per annum. It will thus be seen, that in 1837, the income of this Charity amounted to £58 per annum.

In 1864, the trustees sold and conveyed to the Halstead and Colne Valley Railway Company, the six acres of garden ground, called "Tanners Croft" and "Gerrards Meadow," for £1,500, which, on the 22nd June, 1864, was invested in Consols. In 1868, the trustees, with the consent of the Charity Commissioners, sold "Sparkes Croft," containing twelve acres fifteen poles, to Mr. George de Horne Vaisey, for £1,600, and this sum was subsequently invested in Consols.

The trust property now consists of £3,364 12s. 8d. Consols, standing in the names of the Official Trustees of Charitable Funds, and the before-mentioned piece of land called "Gyles Croft," containing six acres or thereabouts, in the occupation of Jacob Evans, at a rent of £12 per annum, the fee simple of which field is, by virtue of the order of the Commissioners, dated the 15th June, 1887, vested in the Official Trustee of Charity Lands ; but the right to sue for, recover and receive, and to give receipts and discharges for all sums of money, rents in arrear, and choses in action, due to or recoverable for the benefit of the Charity, is vested in the trustees, their executors, administrators and assigns, in trust for the Charity.

By way of scheme, the Commissioners, by the before-mentioned order have directed that—

1. The trustees shall consist of twelve competent persons, residing in or near the parish of Coggeshall.

2. Any trustee who ceases to be qualified as aforesaid, or is adjudicated a bankrupt, or is incapacitated to act, or communi-

M 2

cates in writing to the trustees his wish to resign, or fails to attend any meeting of the trustees for a consecutive period of two years, shall thereupon cease to be a trustee.

3. Future trustees shall be provisionally appointed in each case by the trustees, by a resolution passed at a meeting specially called for the purpose, and of which at least three clear days notice in writing shall have been given to each trustee, and to be held after the lapse of one calendar month from the occurence of the vacancy to be filled up.

4. Every provisional appointment of a trustee shall be forth-with notified by or under the direction of the trustees to the Charity Commissioners, at their office, in London, and no provisional appointment shall be valid until it has been approved by the said Commissioners, and their approval certified under their official seal.

5. There shall be a quorum when five trustees are present at any meeting.

A dispute having arisen between the inhabitants of Great and Little Coggeshall, as to the distribution of the income of the Charity, and the question having been referred to the Commissioners of Charitable Uses, it was by the before-mentioned decree, dated the 30th May, 1613, ordered that the churchwardens and overseers of Great Coggeshall, or the feoffees of the Charity, should for ever pay to the overseers of Little Coggeshall, the yearly sum of £3, at Michaelmas and Lady-day, by equal portions to be deducted out of the profits of the Charity, and to be employed for the relief of the poor in Little Coggeshall, at the discretion of the overseers of that parish, according to the true meaning of the Will of Thomas Paycocke, deceased.

The income of the Trust is usually distributed early in February, in sums varying from 1s. to £1.

By a scheme of the Charity Commissioners, approved by Her Majesty in Council, on the 13th May, 1887, after declaring that it was desirable to apply for the advancement of education a sum of £500, part of the endowment of Paycocke's Charity, it was ordered that, from the date of the scheme, the sum of £500 should be part of the Foundation governed by a scheme made under the name of Sir Robert Hitcham's Schools, at Coggeshall, on condition that, in addition to the scholarships to be maintained by the Governors under the Hitcham School Scheme, those

Governors should maintain three other scholarships, to be called Paycocke's Scholarships, each of a yearly value of £5, tenable at the Boys' School maintained under that scheme, to be competed for by boys who are and have for not less than three years been scholars in any of the Public Elementary Schools, in the parishes of Great Coggeshall and Little Coggeshall, but to be subject to the like conditions as made with regard to other scholarships, in clause 60 of the Hitcham School Scheme, that is to say, that the scholarships are to be given as the reward of merit, to be freely and openly competed for, to be tenable only for the purposes of education, and to be liable to determination for misconduct, idleness, failure to maintain a reasonable standard of proficiency, &c.

Of the before-mentioned sum of £3,364 12s. 8d. Consols, the Charity Commissioners have transferred to the Governors of the Hitcham School, £487 4s. 2d. Consols, equivalent to £500 sterling, to be applied in maintaining the before-mentioned scholarships.

Thomas Guyon's Charity.

THOMAS GUYON, of Great Coggeshall, gentleman, father of Sir Mark Guyon, made his will, bearing date the 21st November, 1664, and thereby, after appointing Sir Mark Guyon sole executor, gave £200 to be laid out in lands and tenements, by Sir Mark, to and for the use and benefit of the most honest, aged poor people of Great Coggeshall, and the yearly rents and profits thereof arising, his mind and will was, should weekly, upon every Lord's Day, after the sermon in the forenoon, be bestowed in bread for their relief. And further, his mind and will was, that the settlement of such lands as should be purchased with the said £200, should be made to the said Sir Mark Guyon and eleven of the chief inhabitants of the said town of Coggeshall (by the nomination of the said Sir Mark Guyon), and their heirs; and that, by such deed of purchase, the trust should be declared to the use aforesaid, and when so many of the said trustees should be dead that there should be but six of them living, his will was, that they should raise a new deed to twelve more of the principal inhabitants of Great Coggeshall aforesaid, for the better continuance of the said trust.

Sir Mark Guyon, of Great Coggeshall, knight, by deed, dated the 22nd of January, 1676, granted to Matthew Guyon, Isaac Hubberd, John Cox, Sen., Richard Shortland, Joseph Drywood, gentleman, John Guyon, Richard Sheppard, William Cox, Thomas Buxton, John Cockerell, Symon Richold, and Thomas Keeble, clothiers, all of them of Great Coggeshall, one annuity or clear yearly rent-charge of ten pounds and eight shillings, to be issuing and going out of all that messuage or tenement, outhouses, edifices, buildings, barns, stables, yards, gardens, orchards, and eight closes or parcels of land and pasture, with the appurtenances, anciently called or known by the name of 'Windmill Fields,' and then (1676) called or known by the several names of 'Garden Field,' 'Great and Little Cross-path Fields,' Windmill Fields,' 'Long Pitch Shott,' 'Potters Field,' 'Middle Eight Acres,' and 'Upper Eight Acres,' all of which premises are expressed to be in Great Coggeshall, and to contain together, by estimation, three-score and fifteen acres, more or less, and were then in the possession of Sir Mark Guyon, his assigns or under-tenants. The annuity was made payable on the four usual quarter days for the payment of rent, and is expressed to be held for the use and behoof of the poor of Great Coggeshall, according to the true intent of the will of Thomas Guyon, viz. :—weekly, upon the Lord's Day in every week, after the sermon or prayers in the forenoon, the sum of 4s. thereof, to be bestowed in good wholesome 3d. bread, and the same bread to be equally distributed and given to sixteen of the most honest, aged poor people of Great Coggeshall aforesaid. The deed contains powers of distress for non-payment after demand, and has also provisions for the appointment of new trustees.

The deed is signed by Sir Mark Guyon, and bears his seal :— a shield with three bends, on a canton a lion passant guardant.

This property belonged to Mr. William Townsend, in 1740, and was occupied by him.

The Rent-charge has from time to time been vested in new trustees, the last appointment being by deed dated the 14th April, 1783, when Osgood Hanbury the elder, of 'Oldfield' Grange, Esq., Richard Meredith White, clothier, and Fisher Unwin, brewer, the three surviving trustees, appointed Henry Du Cane, clerk, Vicar of Great Coggeshall, Osgood Hanbury the younger, of 'Oldfield Grange,' Esq., Richard White the younger, clothier,

William Walford, farmer, Thomas Unwin, gentleman, Stephen Unwin, clothier, Joseph Bott, clothier, Habakuk Layman, gentleman, Ephraim Willsher, farmer, William Dixon, surgeon, John Godfrey, surgeon, and William Potter, Junior, gentleman, all of them principal inhabitants of Great Coggeshall.

The last survivor of these trustees was Mr. Osgood Hanbury, who was living in 1837.

The present trustees are the Vicar and Churchwardens of Great Coggeshall, who were appointed by an order of the Charity Commissioners, dated 4th November, 1862.

Bread of the value of £10 8s. per annum is distributed in 3d. loaves at the church, on Sundays, after afternoon service, among poor parishioners of Great Coggeshall.

As it is important that the identity of the land out of which this rent-charge is payable should be maintained, the following is extracted from a survey made for Morden College, Blackheath, in the year 1740.

No. on Morden Coll. Sur.	Name of Field.	Quantity.			No. on Ord. Survey	Quantity per Ordnance Sur.		
5	Garden Field	6	0	34	310	5	2	21
6	Hither Crosspath Field	7	1	2	304	7	1	21
7	Further ditto	10	1	7	303	10	1	24
8	Lower Eight Acres ...	8	0	32	266	9	0	12
9	Upper ditto	9	1	32	220	9	0	18
10	Thomson's Field ...	13	2	16	267) 268)	14	0	22
11	Loam Pit Field ...	12	2	0	302	12	3	4
12	Windmill Field ...	9	3	2	305	9	0	16
		77	1	5		77	2	18

Sir Mark Guyon's Charity.

BY Deed, dated 1st May, 1678, and made between Sir Mark Guyon, who is described as then late of Great Coggeshall, but afterwards of Dynes Hall, in Great Maplestead, Essex, Knight, of the one part, and Matthew Guyon, Isaac Hubbard, Joseph Drywood, Richard Shortland, gentlemen; Richard Shep-

pard, Ambrose Sutton, William Cox, Thomas Buxton, Thomas
Keeble, George Nicholls, Simon Richold and Jacob Cox, clothiers,
all inhabitants of Great Coggeshall, of the other part ; Sir Mark
Guyon gave and granted one annuity or yearly sum of £13 to be
issuing and going, and to be perceived, received, levied, and taken
out of all that messuage, farm and lands, called Highfields and
Windmill Fields, or otherwise situate and being in Great Coggeshall, and then in the tenure of John Cox, upon special trust and
confidence, and to the intent and purpose that the trustees should
for ever thereafter dispose of the annuity of £13, and employ and
lay out the same in bread, and distribute the same bread upon
every Sunday or Lord's day for ever, after Divine service or sermon, namely, to twenty of the most aged poor and necessitous
persons inhabiting within the parish of Great Coggeshall, to each
of them a three-penny loaf, the same bread to be placed upon a
shelf to be set up for that purpose over or near to the seat of the
said Sir Mark Guyon, then standing in the chancel of the parish
church of Great Coggeshall. The deed contains provisions for
the appointment of nine new trustees when the number should be
reduced to three, such new trustees to act conjointly with the continuing trustees. And it is declared that the annuity should be
payable at or in the south porch of the parish church of Great
Coggeshall, upon Michaelmas day and Lady day, by equal portions
without any deduction. Power for the trustees to distrain when
the rent-charge should be in arrear for twenty days after day fixed
for payment, the rent however, being first lawfully demanded.

By deed dated the 29th June, 1819, Richard Meredith White,
of Great Coggeshall, clothier, the owner of the Highfield's Estate,
granted and confirmed the said annuity of £13 unto Osgood
Hanbury, Esq., Henry Skingley, Esq., the Rev. E. W. Mathew,
clerk, Isaac Brightwen, merchant, Thomas Andrew, gentleman,
William Swinborne, currier, John Durrant, saddler, Robert Brightwen, brewer, Richard Townsend, gentleman, John Godfrey, surgeon, and Francis Eagle, surgeon, all of them inhabitants of Great
Coggeshall.

The present trustees are the Vicar and Churchwardens of
Great Coggeshall, by virtue of their appointment by an order of
the Charity Commissioners, dated the 4th November, 1862.

The annuity is distributed in bread, in the same manner as
Thomas Guyon's Charity.

Swallow's Charity.

I N or about the year 1520, Christopher Swallow, who was
Vicar of Messing, conveyed to the Right Hon. John de Vere,
Earl of Oxford, and other persons, lands at Coggeshall and in
other parishes in Essex, to the intent that from thenceforth for
ever an honest, learned and godly man should be maintained to
execute the office of a schoolmaster at Earls Colne, in Essex, who
should be learned in the Latin tongue and skilful in grammar and
able to instruct children in the grammar there, and that the same
schoolmaster should in respect only of the profits of the said
lands, without any other reward, instruct in grammar the number
of 30 children, whose parents should be dwelling either within
the parish of Earls Colne or in Coggeshall, Ardleigh, Stisted,
Messing and Marks Tey, &c., and that the schoolmaster should
hold and keep the school during the space of three years at Earls
Colne, and *during the space of other three years immediately ensuing at Coggeshall*, and then again at Earls Colne, and so *alternis
vicibus* in each of the said towns.

For very many years, probably centuries, the town of Coggeshall derived no benefit whatever from this Charity, and had it not
been for the unceasing perseverance of the late Rev. William
James Dampier, the beneficent intention of the *quondam* Vicar of
Messing would have been entirely lost to the parish. Under the
direction of Mr. Dampier, a petition to the Lord Chancellor was
drawn up by Mr. Malins (afterwards Vice-Chancellor Malins).

This interesting document sets forth the whole history of the
Charity, and covers five large skins of parchment.

The claim of Coggeshall to participate in this trust was ultimately recognised by the Charity Commissioners, and in their
scheme, dated 13th May, 1887, they directed that a sum of £500
out of the Earls Colne Grammar School Foundation should be
paid to the Foundation known as Sir Robert Hitcham's Schools,
at Coggeshall, and they provided that if there was not room in the
Earls Colne Grammar School for all boys found fit for admission,
preference should be given to such of them as were of poor inhabitants of either of the parishes of Great Coggeshall and Little
Coggeshall.

Goodays⁺ Charities.

BY her will, dated in 1618, Jane Gooday, of Feering, widow, directed her executor to lay out £30 in the purchase of a house, to be estated to some of the parishioners of Great Coggeshall and their heirs, to the intent that the profits thereof should be laid out at the discretion of the vicar and overseers *to buy needful clothing for the aged poor of Great* Coggeshall for ever.

John Gooday, as the executor of his mother's will, in April, 1618, laid out the sum of £30, with £20 of his own money, in the purchase of a house with a garden in Church Street, Coggeshall, called *Pagetts*, and by deed, dated 3rd Oct. 1619, conveyed the same unto the then Vicar of Coggeshall and nine other inhabitants and their heirs upon trust, to permit the vicar and overseers to receive the rents and profits and apply them according to the intention expressed in Jane Gooday's will, with provisions for the appointment of new trustees.

About the year 1714, the house being very much decayed, and part having fallen down, and the rent not being sufficient to keep it in repair, the trustees sold it for £28 to Daniel Cooke, of Coggeshall. The ground is said to have been laid to the Swan Yard.

By indenture, dated 13th February, 1718, made between William Townsend, of Great Coggeshall, of the one part; and Robert Townsend, Samuel Sparhawke, Isaac Buxton, Sen., Isaac Dawes, Thomas Buxton, John Sparhawke, John Armond, Joseph Cox, John Mount, John Gladwin, Isaac Potter, Ambrose Hayward, Jun., and Richard White, all of Great Coggeshall, of the other part; William Townsend, in consideration of £28 paid to him by the said Robert Townsend, Samuel Sparhawke, Isaac Dawes, and John Barnard, of Great Coggeshall, who were the surviving trustees of the old property in Church Street, granted an annuity of 32s. to be issuing and going, and to be received, levied, and taken out of all that messuage or tenement situate in East Street, otherwise Gallows Street, in Great Coggeshall, commonly called by the name or sign of the *King's Arms*, and the garden and yards thereunto, belonging then or then late in the tenure of Robert Sutton, or his assigns, upon trust, that the trustees should dispose of the annuity and employ and lay out the same in linen cloth upon the 24th June in every year, for the benefit of the most aged poor and necessitous persons inhabiting within the parish of Great Coggeshall, with provisions for appointment of new trustees, and with power of distress and a covenant by the grantor to keep the premises in repair.

The last appointment of new trustees was by deed dated 14th April, 1783, the last survivor of whom was Osgood Hanbury, Esq., who died in 1856.

The property, subject to the annuity, was sold by auction in 1870 by the trustees of the will of the late Mr. William Swinborne, and then consisted of a range of five cottage tenements with gardens in East Street, adjoining the Swan public-house towards the east, and then in the occupation of French, Keys, Thurgar and Evans, and one unoccupied.

The cottages were purchased by the late Mr. Matthias Alfred Gardner, whose representatives regularly pay the annuity.

In 1837, the Charity Commissioners suggested that the annuity should be henceforth paid to the vicar and overseers, to be expended as directed by Jane Gooday's will, in needful clothing for the aged poor.

The annual sum of 32s. is received by the vicar and churchwardens, and given away by them in flannel to eleven aged poor persons, chiefly widows.

𝔏𝔞𝔫𝔡 𝔦𝔫 𝔚𝔢𝔰𝔱 𝔖𝔱𝔯𝔢𝔢𝔱.

THERE is a small piece of ground in West Street, lying between the Gelatine Factory on the east and a plot of garden ground (No 316, Ordnance Survey) on the west. It was formerly let at 10s. a year, but 7s. 6d. only is now paid for it by the occupiers, Messrs. Pfander Swinborne.

This may be the site of the "two almes houses at the upper end of West Street, going to Braintree, given by Sir Mark Guyon to this parish in lieu of two alms houses yt were pulled down neare his houses," referred to in Holman's MS.

The income of this small property is generally given to the Clothing Club.

Ann Richardson's Charity.

ANN RICHARDSON, by her will (the date of which in the Parliamentary Returns of 1786 is stated to be 1726) gave to Thomas Wilsher and his heirs, a freehold messuage or farm called *Romans*, with the lands thereto belonging, situate at East Hanningfield and Rettendon, in Essex, upon trust yearly and for ever to pay to the overseers of Little Coggeshall £8, to be by them distributed in bread, weekly, to the poor husbandmen and widows of husbandmen belonging to the said parish, who should take no collection, but there being no church in Little Coggeshall her will was that the bread should be given in the church of Great Coggeshall.

The property, subject to the annuity, belonged, in 1837, to a Mr. William Cook, and was occupied by his tenant, Whitamore.

On the 14th March, 1842, in a suit, the Attorney-General *v.* Cook and others, a scheme was settled by one of the Masters in Chancery and provided *inter alia*, that the overseers and church-wardens of Little Coggeshall shall keep a list in each year of the names of all the deserving poor husbandmen and poor widows of husbandmen who are parishioners of Little Coggeshall not receiving parochial relief, from which list they shall select the persons who are to partake of the charity, but such persons shall and may be removed from such list when and as such overseers and church-wardens shall see occasion, who are to distribute rateably and in rotation to and amongst such persons, so that all on such list may in their turn partake of the advantage of the Charity; that the persons who shall be entitled to partake of the Charity shall be such persons only as are inhabitants or belong to the parish of Little Coggeshall, and are poor husbandmen or widows of poor husbandmen not receiving parochial relief, preference to be given to the most aged and infirm; that there shall be five trustees appointed of the Charity who shall receive the annuity or rent-charge of £8 per annum, and lay out the same in the purchase of bread, weekly, by 3s. at a time, except in Christmas week when there shall be expended 7s., and which bread, when purchased, shall be distributed to and amongst poor husbandmen and poor widows of husbandmen not receiving parochial relief; that if at any time there shall be no trustees of the Charity, the officiating minister for the time being and the churchwardens and overseers shall be considered and taken to be trustees of the Charity, and entitled to receive the annuity and give a receipt for the same, and to distribute the bread until trustees shall be duly appointed.

By a subsequent order on further directions, in the year 1842, the scheme was varied by appointing the officiating minister and churchwardens and overseers of the parish to be trustees of the Charity.

Further information concerning this Charity may be obtained by an inspection of the proceedings in Chancery in 1835, Goodson *v.* Cook.

Mrs. Richardson was probably the same person as Ann, the wife of Mr. John Richardson, and daughter of Mr. John Willsher, of Scripps Farm, Little Coggeshall. John Richardson died, 20th November, 1693, aged 33, and was buried in Coggeshall churchyard, where also was laid his only daughter, Anne, who died, 13th September, 1712, aged 18 years.

The Amalgamated Charities.

COMPRISING

The Market Houses or Wordsworth's Charity, Crane's Charity. The Almshouses or Greenwood's Charity, Johan Smith's Charity, or the Tilbury Bread Money, and Hibben's Cottages.

IT is proposed first to consider each of these Charities in the order indicated above, and subsequently to deal with them as one combined Charity.

The Market Houses or Wordsworth's Charity.

THE site of these houses, for they have long since been demolished, is well known to the inhabitants of Coggeshall. It comprises about twelve rods of ground, lying at the southern extremity of Stoneham Street, and at its junction with Church Street. At the time of the report of the Charity Commissioners, about 1837, there were posts under ground which defined the exact extent of the property. The posts having decayed, the parish in vestry assembled, on the 15th June, 1865, adopted a plan of the property, which (with the concurrence of the trustees of the Charity) was submitted to them by the surveyors of the highways. This plan was reproduced by the writer, in a paper on the Amalgamated Charities, published in 1888.

The first record we find of this property is in the report of the Commissioners, appointed in the 2nd year of King Edward VI., to make enquiries concerning Chantry properties, and in which is the following :—"Item, one old Chapel in the street there, with a little Garden, which is worth by the year, 4s." It may be that this is the chapel to which reference is made in the will of Thomas Halle, of Coksale, dated 15th January, 1499-1500, and proved on 5th February, following :—"I bequeth towarde the edifying and making of a Chapell within the said towne of Coksale, XXˢ to be paid when the said Chapell is in werkyng,"

King Edward VI. gave the old chapel, &c. to Ralph Agard and Thomas Smyth, from whom it passed to Reginald Hollingworth, and descended to his son, Lawrence Hollingworth, and from him it was conveyed to Robert Wordsworth, of Great Birch, Essex, gentleman, who on the 7th October, in the 30th year of Queen Elizabeth's reign (A.D. 1588), for divers good causes, &c., granted the same chapel to certain inhabitants of Coggeshall, by the description of "*Totam illam veterem Capellam modo usitat p le Corne Markett howse ac unu pvu gardinu eid Capelle adiacen cu ptin scituat et existen in Coggeshall pred,*" or to render it in English, "All that old Chapel now used for the Corn Market House, and one small garden to the same Chapel adjoining with the appurtenances situate and being in Coggeshall aforesaid."

From an inquisition, taken by Sir Henry Maxey and Sir Thomas Wyseman, knights, and others, in the 11th year of King James I., it appears that the purchasers from Robert Wordsworth were persons representing the trades of the fullers and weavers at Coggeshall. These persons converted the chapel into a market house or place of mart or meeting, with rooms for stowage and other uses, and a clock and watch-bell were there kept for the better ordering of apprentices of the two trades. The Commissioners, after making enquiries into the charity generally, proceeded to decree the manner in which the charity should in future be administered, which was, to put it concisely, that the property should be let to a fuller or weaver, that the house and rooms with the clock and watch-bell should for ever be kept repaired, renewed and maintained with the rents and profits of the premises, and the surplus profits paid to the fullers and weavers and to the poor of Coggeshall generally.

From 1635 till 1719 the property is referred to as the Corn and Butter Market Houses; in 1774, as the Market Houses. *

In 1776, the trustees of the charity let part of the property to Richard White, by the description of the Wool-hall over the Market Place, reserving to themselves the chamber or room wherein the town clock of the parish then stood, with the staircase to the same belonging, with free liberty to go to and from the same to repair and wind up the town clock.

The trust deed of 3rd August, 1795, records the following facts, viz. :—That the old chapel used for market purposes having become so ruinous and out of repair as to be incapable of being repaired, the trustees (with the consent of the parishioners) caused the old buildings to be pulled down and the material thereof to be sold, and with part of the proceeds they built a turret or clock house upon other premises belonging to the poor of Great Coggeshall (Crane's Charity), and placed therein the said clock and watch-bell for the use of the parishioners of Great Coggeshall. The surplus of the proceeds of sale was employed in building two almshouses on Greenwood's charity land, south of Buttfield, near the church.

The exact date of the pulling down of the Market Houses was recorded by Henry Emery, of Market Hill, who died in 1844, aged 78; his note is, "Began pulling down the Market Cross of Great Coggeshall, 16th June, 1787—23rd, finished pulling."

In Bufton's Diary is the following note anent the clock, "30th September, 1686, a new clock was set up at the Market House, made at London, said to cost £23."

In 1837, the Charity Commissioners directed that the profits arising from this plot of ground, and which consisted of rents amounting to less than £1 per annum, paid for stallage when fairs were held near the spot, should be applied by the trustees in the same manner as the income of Paycocke's Charity. It has not,

---

* 1679—Moses Love, weaver cryer, clerk of the market was buried (Bufton).

however, been so applied for very many years past, but is devoted
to the general purposes of the charity, as to which *see post.*

Crane's Charity.

SAMUEL CRANE, of Great Coggeshall, gentleman, made his
will, in November, 1669, and thereby gave the rents and
profits of his messuage, in Stoneham Street, Great Coggeshall,
then in the occupation of Elizabeth Starling, widow, to the use of
the poor of Great Coggeshall for ever, *to be laid out in bread* and
delivered to them every five and twentieth day of December, and
so continue for ever.   And he authorised his executors to make
a feoffment of the said premises to twelve, at least, of the most
substantial inhabitants of the town of Great Coggeshall, and he
appointed William Cox, the elder, and Isaac Hubbard to be his
executors.

William Cox, the elder, and Isaac Hubbard, as such executors,
on the 8th December, 1671, conveyed the house and premises to
Matthew Guyon, John Cox, the elder, Richard Sheppard, John
Bufton, the elder, John Cox, the younger, Thomas Buxton,
Samuel Sparhawke, Thomas Cox, Paul Pemberton, William
Guyon, William Cox, the younger, John Willbore, the elder, Isaac
Cooke, John Cockerill, John Bower, Roger Mullings, John
Willbore, the younger, Benjamin Sampson, Richard Shortland,
Ambrose Sutton, Simon Richold, Robert Sampson, Thomas
Keeble, George Richold and John Bufton, the younger, all
substantial inhabitants of Great Coggeshall, aforesaid.   The deed
contained provision for the appointment of new trustees when
the number is reduced to seven.

The property was from time to time conveyed to new trustees.

In 1837, according to the report of the Charity Commissioners, the trust premises were divided and let as follows :—Two
rooms were let to James Potter, at £2 per annum ; two rooms to
Henry Emery, the schoolmaster of Sir Robert Hitcham's School,
at £2 10s. per annum ; one large room over the master's
residence, used as a schoolroom for the Hitcham School, the
passage leading to Potter's rooms and the staircase, were let to
the master, fellows and scholars of Pembroke College, Cambridge,
as trustees of Sir Robert Hitcham's Charity, from Michaelmas,

1787, for 500 years, at a peppercorn rent. The consideration for which, however, was not known, but it appeared that £60 1s. 1d. was laid out by the Hitcham School trustees in extensive repairs to this property, about the time the lease was granted. The lease was surrendered upwards of twenty-five years ago.

There was also the clock turret, which, it will have been observed from the preceding account of the market houses, was supplied out of the fund arising from the sale of the materials of the old market houses.

A free rent of 8d. per annum is payable to the lord of the manor of Great Coggeshall in respect of this property.

The trust premises are now in the occupation of John Cook, at a rent of £8 8s. per annum.

One penny per annum was formerly paid by Mr. William Denney, for the use of a pipe laid down in Stoneham Street by sufference of the trustees.

The income of this charity goes towards the general expenses of the amalgamated charities.

The Almshouses or Greenwood's Charity.

As to two of the Almshouses:—

Joseph Greenwood, of Great Coggeshall, by deed, dated 2nd August, 1795, granted to the then surviving trustees of the Market Houses, namely, Thomas Bridge, David Crumpton, William Dixon, Richard Meredith White, Stephen Unwin, Fisher Unwin, Haddon Rudkin, Henry Shetelworth, and William Walford, a piece of ground, parcel of a close of land, called "Buttfield," situate in Church Lane, otherwise Back Lane, in Great Coggeshall, containing in length from east to west, 31 feet, and in breadth from north to south, 14½ feet, and abutting on Church Lane towards the south, upon trust for the poor of the parish for the purpose of erecting thereon two cottages or tenements for the use of the poor.

The trustees spent the sum of £50, part of the fund produced by the sale of the Market Houses, in building two cottages or tenements on the piece of ground before-mentioned, in order as far as in them lay to continue the charitable provision of the decree of the commissioners for charitable uses, mentioned under the preceding account of the Market Houses.

N

As to the remainder of the Almshouses :—

The Joseph Greenwood, before-mentioned, by deed, dated 11th December, 1795, conveyed another part of "Buttfield," containing in length from east to west, 62 feet, and in breadth from north to south, 14¼ feet, and abutting upon Church Lane towards the south, to Osgood Hanbury, upon trust for the parishioners and inhabitants of Coggeshall, to the intent that they should build thereon four cottages, for such poor persons belonging to the parish to reside in, who should be incapable of providing habitations for themselves, to be selected by the churchwardens and overseers in such manner as they should think most beneficial.

Four cottages were subsequently built with some monies left by the will of the late Mr. Osgood Hanbury, and the proceeds of the sale of an old Pest House and perhaps of some almshouses, which Morant, writing in 1768, mentions thus, "There are three almshouses adjoining to the churchyard without endowment."

The six tenements comprise twelve rooms, which are occupied by a corresponding number of old people.

Johan Smith's Charity, or the Tilbury Bread Money.

BY her will, dated 21st April, 1601, Johan Smith, of London, widow, directed her executors to pay to her son, Sir William Smith, £400, therewith to purchase the sum of 40 marks yearly, to be bestowed and employed for the relief of the poor in Coxall and Bocking, the same to continue and be as her free gift unto them for ever; twenty marks (13s. 4d. each) *to be bestowed upon the Poor of Coxall yearly, by 5s. in Bread every Sunday,* the distributors thereof to have for their pains yearly, 6s. 8d. And the other 20 marks to be bestowed upon the poor of Bocking in like manner.

By deed, dated 25th November, 3rd James 1st (1605), Sir William Smith, of Lound, Leicestershire, Knight, in consideration of £400 then come to his hands and in due performance and execution of the before-mentioned will, and in discharge of the confidence and trust reposed in him by his mother, Johan Smith, so far as concerned the town of Coggeshall, did grant unto Thomas Fuller, Thomas Aylett, Henry Warner, George Cockerell,

Thomas Bridges, Thomas Shortland, Nicholas Richold, Thomas Gray, John Gray, Jun., Thomas Guyon, William Gladwin, Thomas Alleston, Robert Fuller, Jun., William Bufton, Clement Gymlett, William Clark, Jun., John Clemence, William Fuller, Jun., Thomas Shortland, Jun., and Robert Crane, all inhabitants of Coggeshall, one yearly rent of twenty marks, to be issuing out of a house and the site of the monastery or priory of Lound, in Leicestershire, and the lands thereto belonging, to be paid at lady day and michaelmas day, upon condition *(inter alia)* that if the said Sir William Smith should convey one other like rent-charge of twenty marks to the trustees, to be issuing out of lands of adequate value near London or Coggeshall, then the rent-charge on the estate at Lound should cease.

By deed, dated 6th June, 15th James I. (1617), the said Sir William Smith and Humphry Smith, the grantees from King James I., of a fee farm rent of £15 issuing out of the rectory and church of East Tilbury, in Essex, conveyed the same fee farm rent to the before-mentioned trustees, as a full recompence and satisfaction of the said yearly rent of twenty marks, charged on the estate at Lound, but upon trust for the poor of Coggeshall according to the true meaning of the said will, and with a proviso for the appointment of new trustees.

In 1837, the rectory of East Tilbury belonged to the Rev. Edwin Lloyd, and at that time the income of the charity (after payment of expenses) was distributed in bread made up into thirty twopenny loaves, which were given away at the Church every Sunday after service, amongst poor parishioners selected by the churchwardens in equal shares.

Thirteen pounds per annum is still given away in bread in thirty twopenny loaves at the church every Sunday.

Hibben's or Weaver's Charity.

FROM the Parliamentary Returns of 1786, it appears that Anthony Hibben, *alias* Weaver, by his will gave to the poor of Coggeshall land then producing £5 per annum.

A deed of appointment of new trustees, dated 14th April, 1783 (after reciting that neither the will of Anthony Hibben nor any title deeds to the trust property could be found, and that Richard White was then possessed of the property thereinafter described), the said Richard White conveyed to Osgood Hanbury

and twelve others, all that messuage or tenement with the yards,
gardens and hereditaments, in Church Street, in Great Coggeshall,
abutting upon Church Street towards the south, upon trust that
they should dispose of the rents and profits amongst poor
inhabitants of Great Coggeshall yearly, upon the 1st of January,
for ever, in such parts as they should think fit. The deed contained provisions as to the appointment of new trustees.

In 1837, the property of this charity consisted of three
tenements under one roof, and a small yard in Church Street,
Coggeshall, then let to William Clarke, John Raven and the
Overseers, as yearly tenants, at rents amounting to £9 4s. per
annum, which was distributed with Paycock's Charity.

The trust property is now (1889) in the occupations of
Robert Evans, Elijah Fairs and Jacob Rowland.

The income is exhausted by the general expenses for repairs,
rates, &c.

The Amalgamated Charities.

THE before-mentioned charities are collectively known by
this name.

The first appointment of trustees of these charities by the
Charity Commissioners, was made by an order, dated 7th August,
1863, and by it the incumbent and churchwardens and their
successors in office, and thirteen other inhabitants of Great
Coggeshall, were appointed trustees, and the legal estate in the
trust properties was vested in the official trustee of charity lands
and his successors in trust for the charity.

The new trustees thus appointed took steps to obtain a scheme
for the future management of the charity; but the scheme, which
was drafted in 1863, was not proceeded with.

The present trustees are :—

The Rev. Hubert Mornington Patch, Vicar of Coggeshall.

Joseph Smith Surridge, } Churchwardens.
George Frederick Beaumont, }

William Gentry Dennis.

John Shuttleworth.

Edward Alexander Applebe, } Appointed by order of the Charity
John Beard, } Commissioners, dated 11th Octo-
Edward Edgar, } ber, 1887, to act jointly with the
John Bruff Frith, } before-named, who were the con-
Thomas Simpson, } tinuing trustees at the date of
} the Order.

By the order of 11th October, 1887, the Commissioners directed that :—

The right to sue for, recover, receive and to give receipts and discharges for all sums of money, rents in arrear, and choses in action due to or recoverable for the benefit of the charities, should vest in the trustees thereby appointed individually, jointly with the continuing trustees, their executors, administrators and assigns, in trust for the said charities.

As there is no scheme for the administration of the charity, it follows that the intentions of the several donors must be observed as far as possible.

1. The income derived from the Market Hill, should be applied for the relief of the poor, for instance, in the insurance and repair of the almshouses.

2. The income from Crane's Charity, after deducting the necessary outgoings, should be laid out in bread for the poor, to be delivered to them every Christmas Day.

3. The Almshouses should be used as such.

4. Bread of the value of £15 per annum, less 6s. 8d. for distributor (Johan Smith's Charity), should be given away every Sunday in equal portions.

5. The net income of Hibben's Cottages should be applied for the benefit of the poor.

The National Schools.

IN the years 1838-9, two pieces of ground on the west side of Stoneham Street, where the old workhouse stood, were conveyed to the vicar and churchwardens of Coggeshall, as a site for a building to be used as a school for the purpose of educating the children of the poor according to the principles of the National Society. In 1847, a site was acquired for the residence of the master and mistress of the schools, and, in 1875, the premises were further extended by the purchase of an adjoining cottage and garden. The buildings consist of two spacious rooms in separate enclosures, one for boys and the other for girls ; there is also a suitable residence for the schoolmistress. The schools are maintained by voluntary subscriptions, government grants, school-pence, and collections at church.

The British Schools.

THESE schools adjoin the Independent Chapel, and are built on a piece of land purchased in 1841. They are held in trust to provide education for the children of the poor, subject to the rules prescribed by those who provide the funds for their support, but no child is to be excluded by reason of any religious or other matters of distinction of sect or party. Their maintenance is provided for in the same manner as the National Schools.

MANUFACTURES.

The Cloth Trade.

ONE of the earliest trades of the country was that of manufacturing wool into cloth, and the statutes of the realm abound with enactments giving encouragement to the clothworkers and regulating the manufacture. Thus, King Henry II. directed that if any cloth were found to be made of Spanish wool mixed with English wool the mayor of London should see it burnt, and in the 11th year of King Edward III. we find it ordained that no cloth should be worn but such as was made in England; and in the same year another statute encourages the foreigner to settle here, by enacting that "all the clothworkers of strange lands of whatsoever country they be, which shall come into England, Ireland, Wales and Scotland within the King's power, shall come safely and surely, and shall be in the King's protection and safe conduct to dwell in the same lands choosing where they will, and, to the intent the said clothworkers shall have the greater will to come and dwell here, our Sovereign Lord the King will grant them franchises as many and such as may suffice them." This statute and the advantages which followed induced many Flemish manufacturers to settle in England, especially in the eastern counties.

Fuller's *Church History* describes the attractions offered by Edward III. to the foreign manufacturers in graphic language :— "Here," says he, "they shall feed on beef and mutton till nothing but their fulness shall stint their stomachs ; yea, they shall feed on the labor of their own hands enjoying a proportionable profit of their pains to themselves, and the richest yeo-

men in England would not disdain to marry their daughters unto
them, and such the English beauties that the most curious foreign-
ers could not but commend them.   Happy the yeomen's house
into which one of these Dutchmen did enter bringing industry
and wealth along with them.   Such, who came in strangers within
doors, soon after went out bridegrooms and returned sons-in-law
having married the daughters of their landlords who first entertained them, yea those yeomen in whose houses they harboured
soon proceeded gentlemen, gaining great estates to themselves,
arms and worship to their estates."

In 1557 (4 & 5 Philip and Mary, c. 5) especial mention is
made of Coggeshall as a cloth manufacturing town, and there is
no doubt that at this date the trade was well established here.
This statute, after reciting that the Act 5 and 6 Edward VI., which
provided for the true and perfect making of woollen cloth, was
oppressive to divers clothiers and could not be observed in all
points, enacted among other things that "Forasmuch as many
persons do counterfeit the making of *Cocksal*, Bocking and Braintree Clothes, commonly called Handywarps, adding thereto such
like lists as the makers of such clothes do, to the great deceit of
the King and Queen's Majesties' subjects, therefore no person or
persons from the first day of May next coming shall add unto any
cloth or clothes any such like list or lists except the warp thereof
be spun upon the rock or distaff upon pain of forfeiture of the
same cloth or clothes or the very value thereof," &c.   The 34th
section of this statute provided that persons dwelling in certain
counties, or in the town of Goddelmine, in Surrey, might make
cloth outside a city borough or market town as they had formerly
done notwithstanding the provisions of this Act, but Coggeshall
and other towns in Essex were not granted this privilege, and,
consequently, the trade was seriously affected in these places and
would probably have become extinct much earlier than it did but
for the statute passed in 1558 (1 Eliz. c. 14), which recites and
enacts that "Forasmuch as the towns or villages of Bocking,
Westharfold, Dedham and Cockshall, in the county of Essex, be
fair large towns and as well planted for clothmaking as the said
town of Goddelmine or better, and few towns in this realm better
planted for that purpose, and have been inhabited of a long time
with clothmakers, which have made and daily do make good and
true cloth to the great commonweal of the country there, and

nothing prejudicial to or for the commonwealth of this realm, Be it therefore ordained and enacted by the authority of this present Parliament that it shall be lawful to all and every such person and persons which now do inhabit and dwell or hereafter shall dwell in the said towns or villages of Bocking, Westharfold, Cockshall and Dedham, or in any of them now using or exercising, or that hereafter shall use or exercise the feat or mystery of making, weaving, or rowing of cloth or kersie by the space of seven years at the least or have been prentice thereto by the said space of seven years to inhabit and dwell in the said towns and villages of Bocking, Westharfold, Cockshall and Dedham, and in every or any of them, and to use the making, weaving or rowing of cloth or kersie as before this time they might have done if the said Act had never been made, anything in the said Act to the contrary thereof made or any other Act, statute or law heretofore made or hereafter to be made to the contrary hereof in anywise notwithstanding."

The following petition *(State Papers Domestic,* Eliz., Vol. 106, No. 47) was presented by the woollen manufacturers of this town in the year 1575 :—" To the Right honorable Lorde and others of her Majesties most honorable pryvie Counsell, Humbly complayning shewe unto your honors her Majesties poore tenauntes of the towne of Coxhall and other poore clothiers inhabyting there aboute   That whereas oppon complaynt lately made by them unto her highness against John Hastinges, Esquior, touching manye wronges and oppressions offred to them by color of her majesties letters patentes granted to him for the making of ffreesadoes after the maner of Harlam yt pleased her Majestie oppon pytie of their poore estate to commytt th' examination and ending of the same cause unto your honors to th' intent that your poore orators might receive some ende of their troubles and more peaceably hereafter use their trade.   Nowe for information unto your honors of the troathe they say that those woollen cloathes called Bayes which they usually make and whereby they and many hundred people lyve and are maytayned be nether within the letter or meaning of the aforesaide letters patentes being an other kinde of clothe differing many wayes from the ffreesadoes of Harlem making as shall appeare; ffirste in name they differ for that th' one are called ffreesadoes and the other broade bayes ; in breadthe they differ one halfe quarter of a yarde for that their bayes conteyne but vij quarters and his ffreesadoeves by the letters patentes muste conteyne vij quarters and one halfe quarter. In lengthe they differ for that his ffreesadowes are dosens and their bayes commonly contayne ffortye yards in lengthe. In waighte they differ greatly for that their bayes being far more sufficiently made doe contayne at the least one pounde waighte in everye yarde more then is in the ffreesadowes. Also bayes are made altogither by hande warpe, but his ffreesadowes were made by rœll warpe ontill nowe of late Maister Hastinges did learne the hande warpe of certayne clothemakers in Essex. Also bayes are nether died nor rottened by your orators to be ffreesadowes but are left whyte to bee wroughte to such use as the Drapers please either for blanckettes, carpettes or otherwise as other whyte cloathes are (for al manner of woollen broade cloathes, being white may be wroughte into ffreesadowes and so all cloathes should be within the compasse of his letters patentes by Mr. Hastinges' pretence) And beside those differences and many others it is very true and so to be proved by the othes of many ancient men of creditt whose names are subscribed that this maner of bayes now used in Essex was usually made in that countrye above Thirtye yeares before the date of his letters patentes. All which said premisses upon occasion of diverse suites of Mr. Hastinges in her Majesties Courte of Exchecker and els where have bene proved and made knowne bothe to him and many others of good calling and creditt and yett notwithstanding your poore orators have been so contynually vexed by the said Mr. Hastinges and his servauntes and their clothes taken from them and some of their clothes torne in pieces by Mr. Hastinges servauntes against all right and equityc so that poore men being undone by that occasion have bene forced to give over their trade and others have bene compelled against their willes to subscribe to articles made according to his will and desire Wherein if by your honors good meanes they be not spedily relieved it will turne to the utter undoing of your poore orators and of many pore men their wyves and famylyes who are sett on worke only by that trade.

NYCKELUS CHASSEY (? Chaffey) hys marke
by me WYLL A. DENE, 65.
JOHN SUTTON being LXXXVIII yers
JOHN BOTHEM being LXX yers
by me ROBERT SANDER being LXXII yeres

WILLIAM TYLL being LXVI yeres
RICHARD EMENG being LXXV yeres."

In connection with the Spanish Armada, it may be mentioned that the bailiffs of Colchester on the 16th April, 1588, presented a petition to Sir Thomas Heneage, Vice-Chamberlain, desiring that the inhabitants of Coggeshall, Dedham and East Bergholt, might not be excused their contribution towards the furnishing of the ship charged upon them for the Queen's service.*

"A true note and certificate (under date 6th July, 1577) of such wull as hath bene bought by the clothiers of Coggeshall aforesayde synce the first day of August, Anno 1576 "† shows that the following persons were at that time engaged in this the staple business of the town :—Thomas Tyll, William Armond, John Gooddaye, John Pierceson, Robert Draper, Robert Lytherland, Robert Jegon, Thomas Annsell, Edmond Tyler, William Trewe, John Sweeting, Richard Larke, Christopher Watson, Thomas Graye, Robert Pitchfourd, William Gyon, Wm. Clarke, John Saunder, Wm. Saunder and Thomas Canon, the last of whom "bought, as is supposed, not lesser than XL toddes, for he being from home we could not know the certaintye ;" and the certificate ends by stating that "all these parcells of wull in ye cast being broken hath bene bought of Mr. Freeman, stapeler, and yet a maker of bayes at Mauldon (to ye hindrance of all clothiers) or of his deputye by those whose names folowe, Thomas Dammat, Robert Larke, Thomas Graye, John Watson, Thomas Cole, Thomas Sutton, Thomas Lawrence."

Coggeshall is mentioned by Norden, in 1594, as one of the "especial clothing towns" of the County of Essex, and he goes on to tell us that " Cogshall is specially famous for the most rare *Whites* there made exceeding any cloth in the land for rare fineness and therefore called Cogshall whites. It is governed by 24 head-boroughs of whom are chosen two constables for the time being chief governors of the town."

The following extracts from the State Papers, Domestic *temp.* Commonwealth (Vol. 25, Nos. 51 & 52) are of sufficient interest to admit of their being set out verbatim, for they give much valuable information, concerning not only the trade here but the times generally :—

---

* State Papers Dom., Vol. 209, No. 93.   † Ibid, Vol. 114, No. 47.

"1652, 29 Oct. To the honble Councell for Trade.
  The Humble Petition of the Clothiers of Coggeshall in
    the County of Essex
  Humbly shewing

That whereas in their General Peticon many Grievances have byn presented to this Honble Councell And yor Petrs had free accesse and diverse hearings with promise of redresse with best expedition

And for that the Ingrossers of wooll are now as active in buying so soon as the same is shorne, or before it is of from the sheepes back as heretofore

Therefore your Petrs. most humbly pray this honoble. Councell to expedite their redresse And also to graunt yor. Petrs. full power to elect officers amongst themselves for regulating the making of manufacturyes in the aforesaid towne And that they may be graunted a distinct *seal with a cocke* upon the same to distinguish their true making for the honor and benefitt of this Commonwealth; not prohibiting other townes or places from making the like sort, they having also their particular seale, or from enjoying the same seale they observing the same Rule and Government with yor. Petrs.

And yor. Petrs. shall pray, etc.

Officers to be chosen yearly by the Inhabitantes (using the trade) successively and first to be established by the persons hereunder written for Rules and Orders :—Thomas Guyon, Wm. Gladwyne, Richard Shortland, John Sparhawke, William Tanner, Sen., Edmond Coxe, Henery Johnston, Ambrose Browning, Robt. Hills, William Guyon, Richard Sheppard, John Cockerell, John Sampson, Wm. Coxe, John Coxe, Wm. Tanner, Jun., John Bufton, Samuell Coxe, John Cooke, John Grey." (No. 51)

"1652, Nov. 3, To the right honourble. the Councell of State for the Commonwealth of England sitting at Whitehall, the humble petition of the Clothiers at Coggeshall in Essex.

Humbly shews that whereas by the making of Coggeshall bayes *many thousands* of poore people are employed, which bayes have been exported by merchants into parts beyond seas called the Straights which for a yeare past have bin obstructed and of late wholly prevented since the Hollander is turned against us insomuch as that without strong Convoyes (to bee granted by this state) the merchants will not adventure their goods whereby for sixe moneths past your Petitionrs. have had no sale for their bayes, their stocks and credits are improved to the uttermost, and without some vent of their goods they are no way able to proceed in their trade or to set their poore on work which are already become so numerous that without worke they must bee kept or starved, which yor petitionrs. are not able to prevent for the charge of collection in this place exceeds all other, every 20 li. per an. paying 5 li. yeerely to the poore and so answerably and the rather because yor petitionrs. have bin and are still much disenabled for that in 1642 in their ardent affection to the Parliamt. they did upon the publike faith lend greater summs of money than any place in the nation (they could ever heare of) even . . . . n times beyond men of equal estates and indeed beyond their own ability joyning together in Bonds for sums of money upon interest, the which for great part is held at interest to this day by which meanes many persons with their families have bin undone, being not able to pay a quarter of their debts and others endamaged by their bonds to pay for their neighbours alsoe the time of ten years being now expired they are necessitated to represent their undoing condition and all the premises considered yor Petitionrs doe humbly pray this honble Councell to commiserate their distresse and to grant them speedy reliefe.

1. That the merchants for trade may have all encouragement, that they may know of forraine nations who are friends and not have their estates suddenly surprised as in Portugale, Holland and Denmark in which hazards the richest merchants have bin caused to surcease merchandizing and to purchase lands.

2. That sufficient Convoyes of ships for warre may be with speed granted to the Straights and other countreys.

3. That forasmuch as your Petitioners in general are so extremely disenabled and discouraged for want of their money lent upon the publicke faith which amounts to above 6000 li. in this poore towne and that yor Petitioners have bin constantly faithfull and usefull by setting out forces at their owne charges to assist the Parliamt. farre beyond their abilities that some way may be prescribed whereby yor petitioners may be paid ther true debts in the first place and that with speed before your Petitioners are wholly undone.

And your Petitioners shall ever pray, etc.

Robert Crane, Thomas Guyon, William Gladwine, John Digby,

John Sparhawke, John Huntsman, Henry Johnson, John Cocke-
rell, Michaell Richolds, Ciprian Streett, John Streete, Nicholas
Street, Thomas Cooke, Josiff Clarke, John Till, Wm. Tanner,
William Cox, John Cox, Samuel Cox, John Bufton, William Ar-
nolds (? blotted), William Costered, Willyam Motos, Paull Pember-
ton, Thomas Shortland, John Lees, Thomas Swan, Edmond Cox,
Richard Shortland, John Gray, John Sampson, Ambrose Sutton,
William Tanner, Thomas Nicholls, Ffrancis Page, Roger Sturges,
John Bowyer, William Raulinson, William Emen (? Ennew),
Richard Pemberton, John Sloman, Edward Bond, Thomas
Nicholls, John Nicholes, Enoch Hinting, Henry Warner, Henry
Hinting, William Asly, Robert Asyle, Robert Mills, John Alegant,
Jacob Watson, Thomas Branwood,* Robert Sebroke, Jeremiah
Perryman, Hennery Frost, John Lyance, John Smith, Sen.,
Thomas Braddye, John Brightwen, Robert Barwell, William
Dimbleby, William Hills, Abraham Cooke, Thomas Bringest,
Edward Lees, John Till, Jun., John London, Robert Wheeler,
John Royce, George Irland." (52)

In or about 1664, certain orders were drawn up for the trade
and mystery of the clothiers, fullers, baymakers, and new drapers,
in the town of Coggeshall, and were confirmed by the Quarter
Sessions of the Peace. These orders provided that none should
use the trade unless they had been apprenticed seven years, that
none should be apprenticed unless one of their parents had 40s.
a year freehold, that one journeyman should be kept for every
three apprentices. Fines were imposed on those who absented
themselves from the guild; and warrants were issued by the
magistrates requiring the wardens of the company, and the constables of the town to prosecute all intruders into the trade, and
offenders against the orders. The signatories to the orders were
Richard Shortland, Mathew Guyon, Mark Guyon, John Guyon,
William Gladwin, William Cox, Jo Cox, Jo Gray, Jo Sampson,
Sen., Benjamin Sampson, Paul Pemberton, Robert Nicholas,
Peter Pridmore, K. Neele, T. Purcas, J. Rodley, Sen., T. Keeble,
R. Sheppard, W. Clarke, S. Harvey, Ambrose Sutton.

The warders for the fullers, in 1659, were N. Gladwin and
Wm. Hatton; in 1698, Robert Nicholas and John Andrews; in

---

* A query appeared in *East Anglian Notes*, N.S., Vol. II., p. 255, as to
this family, a member of which, tradition says, settled in Hartford, Connecti-
cut, U.S.A., about 1650.

1710, John Hatten, Jun. and John Philbricke; and in 1799, William Mayhew and Mark Cowell.

The feoffees for the fullers, in 1659, were John Rodley and Willm. Clark, Junr., and the stock £22 11s. 6d.; in 1799, F. Lay and J. Seex, who are the last-named feoffees in the book of orders, divided the remaining stock among about thirty persons, on 14th November, 1800.

The old Wool Hall is noticed elsewhere, under the head of 'The Charities.'

The Guild Hall, which was probably connected with the woollen manufacture of the place, may be referred to here. The earliest record concerning it is contained in the Certificate of Chantry Land for Essex, 2 Edward IV., under Coggeshall in Lexden Hundred—"Item, one house then called the Yield Hall, and is worth by the year, 5s." The situation is ascertained by an abuttal reference in the Court Rolls of the Manor of Great Coggeshall, contained in the admission of Thomas Ludgater, who, A.D. 1693, on the surrender of William Till, and Maria, his wife, became possessed of the property which adjoins the site of the Guild Hall towards the west, and is described in the abbreviated Latin of those days which, for the benefit of the general reader, may be translated and rendered in the following anglicised form: All that his parcel of customary land with the house or cottage thereupon built lying and being in Church Lane in Great Coggeshall, abutting upon a tenement sometime since called the Guild Hall over against the west ("on the part of the east" in subsequent admissions), which premises were sometime in the occupation of George Ireland and are now in the occupation of the said William Till.

The Guild Hall may be found on the south side of Church Lane, commonly known as Back Lane, about 80 feet or thereabouts eastward of Wayne Lane. It is a dwelling in two tenements, measuring about 36 feet by 14 feet. It was probably originally devoid of partition wall or flooring, and thus adapted for an Assembly Room or Hall, and that it was used for this purpose is somewhat confirmed by the fireplace, which consists of an opening on the east side, and measures 6 ft. 10 in. in width by 4 ft. 7 in. in height. In the north wall of the fireplace is a recess 2 ft. wide and 9 in. deep, with an oak seat almost concealed by the layer or two of brickwork above it; on the left (*i.e.* on the east wall), in immediate proximity to the recess and 3 ft. from the floor, is a niche with an angular top and having a base 6 in. in width ; from base to apex it is 11½ inches and it recedes into the wall to the extent of 8 in. This small aperture may have been originally intended for the crucifix or the image of the patron saint of the guild ; in later days, however, it has doubtless served as a receptacle for the host's refreshment.

It was the custom of the clothiers to have an annual procession in honor of Blaize, or Blasius, Bishop of Sebaste, in Armenia, who is said to have invented the art of wool-combing, and was put to death in the persecution under Diocletian, in the year 289, and orations were delivered on these occasions. Thus we find, in 1699, our local poet, Bufton, writing the following verses for the *Bellman* for the *Guilding Morn :—*

> " This day there will a noble feast be made
> For all amongst us of the Fuller's trade
> This ancient custom they do still uphold
> Which hath been used from the days' of old :
> Their wardens for next year will chosen be
> By voice of those who of the trade are free."

And again he tells us that in August, 1688, he wrote the following verses of his own composing :—

> " As in all ages have been some that stood
> Most nobly to promote the public good
> So in the present age some are inclined
> The good of this our Fulling trade to mind."

    *   *   *   *   *   *

The processions appear to have been continued till the close of last century, and below is given the Programme of a Procession exhibited by the Weavers of Coggeshall, on Wednesday the 15th of June, 1791.

" Order of the Procession—

		Two Leaders		
		Two Ensign Bearers		
		Flemings two and two		
Two Orators		The Union Jack		Two Orators
		Two Garlands		
		Drums and Fifes		
		Captain of the Guards		
		Guards two and two		

Lieutenant of the Guards
King Henry the Second with his attending Lord on horseback
Guards two and two
Band of Music
The Shepherd and Shepherdess
A Slay-maker
A Shackle-maker and Loom-maker
Two Ensigns of the Trade
Jack of Newberry and Fleecy care
Two Pappers
Platform
With Britannia and her children, Bezaleel and Aholiab, with
several branches of the trade at work, viz.:—Spinning, Winding,
Warping, and Weaving and the Weavers' Arms
Two Pendents of the Manufacture
Lads and Maids two
Attending two with Garlands
Lads two and Maids two
Attending two with Banners
Lads and Maids two and two
Two Orators
Followed by the Cavalcade two and two

☞ The Procession will set out precisely at Eight o'clock from
the *Bird-in-Hand*
The Procession will not move out of town."

One of the original orations is headed by prints representing
A Woman Spinning. King Henry II. A Man at the Loom.
Then follows :—

"An Oration
For the Procession of the Weavers at Coggeshall
On Wednesday, the 15th of June, 1791.

From ancient Times our useful Art we trace
As sacred Writ records in many a Place ;
All those whose Skill could curious work devise
Wove Coats for Aaron and his Sons likewise ;
The Ephod's Robe was woven all of blue
For Israel's Priest, who holy was and true.

Wise-hearted Women too spun with their hands,
The various Ornaments (by GOD's commands)

o

To inclose the Ark Divine with Curtains made
Of cunning Work, as 'tis in Scripture said
Britons were once a naked, painted Band
But since the nimble Shuttle bless'd the Land
By just degrees the social Arts arose
Polish'd our Hearts and taught the use of Clothes

Long, long may peace extend her pleasing smile
And commerce flourish in our happy Isle
Long may the labors of the British Loom
Clothe distant climes and ages yet to come.

In the latter half of the 17th century tokens, or small copper coins, payable at the place of business of the issuer, came into vogue in Coggeshall and other places. The following is believed to be a complete list of those which were issued by the clothiers and other traders of this town :—

Obverse, * Benjamin Samson—   Samson.†
Reverse, In Coggeshall, 1665—   B. E. S.

Obverse, * Samuel Cox of—   In centre a hand holding a quill.
Reverse, Coggeshall, In Essex.—   S. C.

Obverse, * Robert Purcas—   The Grocer's Arms.
Reverse, In Coggeshall—   R. A. P.

Obverse, * Thomas Guyon In—   A. Rose.
Reverse, Coggeshall, 1667—   T. G.

Obverse, William Guyon, 1670—   A fleur-de-lys.
Reverse, In Coggeshall, In Essex—   His Half Peny. W.R.G.

Obverse, Thomas Beckwith, In—   The Tallow Chandler's Arms.
Reverse, Coggeshall, In Essex—   His Half Peny. T. A. B.

Obverse, * Henry Benyan of—   A Griffin holding a key.
Reverse, Coggeshall in Essex—   H. B.

Obverse, John Digby—   A fleur-de-lys.
Reverse, Cogsall Grocer.—   J. D.

Obverse, John Lark, of—   St. George and the Dragon.
Reverse, Coggeshall, 1667—   J. M. L.

---

* In the possession of the writer.

† Samson is represented holding the jaw-bone of an ass in his right hand and with a robe over his loins and left shoulder.

Obverse, Francis Lay, at the—   a Swan.
Reverse, In Coxhall this for—   Half-a-Peny.   F. D. L.
Obverse, Moses Love, Slay—   a shuttle
Reverse, Maker, of Coggeshall—   M. L.
Obverse, Edmond Spicer—   a sugar loaf
Reverse, In Coggeshall—   a device of two interlaced ovals
Obverse, Ambros Sutton— a greyhound's head collared with a
                              coronet.
Reverse, In Coggeshall, 1665—   A. S. S.

Tambour Lace.

TAMBOUR Lace, or the embroidering of net in cotton, silk, beads, and gold and silver tinsel, is manufactured here, several hands being engaged in the trade, working generally in their own homes. Some of the workers are remarkably skilful and their laces find a ready sale in London and on the Continent. Exquisitely wrought dresses and shawls have been manufactured by the Coggeshall toilers, and have been worn at Her Majesty's Drawing-rooms and at other state assemblies.

Silk Throwsting.

THIS trade, which once found work for several hundreds of men, women and children, has now become extinct. It is said that there were 700 hands employed at the principal mill in the year 1863. This mill belonged to the well-known firm of Durant & Co., the business there being carried on by Messrs. Hall & Son. About twenty years ago this large establishment, which cost many thousands of pounds to erect and furnish, was closed and since then a great part of the population has migrated to find work in the neighbouring towns of Halstead, Braintree, Bocking and elsewhere. Silk velvet is manufactured in the town, but this trade has not been extensively adopted.

Isinglass.

ISINGLASS and Gelatine works were established here many years ago by Messrs. Swinborne, Wallington & Co., and the business is now carried on by the Messrs. Pfander-Swinborne. The articles manufactured by this firm have now a world-wide

O 2

reputation, and Lord Coleridge in a recent case in which the Coggeshall manufacturers were called upon to justify their use of the words, " Patent Isinglass," in giving judgment remarked, that it had been found that the isinglass sold by the Messrs. Swinborne was the most concentrated and perfect form of isinglass, and was well known in the trade having been used for over 30 years.   The works are at the upper end of West Street, and many hands are there engaged.

Brewing.

COGGESHALL is noted for the remarkable quality of its ales.   This is due to the excellent supply of water obtainable here.   There are several important breweries, the beers from which are carried over an extensive area.   The principal businesses taking them in alphabetical order, are those of Mr. John Beard, Messrs. Beard & Bright, Messrs. E. Gardner & Son, and Mr. John Kemp King.   Messrs. Gardner's firm had the satisfaction of being awarded a Diploma of Honour for their pale ale, or bitter beer at the National Brewer's Exhibition, in 1888.

Seed-growing.

THE seed-growing industry is extensively carried on in this neighbourhood, and in the spring and summer months of the year the fields of garden-flowers, including acre after acre of sweet pea, nasturtium, aster, mignionette, &c., contrasting with the green and yellow corn, are the subject of frequent comment by the traveller in the district.   The seed-growing business established by the late Mr. John Kemp King is now well known throughout the country.

The Coggeshalls.

THE arms of this ancient family are Argent ; a cross between four escallops sable. The family does not appear to have had a crest until John Coggeshall, of Fornham, St. Genovese, Suffolk, procured of Robert Cooke, Clarencieux, on the 5th September, 1576, the right to bear " Upon the helme on a wreath argent, a buck couchant sable horned and cleved or., mantled gu., dubled silver " (see Holman's MSS.) ; a boar's head is given as the crest of the family, in Add. MS., 1746, page 23, and in the Rhode Island Magazine, Vol. V., p. 173, the crest appears as a dexter arm embowed holding a sword.

The arms are decidedly typical of pilgrimage, one of the emblems of which is the escallop shell, and another the cross. Carrying the mind back to the days of Richard I., may we not picture an early knight of this family at the Crusades clad in his coat of mail, bearing on his breast a cross, in the beautiful language of Spencer :—

> " The dear remembrance of his dying Lord
> Upon his shield the like was also scored."

The following is the pedigree of the early members of this family :—

1. Sir Thomas Coggeshall, of Coggeshall, Knight, was living in the reign of King Stephen (1149), and had a son,

2. Sir Thomas Coggeshall, also of Coggeshall, Knight, who was living, 1188 and 1194. He had issue Sir Ralph (3) and Sir Roger, who was living 28 Henry III.

3. Sir Ralph de Coggeshall, of Codham Hall, Wethersfield, Knt., was living 1233, died 1305. By his wife, Elizabeth, he had issue—

4. John de Coggeshall, who died, 1296, leaving (in addition to the son from whom descended the Coggeshalls of Hundon, Fornham, &c., Suffolk),

5. Sir John de Coggeshall, of Coggeshall, Knight, who was living in 1302, and married Sara, daughter of Jordan le Brun, Knight. Sir John died 1319, leaving—

6. Sir John de Coggeshall, Lord of Coggeshall, knighted 1337; High Sheriff of Essex for several years. Aged 18 in 1320, proved his age, 1322, died 1361; married Mary (? Margery), daughter and heiress of Henry (? Humphrey) de Stanton of Essex. She died, 1342. (It is this Sir John's monument that is given in Weever.—See Holman's MS.) He had issue Sir Henry and Thomas.

7. Sir Henry Coggeshall, Knight, was 30 years of age in 1361, died 1375, buried at Coggeshall; married Joane, daughter and heiress of William de Welles of Exning; she died 1375. They had issue Sir William, of whom hereafter, and Thomas of Sandon, who held Newhall, in Boreham, in 1391, and died in 1422, having had issue one son and one daughter, Richard the heir, aged 13 in 1422, and died without issue in 1432, and Elizabeth, the daughter married Thomas Philip.

8. Sir William de Coggeshall, of Codham Hall, Wethersfield, Knight, was aged 18, in 1375 and died 1424. High Sheriff, 1391, he married Antiochia, daughter and heiress of Sir John Hawkwood, Knight, the celebrated Captain of Condottien, whose residence was at Sible Hedingham, Essex. Her second husband was Sir John Tyrrell, Knight, of East Horndon, Essex. Sir William, by his wife, Antiochia, had issue no sons but four daughters—

9. i. Blanch, who married John Doreward, Esq., of Bocking.

   ii. Eleanor (? Alice), who married Sir John Tyrell, of Herons, Knight.

   iii. Margaret, who married, first, William Bateman, Esq., of Little Samford, and, secondly, John Roppeley, Esq.

iv. Maud, who married, first, Robert Dacres, Esq., and, secondly, John St. George.

This Sir William Coggeshall held considerable estates in Essex, which for want of male heirs were divided amongst the daughters. He was living at Coggeshall in the 6th year of the reign of King Henry V., as the lease of his Manor of Codham Hall, Wethersfield, is tested at Coggeshall.

The Manor of Coggeshall Hall, as has been noticed (p. 125), was for several generations one of the possessions of this family, and it is probable that it was their principal seat. There were also branches of the family settled at Boreham and Sandon, some of whom were buried at Maldon and others in Boreham Church. Weever preserves the following inscription, which was formerly on a gravestone in the body of All Saints' Church, Maldon :—

"Here lies Richard (Henry) Coggeshall, son and heir of Thomas Coggeshall, son of Thomas Coggeshall, Esq. who died 9 Jan. 1427.'

Others were citizens of note in London, and were buried in the Parish Church of St. Margaret, on Fish Street Hill, and in St. Nicholas, Cold Abbey (*see* Weever's Funeral Monuments). Considerable information relating to the Coggeshalls, chiefly of a genealogical nature, is contained in the Davy MSS., vol. 48, in the British Museum, and some notes may be looked for in the Histories of Essex by Morant and Wright, also as to the later members of the family in 'Suffolk Records.'

From a younger brother of Sir John Coggeshall descended John Coggeshall, of Hundon, in Suffolk, whose posterity lived at Gosfield and then at Fornham Saint Genovese, in Suffolk ; of this branch was Henry Coggeshall, a man of great ingenuity. He improved the art of mensuration, and in 1677, published a work, " Timber Measure by a line of more ease and exactness than any other." He also invented a Sliding Rule which was called after his name. He had a son, William Coggeshall, of Diss, in Norfolk, and a stone in Diss Church records that this William was born at Stratford, Suffolk, and died, Aug. 9th, 1714, aged 48, and that he, by Elizabeth his wife, had a son, John, who died, April 13th, 1706, aged 6.

In Framlingham Church, level with the floor of the aisle, at the head of Sir Robert Hitcham's tomb, there was, when Green wrote his '*History of Framlingham*,' in 1834, a range of three marble slabs to the memory of John Coggeshall, two of his wives

and a daughter. Above the inscription on his slab were Quarterly
Coggeshall 1 and 4, a cross between 4 escallops ; Dover, 2,
ermine, a cinquefoil ; Sheppard, 3, a fess between 3 talbots passant, in their mouths a bird bolt, impaling Cotton, a chevron
between 3 cotton hanks. Helmet, mantle, crest,—a stag couchant.

> " Here lieth the body of John Coggeshall, Gent., who died
> 13th of Novem., 1752, aged 86 years. Also the body of
> Mary his second wife, who died 21st October, 1729, aged
> 41 years."

In a lozenge, the arms of Coggeshall as before, with helmet,
mantle, and crest as above.

> "Here is interred the body of Mary, the daughter of John
> Coggeshall, Gent., by Mary his wife, who departed this life
> the 1st. of August, Anno. Dom., 1726, ætat 17."

On the third stone—

> "Here lieth the body of Elizabeth, the third wife of John
> Coggeshall, Gent., who died 29th of October, 1741, aged
> 48 years."

John Coggeshall, Gent., in 1742, gave to the Church of Framlingham, a large silver flagon, weighing about 53 ounces, also a
brass branch for 20 lights.

The following notes are from the Herald's College, "John
Coggeshall, of Gosfield, in Essex, Gent., married and had issue :
Roger, sone and heire ; Richard, 2 ; John, 3 ; William, 4 ;—Roger
Cogshall, of Fornham St. Martin, in Suffolk, married Elizabeth,
ye daughter of — Smith, of Boxley, in Essex, and had issue :—
John, sone and heire.

"John, sone and heire of John, married to his first wife,
Elizabeth, ye daughter of George Bacon, of Hesset, in Suffolk,
and had issue :—Edmond ye first who died yonge, 2nd after he
married to his 2nd wife, Ann, ye daughter of John Bene (? Reeve)
of Thwaite in Suffolk, and by her had issue : Elizabeth, married
to John Bacon, ye younger, of Hesset.

"George, ye sone and heire of John, married Ann, ye daughter of Edmond Orange, of Berry St. Edmonds, and as yet hath
no issue. Died without issue, 1615."

From another pedigree in the same College we learn that a
Roger Coggeshall, of Fordham, Suffolk, had a son, John, who
resided at Orford, Suffolk, and married Elizabeth, daughter of
Robert Beversham, of Orford. They had issue :—Thomas (4th

son), who married Sarah, daughter of Edward Scott, of Glemsford, Suffolk ; Henry, of Benham (? Benhall), Suffolk (2nd son), 1664, married Ellinor, daughter of John Geoffrey, alias Spooner, of Tanington ; James, of Carson, married Barbara, daughter of Anthony Yorke, and John of Melton, Suffolk, Gent., 1664, who married Elizabeth, daughter of Philip Boone, of Saxted, Suffolk. Henry and Ellinor Coggeshall had issue John, sone and heire, aged about 9, anno 1664, Henry, Thomas and Mary.

There is among the *Harl. MS.S.* (1136, p. 62), this pedigree : "John Coggeshall of Hundon, Co. Suffolk, had issue John Coggeshall, of Gosfield, Co. Essex, who had issue : Richard, John, William and Robert (? Roger) of Fornham St. Martyn, Co. Suffolk, who married Elizabeth, daughter of — Smith, of Burley. They had a son, John, who married Anne, daughter of John Reeve, of Suffolk, and Elizabeth, daughter of George Bacon, of Hesset. By his marriage with Elizabeth he had a son, Edmond."

The following extracts are from the Coggeshall Registers :—

MARRIAGES.

1572—Aug. 11. John Coxill (? Caxill) and Joan Damat.
1574—April 22. Thom. Coxill (? Caxill) and Cicelie Freeman.
1603—Feb. 2. William Hull and Sarah Coxall.
1610—Feb. 25. Jhon Rogers (? Keyes) and Annis Coxall.
1626—July 3. Nathaniel Greeve and Annis Coxal.

BURIALS.

1585—Oct. 8. Anne, daughter of Jo. Coxill.
1600—Jany. 9. Joane, wife of Ralphe Coxall.

A search of the Register of Baptisms, Marriages and Burials from their commencement down to the present time has been made, but no other entries than the above have been found.

There is only one entry under this name in the Gosfield Registers, and that is of the marriage of Alice Coggeshall with Robert Wilton, in 1548. This information was kindly furnished by the Rev. Elliot, Vicar of Gosfield, who also wrote that the arms of Coggeshall are found quartered with those of Baker Cotton, Gent, Greene, Ingowe, Strangman, Thursby, Tyrell and Wentworth.

At St. Andrew's, Halstead, there is a mural brass to "Elizabeth, the wife of John Watson, the daughter of John Coggeshall, Gent., who was buried, February the 23rd, Anno Dmi. 1604." There is the figure of a lady kneeling at a desk facing, to the left

in front of the desk two boys, and behind her three girls all facing
as the mother; and, in the foreground, under the daughters a
chrysom child, but there are no armorials.

The Re-union of the Coggeshall Family.

ON the 9th September, 1884, some 400 or more descendants
of one, John Coggeshall, assembled at Newport, Rhode
Island, America, to hear the address of the Hon. Henry T. Coggeshall, of Waterville, New York, upon their family history. This
John Coggeshall appears to have been born in England about
1591, having died on 27th November, 1647, aged 56 years, at
Newport, Rhode Island. He was a puritan and was among those
who, seeking to escape the persecution of the times, sailed from
their native country in the ship "Lyon," on the 23rd June, 1632,
arriving at Boston on Sunday, the 16th September following.

His business is believed to have been that of a silk merchant,
and it is probable that he was born in Essex or Suffolk, and
although his father's name is not known we know that his mother's
name was Ann, and that when she made her will, on 16th April,
1645, she was residing at Castle Hedingham. By her will, she
gives to her son, John Coggeshall "now," as she says, "dwelling
in New England, my house and lands at Sible Hedingham, together with the legacy given him by his uncle, John Batter, with
remainder in event of John's not claiming them to Henry Raymond, my grandchild, son of Richard Raymond, deceased. She
also gives certain parts of her property to John, Anne, Mary,
Joshua, and James Coggeshall, children of her son John. Her
will was proved in the Prærogative Court of Canterbury, 171
Essex, on 16th April, 1645. The emigrant wife's name was Mary,
and when they left England they took with them their three children, John, born about 1618, Joshua, born 1623, and Ann, born
1625 ; and from the records of the First Church, Boston, Massa-
chusets, it appears that they subsequently had daughters, Hana-
niel, baptised 3rd May, 1635, and Wait, baptised 11 Sept. 1636,
and a son, Bedaiah, baptised 30th July, 1637.

Shortly after his arrival at Boston, John Coggeshall was made a
freeman of the colony, and was about the same time elected a
member of the church in Roxbury. He afterwards settled at
Portsmouth, Rhode Island, where, after starting a settlement, he
with others removed to the southern part of the island of Aquid-

neck, where the town of Newport now stands. When the four towns of Newport, Portsmouth, Providence and Warwick were united, John Coggeshall was elected to the honourable position of first President. He died on 27th November, 1647, aged 56, and was buried on his own land in Newport, where his descendants have erected a monument to his memory, and enclosed the little family burial ground with a neat and substantial stone wall.; it is situate in Coggeshall Avenue, near Victoria Avenue. His son, John, who was, as we have seen, born in England, was a Major of the Militia in the new country.

For further information as to John Coggeshall, the emigrant, and his descendants, the reader is referred to the *Rhode Island Magazine* for October, 1884, which contains, in addition to the address of the Hon. H. T. Coggeshall, occupying 28 pages, a contribution towards a genealogy of the family extending over 17 pages, the greater part of which is fraught with interesting narrative or detail.

The address of the President of the Re-union concluded in this appropriate strain : "Thus have we reviewed the Coggeshalls of the past. Their high aspirations and proud achievements illumine with credit the page of your family history. That the Coggeshalls of to-day deserve honorable mention it is needless here to say. * * * * Of the Coggeshalls yet to come, could the future be unfolded, we should see—whether distinguished by science or art, literature or politics—a long line of deserving men and women, law, abiding, liberty loving, trusting in man, brave. in war, sincere in friendship, fond of home and its associations, for these are characteristics which do not die."

The name of Coggeshall as a personal name is almost extinct in England, but there are Coxalls in Essex and elsewhere, and the persons with this corrupted patronymic are doubtless derivatives from the former possessors of Coggeshall Hall.

The Du Canes.

THE arms of this family are argent, a lion rampant sable, crowned or. ; on a canton azure, a chevron between three acorns of the 3rd, crest—a demi lion rampant sable crowned and supporting an anchor erect or.

The first English representative of the present Lord of the Manors of Great and Little Coggeshall was—

1. John Du Quesne, of Canterbury, afterwards of London, who came out of Flanders on account of the persecution of the protestants by the Duke of Alva, *temp*. Elizabeth. He had a son,

2. John Du Quesne, born in London; married 22nd January, 1599, Sarah de Francqueville, and died in 1612. He had a son,

3. Peter Du Quesne sometimes called Du Cane, of London, Esquire, born 1609; was elected Alderman, 1666, and discharged upon payment of a fine of £500 and 20 marks. He died, 7th February, 1671, aged 62. Buried in a vault at east end of St. Pancras, Soper Lane. He married Jane, daughther of Elias Maurois, of Canterbury, by Elizabeth, daughter of Laurence Desbouverie, of Sandwich, Kent. They had a son,

4. Peter Du Cane, of London, Esquire; born the 17th March, 1645; married on 6th January, 1675, Jane, eldest daughter of Richard Booth, Esq., who was elected Alderman of London in 1668, and discharged on payment of £520. Peter Du Cane died, 16th September, 1714, and was interred in the family vault at St. Pancras, Soper Lane. He had an only child

5. Richard Du Cane, of London, Esq., born, 13th October, 1681, served in the first Parliament of George I. for the Borough of Colchester; arms granted to him 6th February, 1730; married, in 1710, Anne, only daughter and heiress of Nehemiah Lyde, Esq. Lord of the Manors of Great and Little Coggeshall. She died 21 Sept. 1722, aged 33. Her husband died 3 Oct. 1744, aged 63, leaving issue,—
Peter, of whom hereafter. Richard, who died, 4 Feb., 1743. Jane, only daughter, born 22nd June, 1711; married 27 March, 1735, Charles Boehm, Esq., son of Clement Boehm, Esq., one of the Directors of the Bank of England. She died 9 January, 1756, aged 45. Had issue (i.) Jane, born 8 Aug. 1737, died 19 May, 1738; (ii.) Elizabeth, twin sister of Jane, died 26 Sept., 1738; (iii.) Jane, the 2nd, born 4 Dec., 1738, died 13 April, 1740; (iv.) Richarda, born 26 June, died 27 Sept., 1742 (issue buried at Coggeshall, see p. 50).

6. Peter Du Cane, eldest son and heir, born the 22nd of April, 1713; married 27th March, 1735, Mary, only daughter of Henry Norris, Esq., of Hackney, Middlesex. Died 28th March, 1803, buried at Braxted, Essex. He was High Sheriff of Essex, a Director of the Bank of England, and of the East India Company. They had issue among others, Peter, of whom hereafter, and Henry, Vicar of Coggeshall, who was born 21st Sept., 1748; married Louisa Desmadrill, and had issue (i.) Rev. Henry Du Cane, of Witham Grove, Essex, born in 1785, and had issue, (ii.) Richard, a Major in 20th Regt. of Dragoons, born in 1788, died leaving issue, Col. Sir Edmund Frederick, K.C.B. *vide Debrett;* (iii.) Charles, born 1789, of whom hereafter; (iv.) Louisa, born 1781; (v.) Anna, born 1783; (vi.) Sarah, born 1791; (vi.) George, who died without issue.

7. Peter Du Cane, Esq., of Braxted Lodge, Essex, born the 20th April, 1741, died in 1822, buried at Braxted; married in 1769, Phœbe Phillips Tredcroft, eldest daughter of Edward Tredcroft, Esq., of Horsham, Sussex. They had issue, Peter, of Braxted Lodge, Esq., Sheriff of Essex, and M.P. for Staining, Sussex, born 19th August, 1778, died 23rd May, 1841, without having been married; Henry, who died young; Mary, born 7th September, 1770; married Edmund, son of William Smith, Esq., of Horsham, and had issue (i.) Edmund Smith, died aged about 23, unmarried; (ii.) Rev. Percy Smith, Rector of Pattiswick, Essex (iii.) Frederick Smith, Esq., married Isabella daughter of Rev. James, and five other children; Sarah, born 16th June, 1772, died 21st June, 1782; Charlotte, born October, 1774.

8. Charles Du Cane, a Commander of the Royal Navy (cousin of Peter No. 7, son of Henry and grandson of Peter, No. 6) born 1789, died 17th November, 1850; married Francis, daughter of the Rev. Charles Prideaux Brune, of Prideaux Place, Cornwall. Had eight children, of whom was,

9. Sir Charles Du Cane, K.C.M.G., of Braxted Park; he was born 1825, educated at Charterhouse and at Exeter College, Oxford, B.A. 1847, Hon. 4th Class Classic and Mathematics M.A. in 1864; was a Civil Lord of the Admiralty, 1866-8; Governor of Tasmania, 1868-74; and a Royal Commissioner to inquire into the Factory and Workshop Acts, 1875;

in 1878 he was appointed Chairman of the Board of Customs, which position he retained till his death. He was a staunch Conservative and was M.P. for Maldon, 1852-3, and for North Essex, 1857-68; a Justice of the Peace and a Deputy-Lieutenant for Essex. He married in 1863, the Hon. Georgiana Susan Copley, daughter of the 1st Baron Lyndhurst, and died 25th February, 1889, leaving two sons and three daughters, the eldest son being (i.) Charles Henry Copley Du Cane, born 25th May, 1864 (ii.) John Philip Du Cane, born 5th May, 1865 (iii) Edith Georgiana Sophia, born 4th February, 1867 (iv.) Florence Gertrude Louisa, born 21st May, 1869, and (v.) Ella Mary, born 4th June, 1874.

An account of the family Du Quesne and especially of the branch which settled in England in the reign of Queen Elizabeth, has been compiled by Lieut.-Colonel Edmund Frederick Du Cane, C.B., and is a remarkably complete genealogical record. It was published by Messrs. Harrison and Sons, in 1876.

The Hanburys.

THE Hanbury family for upwards of a century and a half have been settled at Holfield or Oldfield Grange, Coggeshall. The first of the name who settled here was John Hanbury, who, Morant says, was a rich Virginian merchant. He married Anna, the daughter of Henry Osgood, the owner of this estate, who was probably a descendant of John Osgood a merchant of the city of London in the latter part of the seventeenth century. John Osgood had two sons, the eldest Salem married Ann, who was afterwards the wife of Joshua Gee, of London citizen. Salem had two daughters, Rebecca and Ann. He made his will on 10 June, 1703, and when he died he was possessed of a share of a 200th part of New Jersey, in America, which he inherited under the will of his father, dated 17 May, 1694. Burke, in his *Armory*, speaks of the Hanburys, of Holfield Grange, as 'a great commercial family of the City of London,' and gives the arms as or., a bend engrailed az, cotised sa ; crest, out of a mural crown gules charged with two estoiles or, a demi lion ramp guard erm holding in the dexter paw a battle axe ppr. This family, as bankers, brewers and merchants, is allied to business firms of great repute.

The John Hanbury before mentioned appears to have died about 1750 ; on his death the estates passed successively to his son, grandson, and great-grandson, all of whom bore the Christian name of Osgood. The great-grandson died on the 3rd May, 1882, at the age of 56, leaving an only son, Osgood Beauchamp, and three daughters. Mr. Osgood Beauchamp Hanbury attained his majority in 1888, and then succeeded to the estates. On the 17th October, 1889, he married Flora, the only daughter of Major Francis Tower, of Thremhall Priory, Takeley, Essex, but hardly had the "mellow, wedding-bells—golden bells"—rung out their joyous peal than the tolling of the "iron bells" announced that the young squire had passed away. His death, resulting from an attack of scarlet fever, took place, on the 25th October, 1889, at Leamington, where he was spending his honeymoon. He was buried in the vault at Pattiswick, in which his grandfather and father were laid to rest in 1873 and 1882. (The father of the former having been buried in 1852, and the grandfather in 1784, in the Friends' Burial Ground, at Coggeshall.) With the demise of the youthful bridegroom the name of Osgood Hanbury has become extinct, and the estates have passed to the Tower family. Mr. Hanbury had three sisters, one of whom was married on 26 February, 1884, to Capt. Heron-Maxwell; another sister, Constance, was married on 26th September, 1888, to Henry Charles Sloane Stanley, Esq.; and the third sister, who was unmarried, died of fever at Cairo, on 7th March, 1886, aged 22.

The old residence (Holfield Grange) was pulled down by the late Mr. Osgood Hanbury about ten years ago, and a large red brick mansion with stone facings erected on the same site. This estate, which was formerly one of the granges of the monastery, shortly after the dissolution was granted to Sir Clement Smith, of Little Baddow, Essex, on whose death it descended to John, his son and heir, who sold it to Robert Gurdon ; he, dying in 1578, was succeeded by his son, John Gurdon, who sold the property to Henry Osgood, whose daughter became allied in marriage to John Hanbury, and in this family the estate continued till 1889.

The Paycockes.

MEMBERS of this family will be found noticed in several parts of this work. Their name is variously spelt Pecock, Peacock, Paycock, Peaycocke, &c. The first of the family of whom we have touch was the Thomas Paycocke who died 21st May, 1461, and whose memorial inscription is recorded in Weever's '*Funeral Monuments (ante p. 42)*.

John Pecok (presumably the son or grandson of Thomas Paycocke above-mentioned) made his will on 20th January, 1505-6, a great part of which appears on pp. 75 and 76, but there are a few genealogical items which more appropriately find a place under this general reference to the family. From this will we gather the following facts, namely that John Pecok had two sons, Robert and Thomas, and a daughter Alice, and his wife's name was Emma; he left his house in Church Street. and the house he dwelt in, and the land called 'Braziers' (No. 355, Ord. Sur.), also his house between the Bridge and Little Coggeshall to his wife for life, and then to his eldest son John.

Some part of the will, dated 1518, of Thomas Paycocke, son of John Paycocke above-mentioned, has been set forth on pp. 76 and 77. The document itself is of considerable length, but the genealogical items have been summarised by Mr. H. W. King, and the following notes are derived from his paper read before the Essex Archæolgical Society, at Coggeshall, 19th October, 1888 :— Testator mentions "Anne my wife, my brother John Paycocke, Thomas Paycocke, son of my brother Robert Paycocke, and Robert his brother, Robert and Margaret Upcher, my sister's children"; he gives directions for the laying down of his sepulchral memorial, with the brass effigies of himself and his two wives, in Coggeshall church (*see p. 43*), and the cost of it; and of another in memory of his father-in-law, with brass effigies in Clare church, Suffolk, his wishes being expressed in this manner :—"My executors to purvey a marbill stone with myne image and both my wif's, and they to bestow £5 thereon. I will also that they purvey and order a stone to be laid in Clare church, and laid on my father-in-law, Thomas Harrold, with his pycture and his wife and children thereupon." The testator gives several legacies to the Goodays, a family whose name is of constant recurrence in the Coggeshall Parish Registers. These entries have been extracted, and with the information contained in Mr. King's paper, would enable any one interested in the family to construct a fairly good pedigree. It is hoped that Mr. King's valuable paper will appear *in extenso* in the *Transactions of the Essex Archæological Society*. In Messing church the arms of Peacocke are quartered

with those of Haselfoot; 1 and 4 quarterly, or. and sa., a cross
of four lozenges counterchanged, Hazelfoot; 2 and 3 gu, on a
fess engrailed arg. between 3 bezants, each charged with a peacock's head erased proper impaling arg., on a fess gu., 3 eagles
displayed wings inverted or., Peacock : Crest, a demi-peacock or.,
wings expanded az., holding in the beak a snake proper entwined
round the neck. [*East Anglian Notes and Queries*, Vol. II, 244.]

The following notes from the Coggeshall Registers, up to the
year, 1653, are believed to be the only entries relating to the
family, at any rate the only items that are legible : Baptisms, none.
Marriages—1563, June 24, Thomas Till and Joan Peaycocke ;
1563, Nov. 6, Edward Rand and Margerie Peaycocke. Burials—
1562, June 14, Grace Peaycocke, 1580; December 28, "Thom.
Peaycocke, who gave ijc li. (£200) to buy lands for the use of the
poore of Cogshall for ever ;" 1584, Sept. 7, Margaret, wife of John
Peaycocke ; 1584, Feb. 14, "John Peaycocke, the last of his
name in Coggeshall ;" 1590, Nov. 30, Joan Peaycocke, wid.

The Guyon Family.

THIS family was very numerous here in the 16th and 17th
centuries, as appears from the Parish Registers. Some of
them attained great wealth, notably Thomas Guyon, the rich
clothier, who, it is said, amassed no less a sum than £100,000.
He was probably the same person as Thomas, son of Thomas
Gyon, who was baptised here on 24th, Dec. 1592; as it will be
seen from the memorial inscription on his tomb, that he was 72
years of age at the time of his death in 1664, and his mother was
doubtless a daughter or the widow of one Gray, as the marriage
register has—"1591, January 23, Thom Gyon and Margerie
Graie." His wife's name was Annis, by whom he had several
children ; among them George, baptised, 3rd. Aug., 1628 ; Richard, baptised 14th Nov. 1630 ; Mathew, baptised, 10th March,
1632, and Mark, baptised 15th Nov. 1635.

The Guyons were possessed of considerable estates at Coggeshall and elsewhere in Essex. In 1667, Sir Mark Guyon bought
Dynes Hall, Maplestead, and made it his residence. Morant says
he took down a great part of the old house and rebuilt it in a
very substantial manner, but did not live to see it finished.

With this family the families of the Bullocks, the Abdys and the Skingleys are connected. The first two are mentioned by Bufton in the following notes relating to Sir Mark Guyon :—

"1678, July—Sir Mark Guyon was made Justice of the Peace.

"1679, June 19—The Lady Abdy, of Kelvedon, died. June 24—The Lady Guyon, Sir Mark's second wife, daughter of Sir Thomas Abdy, died, and was buried on 26th late in the evening, by torches without a sermon.

"1682, Dec. 14—Sir Mark Guyon was married to Mrs. Augurs, his waiting maid, and kinswoman of Mrs. Andrews, of Feering.

"1690—Squire Bullock married Sir Mark's eldest daughter. 1691—Mr. Thomas Guyon married Sir Mark's second daughter. 1693—Mr. T. Guyon was brought down from London and buried here. Mr. John Bullock married to Mr. T. Guyon's widow."

The Skingleys became allied to this wealthy family by the marriage, on the 25th May, 1765, of Henry Skingley, Esq. (great-great-grandfather of Henry Percy Chevallier Skingley) with Mary Guyon, daughter of John and Ann Guyon, born 5th March, 1739.

The extracts from the Parish Register, Court Rolls and other documents which the writer has made from time to time would, with a little patient research of the old wills at Somerset House and at the Ipswich and Bury Registries, enable anyone interested to construct an elaborate pedigree of the Guyon family.

The Fabians.

THE Fabians were a family of some note in this county and in the city of London in the 15th and 16th centuries. Stephen Fabian held under lease from Robert Sewalle, of Cogges-hall, a water mill in Stisted, as early as 1404. In 1426, he purchased from Sewalle the manor of Jenkins, in Stisted. Morant says this Stephen Fabian was a cordwainer at Coggeshall, but undoubtedly a man of substance ; his posterity became consider-able and flourished in Stisted parish in plentiful circumstances. Stephen had a son, John, who was succeeded by his son bearing the same name. The last-mentioned John had a son, Edward Fabian, Esq., who died on 4th February, 1561, possessed of the Manor of Jenkins, and other lands in Stisted, Pattiswick and Coggeshall. He was succeeded by his son William. In 1462, Robert and John Fabian were living at Coggeshall. This family gave name to a farm lying north of the church *(see Ordnance Survey)*. There are but few entries relating to them in the Registers ;

among the marriages these occur : 1569, May 14th—John Fabian and Elizabeth Ambrose ; 1570, Nov. 5th—John Fabian and Joan Daniel ; 1591, May 16th—John Sweeting and Joan Fabian ; no baptisms, but these burials : 1565, Feb. 17th—Agn Fabian ; 1570, June 10th—Elizabeth, wife of Jo. Fabian ; 1590, Feb. 6th—John Fabian.

The Ayletts.

IN the latter half of the 16th century, and in the beginning of the 17th, some members of this family were resident here ; the earliest record relating to them is the registration of the birth of William, son of Robert Aylett, on 7th February, 1584. As the baptismal register commences in this year it is not possible to say definitely whether or not was born here Robert Aylett, LL.D., the English poet, who is supposed to have been born about the year 1583. This Robert Aylett was educated at Cambridge where he took his degree ; he was afterwards appointed to a Mastership in the High Court of Chancery. In the year 1654 he published "Divine and Moral Speculations in Metrical Numbers upon various subjects." He is said to have been buried at Great Braxted.

Boydin Aylett is the earliest ancestor of the family who can be traced in this county. He had lands at Bradwell, near Coggeshall, in the reign of Henry II. Richard Eylotte, who was returned among the chief gentlemen of Essex in 1433, was of this family. Some of the descendants of Boydin Aylett settled at Rivenhall, then at Hovells, in Coggeshall, and from them sprung the Ayletts of Braintree, Stisted and Braxted.

The Coggeshall Registers record the marriage, on 2nd Sept., 1595, of Dorothy Aylet with Robert Riddlesdale. She was probably the daughter of Robert Aylett, who married Miss Thorowgood and who died in 1603 ; her grandfather appears to have been William Aylett, Gent., of Stisted, who died in 1583, leaving as his eldest son and heir, Richard, then aged 40. She had a brother, Thomas, who resided at Hovells. Thomas had issue, who were baptised at Coggeshall on the following dates :—Anne, 31 August, 1600 ; Dorothy, 24 May, 1604 ; John, 8 September, 1607 ; Elizabeth, 25 May, 1613 ; Nicholas, 16 March, 1614 ; James, 10 June, 1617 ; Alice, 10 June, 1619 ; and Jeremy, 6 August, 1621 ; the last entry has the mother's name Anne

A Robert Aylett had three children baptised here between 1584-9; there are also records of the burials of some of the family at Coggeshall.

One of the possessions of this family, as we have seen, was Hovels, an estate which has several synonyms such as Holvill, Holfield, and Holvil. It was, according to Morant, the Manor House of Great Coggeshall. This seems very probable, for the name appears to imply that it is the site of the *old-ville* or the *old-field*, an allusion to which has already been made (p. 10). The estate belonged to the Abbey prior to its suppression, since which time the seignorial rights, which are incident to the freehold and copyhold lands of the manor have been severed from the demesne lands.

Thomas Aylett, of Great Coggeshall, gentleman, purchased the demesne lands of the manor from King Charles I. and re mained in possession of them until his death on the 19th October, 1650, at which time he was 80 years of age. He lies buried in Coggeshall Church, and on his gravestone, not now extant, he was described as Lord of the Manor of Coggeshall.

The family did not long possess Hovells, for one of them shortly after the death of Thomas, in 1650, sold the estate to Thomas Lovett, Esq.; who sold it to Thomas Guyon, the wealthy cloth manufacturer, who gave it to his grandson, George Guyon, captain of a company of the Trained Bands, who died at Hovells, in October, 1676 ; on whose death it passed to Anne, the wife of Thomas Forster, Esq., ancestor, it is believed, of the late noted politician, William Edward Forster, Esq. ; and from the Morden College Rentals it is found that the estate belonged to John Forster, in 1740 ; Susan Forster, in 1749 ; Elizabeth Forster, and the widow Lamplow, in 1750-3 ; Catherine Forster and the widow Lamplow's son, John Foster Lamplow, in 1766-8 ; Elizabeth Burder and J. F. Lamplow, in 1772 ; Elizabeth Burder and Osgood Hanbury in 1776-9. From 1782 to 1889 it was possessed by successive Osgood Hanburys. The connection between the Hanbury and Forster families has already been noticed (p. 146).

𝕿𝖍𝖔𝖒𝖆𝖘 𝕳𝖆𝖜𝖐𝖊𝖘, 𝕸𝖆𝖗𝖙𝖞𝖗.

THOMAS HAWKES, gentleman, was one of the retainers of John, Earl of Oxford, at Earls Colne Priory. It is probable that he resided on part of the property called 'Constantines,' abutting upon the Market Hill. He was first brought into trouble by his refusal to have his child baptised in accordance with the ceremonies of the Roman Catholic religion. The dialogues which ensued upon this and other questions, between Bonner, Bishop of London, and Hawkes, are fully set forth in *Foxe.* Hawkes, notwithstanding the Bishop's persuasions

BURNING OF THOMAS HAWKES.

remainded firm, and replying to the exhortation to return again to the bosom of the mother church, said "No my lord, that I will not, for if I had a hundred bodies I would suffer them all to be torn in pieces rather than I will abjure and recant." Hereon followed the sentence of death and though condemned on the 9th February, 1555, he was not committed to the flames till 10th June following, on which day having been consigned to the charge of Lord Rich, he was brought with six other fellow prisoners down to Essex to suffer martyrdom. Of these Hawkes only was burned at Coggeshall, tradition says in the Vicarage field, in West Street, and it is related, that "when he was led to the place appointed for the slaughter, he there mildly and patiently prepared himself for the fire, having a strait chain cast about his middle, with a multitude of people on every side unto whom he spake many things. At length after his fervent prayers first made and poured out unto GOD, the fire was set unto him ; in the which when he had continued long and when his speech was taken away by the violence of the flame, his skin was drawn together and his fingers consumed, so that now all men thought that he had expired, when suddenly this blessed servant of GOD (being mindful of a promise secretly made to his friends) reached up his hands, burning on a light fire over his head, to the living GOD and with great rejoicing as it seemed struck or clapped them three times together, and so the blessed martyr of CHRIST straightway sinking down into the fire gave up his spirit, June 10th, 1555."

Other Martyrs.

BESIDES Hawkes there were others of this town who were sufferers during the Marian persecutions.   Three of them, Thomas Osmond, a fuller, William Bamford *alias* Butler, a weaver, and Nicholas Chamberlain, also a weaver, were sent down from London to Essex to be burned; Osmond, at Manningtree, Bamford, at Harwich, and Chamberlain, at Colchester. It is said that they were not executed at the place where they lived for fear of an insurrection among the people. Chamberlain perished on the 14th June, 1555, and Osmond and Bamford on the following day.

Cicely Warren and Christianna Pepper, of this town, were sent with about twenty-two others from Colchester, and it is said that they also would have been burnt had it not been for the clemency of Cardinal Pole.

William Flower, of Snow Hill, in Cambridgeshire, who for some time was a schoolmaster in this town, was burnt at Westminster, on 24th April, 1555.

Thomas Brodehill, a weaver, Richard Web, a weaver, and another Thomas Osborne, a fuller, residents here, recanted and did penance.

John Jegon, Bishop of Norwich.

JOHN JEGON was born at Coggeshall on the 10th December, 1550, probably in a house now demolished on the east side of Wayne Lane and in the rear of the Cloth Factory, for 'Dr. John Giggings' was the occupier of this house in the reign of Queen Elizabeth. He was the son of Robert Jegon by Joane his wife, daughter of — White, whose family had flourished in this county since the reign of Edward III. John Jegon received his early education in this town, and was afterwards sent to Cambridge, where he was chosen fellow of Queen's College, and so continued twenty-five years. On 10th August, 1590, he was elected Master of Corpus Christi College, an office which he held twelve years. He was four times Vice-Chancellor of his University, Chaplain in Ordinary to Queen Elizabeth; Installed Dean of Norwich 22nd June, 1601, and subsequently elected Bishop of that See (June 18), and was consecrated at Lambeth 20th February, 1602, was Bishop fifteen years, died March 13th, 1617, and was buried in the chancel of Aylesham church, Norfolk. His widow, Lilia by name, married Sir Charles Cornwallis.

Dr. Jegon is said to have been a most serious man and grave governor, yet withall of a most facetious disposition, that it is hard to say whether his counsel was most grateful for the soundness or his company for the pleasantness thereof, take one eminent instance of his ingenuity :—Whilst Master of Bennet or Corpus Christi College he chanced to punish all the undergraduates therein for some general offence, and the penalty was put on their heads in the buttery, and because he disdained to put the money to any private use it was expended in the new whiting the walls of the college, whereon a schollar hung up these words on a screen :—

> " Dr. Jegon, Bennet Colledge Master,
>   Brake the schollars heads and gave the wall a plaister."

But the Doctor had not the readiness of his parts any whit impaired by age, for perusing the paper he extemporarily subscribed :—

> "Knew I but the wag that writ these verses in a bravery,
>   I would commend him for his wit, but whip him for his knavery."

He had a brother named Thomas ; born at Coggeshall ;

Master of Corpus Christi, Camb.; Rector of Sible Hedingham;
Archdeacon of Norwich; Vice-Chancellor of Cambridge University; buried in the chancel of Sible Hedingham church, in
1617.

There are several entries under this name in the early Coggeshall registers of baptisms, marriages and burials.

Of this family was probably Robert Giggins, who Bufton says,
distinguished himself by coming from Colchester in the road
backwards on 21st October, 1679.

Bisꟳop Mant.

THE Right Reverend Richard Mant, Bishop of Killaloe and
Kilfenora, and afterwards Bishop of Down and Connor,
has been noticed under the head of the Clergy, as he was vicar
here in the early years of the present century. His portrait,
from which the above reproduction is taken, was not received in
time for its insertion in the short biographical notice of the
bishop, on *page 65.*

John Godard.

JOHN GODARD, "wherever born, had his best being at Coggeshall, where he became a Cistercian monk. Great was his skill in arithmetic and mathematics, a science which had long lain asleep in the world and now first began to open its eyes again. He wrote many treatises thereof and dedicated them unto Ralph, Abbot of Coggeshall. He flourished Anno Dom. 1250 "—*(Fuller's Worthies, p. 333).* One of his works was entitled, ' *Concerning the threefold method of calculating.'*

Nathaniel Rogers.

THE Rev. Nathaniel Rogers was the son of the Rev. John Rogers, a man, says Col. J. L. Chester [*Essex Archæological Journal, Vol. IV., p. 189.*] "of extraordinary oratorical powers, and familiarly known two centuries and a-half ago as the famous preacher of Dedham, and his bust in his peculiar pulpit attitude still adorns the chancel of that church. The son, Nathaniel, emigrated in 1636 with his wife Margaret, who was the daughter of Robert Crane, of Coggeshall. The descendants of this one pair are supposed to be more numerous in America at the present day than those of any other early emigrant family, and I am happy to say they have generally done honor to their origin. The eldest son John was born at Coggeshall ; became 5th President of Harvard College, the University of America *par excellence ;* and to pass to the other extreme end of their line, one of their descendents (Col. Chester) has at this moment the honor to address you. Cotton Mather, in his famous '*Magnalia,*' counts this Nathaniel Rogers among the fathers of the New World." From the registers we learn that Nathaniel Rogers and Margaret his wife had three children baptised here, John, on 17th June, 1627 (buried 21st June, 1627); Mary, on 8th February, 1628 ; and John, on 23rd January, 1630.

John Carter, the Lip Artist.

JOHN CARTER, the son of a labourer, was born on the 31st July, 1815, in this town. He was educated at the Hitcham School, but instead of devoting his attention to the subjects set by his instructor, he was frequently to be found depicting on his desk or in his copy book the figure of a man, a horse or other animal. His natural talent might never have developed had it not been for the accident which befel him in his early years. On Saturday night, as the Rev. W. J. Dampier relates, in the month of May, 1836, John Carter, with some of his companions, was attracted to the rookery at Holfield Grange. Ascending one of the tall trees in search of birds he reached a height of about 40 feet, the limb of another tree, to which he is said to have been crossing, yielded more than was calculated upon or deceived him by its distance, he missed his hold and fell to the earth upon his back. He was taken up senseless and from that time never moved hand or foot. He was conveyed home to his wife on Sunday morning upon a hurdle by his affrighted companions, but a serious injury to the spine had deprived him of all power of voluntary motion below the neck; the mischief, which was at the fifth, sixth, and seventh vertibræ, paralysed the whole body downwards. The muscular power of the neck was retained, no permanent mischief was sustained by the organs of the head, and the faculties were unimpaired.

JOHN CARTER (FROM A DRAWING BY THE REV. W. J. DAMPIER).

Having read of one, Elizabeth Kinning, an inmate of an asylum in Liverpool, who, having lost the use of her hands, had learnt to draw with her mouth, it occurred to him that he might do the same, and he set to work accordingly. The posture in which he drew was lying on his side with the head a little raised by pillows. A small, light desk of deal, made under his own directions, was adjusted for him ; on this desk his drawing paper was fastened with brass headed pins, the drawing to be copied being placed in a convenient position, he first sketched in his subject with a lead pencil which he held between his teeth ; a saucer of Indian ink was prepared and the brush was moistened by his attendant and placed in his mouth and secured firmly by his jaw teeth ; by the motion of his head he produced the most marvellous results, his strokes being most accurate and delicate. He was accustomed to work with very fine hair pencils (some almost as fine as needle points) about 6 inches long. His death was occasioned by the overturning of his invalid carriage. He expired on the 2nd June, 1850. A catalogue of his works with copies of many of his illustrations, is contained in the beautiful '*Memoir of John Carter,*' by the Rev. W. J. Dampier, from which the preceding account has been derived.

Joseph Bufton.

JOSEPH BUFTON, the Coggeshall Diarist of the 17th century, was baptised at Coggeshall on the 30th December, 1650, and was the son of John and Elizabeth Bufton. He had a brother John, baptised on the 15th November, 1646, and three sisters who were baptised at Coggeshall, Mary, 8th May, 1636 ; Elizabeth, on 6th June, 1644 ; and Rebecca, in 1649. His sister Elizabeth was buried on 16th April, 1666, and his mother on the 27th June, 1675. This is all the information which can be gathered from the registers concerning the family. Bufton appears to have been engaged in the staple trade of the town, and he tells us that when he lived with Mr. Hedgthorne, his master took in 23 weavers, and that when Mr. Hedgthorne died, he had 8 combers and 60 weavers. Bufton's father, also a woollen manufacturer (*ante p.* 188), was buried on 7th January, 1694, having reached the ripe old age of 86. His funeral sermon was preached by Mr. Boys, the vicar, and we are told that £1 was paid for the sermon ; the gloves given away at the funeral cost £1 11s. ; the burying suit, 12s. ; but the most costly items of all were the liquors consumed, viz. :—£1 12s. for 4 gallons of sack, and 17s. for 27 gallons of beer.

The following extracts are from the original diaries and note books, which the author purchased from Mrs. Kirkham, widow of the late Mr. Richard Meredith Kirkham. The writing is most beautifully neat and the way in which the work is executed shows that the scribe was a man of considerable industry and possessed of more than ordinary ability, in fact the notes are marvellous specimens of penmanship considering the times in which they were written. The subjects which he transcribed and noted, show that he devoted a great part of his time to religious matters. The following extracts, however, tell us something of the principal dwellers here toward the close of the 17th century. Other notes will be found interspersed throughout this work.

DIARY.

Notes entered in a *Goldsmith Diary* of 1672. " An account of the funeral sermons which Mr. Jessop preached at Coggeshall, which were in all thirty."

" The *first* was at the buriall of *John Sudbury*, clothier, upon Wednesday, the first of April, Anno 1663. [Here, as after all the following, is appended the text of the sermon.]

The *second* was at the buriall of *Old Edmond Cox*, clothier and farmer, at last, upon Saturday, January 23rd, Anno 1663-4.

The *third* was at the buriall of the *Widdow Hills*, who lived at West Mill, upon Friday, July the eighth, Anno 1663-4.

The *fourth* was at the buriall of Old *Mr. Thomas Guyon*, the great clothier, upon Satterday, in the evening by candlelight, November ye 26th, Anno 1664.

The *fifth* was at the buriall of *Mr. William Gardner*, lawyer, who lived at Kelvedon, but dyed a batchelor at his mother's, Mrs. Merrills. This was upon Friday, February the 8th, Anno 1666-7.

The *sixth* was at the buriall of *Mr. Richard Shortland*, clothier, upon Friday, December the 13, Anno 1667. This sermon was finished by candlelight.

The *seventh* was at the buriall of *Mrs. Brockwell*, first wife to Mr. John Brockwell, physitian, and daughter to old William Gladwin, upon Tuesday, May the 19th, Anno 1668.

The *eighth* was at the buriall of *Elizabeth Guyon*, maid, daughter of William Guyon, clothier, she died at Michaell Richolds, about 20 years of age. This was on Thursday, June the 25, Anno 1668.

The *ninth* was at the buriall of *Robert Todd*, of Little Coggeshall, who there held a great brewing office. This was on Wednesday night by candlelight, September the 30th, Anno 1668.

The *tenth* was at the buriall of *Robert Sach*, ffarmer, upon Thursday, Aprill the ffirst, Anno 1669.

The *eleventh* was at the buriall of *Michaell Richolds*, clothier, upon Munday, March the 14th, Anno 1669-70.

The *twelfth* was at the buriall of *Mr. Robert Merrills*, of Little Coggeshall, upon Wednesday, February the 7th, Anno 167½.

The *thirteenth* was at the buriall of *Mary Phillebrowne*, maid, daughter of Thomas Phillebrowne, ffarmer, upon Friday, June 21st, Anno 1672.

The *fourteenth* was at the buriall of *John Wilbore*, a young lad, sonne of John Wilbore, carpenter, upon Thursday, October the 15th, Anno 1674.

The *fifteenth* was at the buriall of *Charles Binion*, brother of Mr. Henry Binion, he dyed at Mr. Thomas Staffords, of Inworth, but was buried at Coggeshall, upon Friday, December the 11th, Anno 1674. The sermon was preached by candle-light.

The *sixteenth* was at the buriall of *Simon Richold's* ffirst wife, who was daughter of Mr. Robert Merrills, of Little Coggeshall. This was upon Tuesday, January the 26, Anno 1674-5.

The *seventeenth*, was at the buriall of *My Deare Mother*, upon Sunday, June ye 27th day, Anno 1675.

The *eighteenth* was at the buriall of *Ambros Armond*, inn-holder, who lived at the *White Hart*, upon Munday, November the 8th, Anno 1675.

The *nineteenth* was at the buriall of young *John Brockwell*, who dyed a batchelor, and lived but a little while after his father. This was upon Tuesday, December the 7th, Anno 1675.

The *twentyeth* was at the buriall of old *Mrs. Raven*, widdow, she was about 92 yeares old, *and grandmother to Mr. Matthew Guyon's Wife*. This was upon Munday, January 31, Anno 1675-6.

The *one-and-twentieth* was at the buriall of *Ambros Sutton's First Wife*, she was a Surry woman. Upon Satterday, the third of June, 1676.

The *two-and-twentieth* was at the buriall of *Mr. George Guyon's Wife*, who lived at *Hovills*, she was Mr. Plumb's daughter,

of Yeldham, her name was Rachel, upon Tuesday, June the
13th, Anno 1676.

The *three-and-twentieth* was at the buriall of *Richard Shortland's
first Wife*, she was daughter of John Grimes, who was
called *Major Grimes*, upon Tuesday, October the 3rd, Anno
1676.

The *four-and-twentieth* was at the buriall of *Mr. George Guyon*,
of *Hovills*, who was *Captain of a Company of ye Trained
Bands*, upon Friday, October the 6th, Anno 1676.

The *five-and-twentieth* was at ye buriall of *Old Mr. William
Gladwin*, clothier, he was almost 93 yeares old, upon
Munday, January the 15th, Anno 1676-7.

The *six-and-twentieth* was at the buriall of *Mr. John Cox*,
clothier, who lived at the *Mount*, but dyed at another house
neare by, upon Ffriday, June the 29, Anno 1677.

The *seven-and-twentieth* was at the buriall of *John Joyce*, comber,
but lat-ward sold cheese, butter, bacon, &c., upon Tuesday,
September the 4th, Anno 1677.

The *eight-and-twentieth* was at the buriall of *ffrancis Lay's Old
Wife*, who lived at the Swan, who before he married her was
the widdow Moore, upon Munday, March the 18th, Anno
1677-8.

The *nine-and-twentieth* was at the buriall of *Francis Lay*, who
lived and dyed at the Swan, upon Munday, November the
11th, Anno 1678.

The *thirtieth* was at the buriall of *Mr. Matthew Guyon*, clothier,
a rich man, who left 4 sons and 2 daughters, upon Friday,
March the 7th, Anno 1678-9."

"Here followes also an account of *the Funerall Sermons*
which were *preached at Coggeshall by Mr. Boys* :—

"The *first* was at the funerall of *Goodman Wilshier*, ffarmer, of
Little Coggeshall, upon Satterday, July the 24th, Anno 1680.

The *second* was at the ffunerall of *Mris. Guyon, Mr. Matthew
Guyon's Widdow*, upon Tuesday, August the 31st, Anno
1680.

The *third* was at the ffunerall of *Mr. Richard Rayment*, who had
been exciseman, but of late a maultster, he lived in ye Hamlet, upon Munday, May the 30th, Anno 1681.

The *fourth* was at the ffunerall of *Old Mistress Hills, old Robert
Hill's Widdow*, upon Friday, November the 4th Anno 1681

The *fifth* was at the ffuneral of young *Edmund Atkinson*, barber, called the *young gold*, because his father was called *the gold*, upon Friday, October the twentyeth, Anno, 1682.

The *sixth* was at the ffunerall of old *Mr. Ambros Sutton*, clothier, he had no child, he was I think above 60 yeares of age, upon Friday, May the eighteenth, Anno 1683.

The *seventh* was at the ffunerall of old *Mrs. Merrills*, old Mr. Robert Merrills' widdow, upon Friday, September the 28th, Anno 1683.

The *eighth* was at the ffunerall of the *Wife of Thomas Levitt*, butcher, she was Thomas Tunbridge's widdow before he married her, upon Thursday, December the 13th, Anno 1683.

The *ninth* was at the funerall of *Robert Groome*, a young man that dyed at Mr. John Digby's, he was his nephew, on Friday, January the 4th, Anno 1683-4.

The *tenth* was at the ffunerall of *Old John Cooke*, carpenter, he was near four score yeares of age, upon Wednesday, May the 14th, Anno 1684.

The *eleventh* was at the ffuneral of ye *first Wife of William Cox*, son of *Mr. Thomas Cox*, minister, she was *Dr. Harrison's* daughter, she dyed in childbed of her first child and the child was buried with her, upon Munday, July the seventh, Anno 1684.

The *twelfth* was at the funerall of *Mr. Thomas Stafford*, lawyer, sonne of old Thomas Stafford, glover, upon Friday, August the 15th, Anno 1684.

The *thirteenth* was at the ffunerall of the wife of *Mr. David Battey*, at the *White Hart*, she was 3rd sister of *Mr. Jeremy Ayletts* wife, upon Monday, September the 15th, Anno 1684.

The *fourteenth* was at the ffunerall of the wife of *Mr. John Wood*, tanner, she was the daughter of *Mr. Glasscock, schoolmaster*, of Felsted, upon Satterday, October the fourth, Anno 1684.

The *fifteenth* was at the funerall of the wife of *Mr. John White*, apothecary. She was one of *Mr. Harrison's daughters*. She kept her chamber about half-a-yeare before she dyed, upon Monday, Aprill the 13th Anno, 1685.

The *sixteenth* was at the ffunerall of old *Mrs. Mount, widow*. She kept schollars, her husband lived at Tollsbury, upon Sunday, June the twentieth, Anno 1686.

The *seventeenth* was at the ffunerall of *old Mr. John Digby*, a lame man, who had formerly been a shopkeeper, upon Fryday, January the 14th, Anno 1686-7.

The *eighteenth* was for young *Mr. Andrews*, a kinsman of Mr. Andrews's, of Feering, who dyed and was buried at Feering, about July 2, 1687, but this ffunerall sermon was preached at Coxall, upon Wednesday, July 13, Anno, 1687.

The *nineteenth* was at the ffunerall of *Mrs. Judith Shortland*, an ancient maid, daughter of Mr. Richard Shortland, upon Thursday, November the 24, Anno 1687.

The *twentieth* was at the ffunerall of the *Wife of old Thomas Strafford*, glover, she was a very ancient woman, it is said had lived 60 yeares with her husband, upon Wednesday, May the second, Anno 1688.

The *twenty-ffirst* was at the ffuneral of *old Mrs. Shortland*, widdow of old Mr. Richard Shortland, she was a very ancient woman, upon Fryday, June the ffirst, Anno 1688.

The *twenty-second* was at the funerall of the *second Wife of Mr. John Wood*, tanner, upon Wednesday, September ye 18th, Anno 1689.

The *twenty-third* was at the ffunerall of *Mr. Robert Merrils*, singleman, who lived in the Hamlet, upon Tuesday, February the 11th, Anno 1689-90.

The *twenty-fourth* was at the ffunerall of *Michael Miles*, butcher, singleman, eldest son of John Miles, upon Wednesday, February the 17th, Anno 1691-2.

The *twenty-fifth* was at the ffunerall of the *second Wife of John Cox, esquire*, she was Major Haine's daughter, she dyed in childbed, upon Wednesday, September the 28th, Anno 1692.

The *twenty-sixth* was at ye ffunerall of *my dear Father, John Bufton*, who dyed in the 86th yeare of his age, upon Munday, January the 7th, Anno 1694-5.

The *twenty-seventh* was at the ffuneral of *William Stokes*, a carpenter, who wrought with John Cook, he was a batchelor, upon Sunday, March the 17th, Anno 1694-5.

The *twenty-eighth* was for *Henry Ireland*, comber, who dyed suddenly July the 8th, and was buried July the 9th, but this sermon was preached upon ye Sunday after, July the 14th, Anno 1695.

The *twenty-ninth* was at the ffuneral of an ancient widdow, who was the mother of young *Isaac Potter's Wife*, upon Tuesday, April ye 14th, Anno 1696.

The *thirtieth* was at the ffunerall of *old John Willbore*, carpenter, he was very ancient, upon Munday, June the 29th, Anno 1696.

The *thirty-first* was at the funerall of *Mr. William Cox*, who lived in ye Back Lane, but was lately removed, and dyed at his daughter Mulling's, upon Fryday, July the 31st, Anno 1696.

The *thirty-second* was at the funerall of *Goldin Mullings*, butcher, a young man, upon Satterday, September the 12th, by candlelight, Anno 1696.

The *thirty-third* was at the funerall of *Mr. Matthew Guyon*, a singleman, who was the son of Mr. Matthew Guyon, he died at Pattiswick, at his brother's, Mr. Charles Guyon, upon Thursday, May the 20th, Anno 1697.

The *thirty-fourth* was at the ffunerall of *Edward Miles*, carpenter, son of John Miles, upon Thursday, June the 10th, Anno 1697.

The *thirty-fifth*, was at the ffunerall of the *first wife of Mr. William Armond*, she was Councellor Coxe's sister, upon Satterday, September the 11th, Anno 1697.

The *thirty-sixth* was at the ffunerall of old *Mrs. Cox*, the widow of Mr. John Cox, she was an ancient woman, upon Fryday, August the 19th, Anno 1698.

The *thirty-seventh* was at the ffunerall of the first wife of *Edmund Tanner*, who was Mr. Gale's daughter, she had a cancer in her breast, upon Tuesday, November the 22nd, by candlelight, Anno 1698.

The *thirty-eighth* was at the funerall of old *Mrs. Peirson*, a very ancient gentlewoman, she was Mrs. Livermore's mother, it was preached at Markshall church, upon Wednesday, February the 1st, Anno 1698-9.

The *thirty-ninth* was at the ffunerall of *Robert Cornill*, a ffarmer, who lived at Grigg's, and had lain lame and sick about four or five yeares, upon Fryday, March the 3rd, by candlelight, Anno 1698-9.

The *fourtieth* was at the ffuneral of *Anthony Blackbourne*, farmer, a singleman, who lived in ye Hamlet, it was preached at Bradwell church, upon Friday, April the 21st, Anno 1699."

Q

"I left Coxall, January 1st, 1699, and so kept no further account of funerall sermons."

After giving "an account of what books which came to my hand I wrot things out of into more books than one :" he proceeds—

"Aug. 8, 1766.—I reckon I have here 22 almanacks, 13 Riders and Gellen, pretty broad, 6 Goldsmith narrow ones, 1 Partridge, very large one, 1 Raven's, of a particular sort, 1 Tanner is a stitched one. Of the 13 of Riders, &c.—5 filled up chiefly with things taken out of other books, 2 old accounts, one for Lon., 1 for Colc. 1 filled chiefly with buriall and marriage, 1 with the monthly account I kept, 1 field up with notes of sermons, 1 has account of household stuff, &c., 1 I kept some accounts in, 1 I keep on my board and write in dayly. Of ye 6 of Goldsmith's— 2 fill'd up chiefly out of other books, 1 fill'd great part with Bellman's verses, 1 greatest part with Irish letters, 1 has an account of funerall sermons,* 1 has the orders in Comber's book, &c. Partridge's —writ most out of other books and Irish letters. Raven's —out of Irish letters, &c. Tanner's—out of a dictionary."

Extracts from one of Bufton's Note Books, marked on cover 'VI.' and commencing "These are the notes of 39 funerall sermons in this book." Then follows the order of the sermons, the name of the preacher, and the text.

"The heads or notes of ye sermon preached at the ffunerall of *old Mr. Thomas Guyon*, November the 26, 1664, by Mr. Jessop :—

"I now come to ye occasion. My worthy friend as when he was alive he was above your censures, so now he is deceased he is not concerned in your commendations. He was a person of great wisdom and judgment ; he was a person of sober conversation ; he was diligent in his employment ; he was surpassingly compassionate to ye poore. I fear, now this great man is fallen among you, many mourners among the poore will go about the streets. He was of a peaceable disposition to the neighbourhood, and I persuade myself he was a religious attender on God in his ordinances and had a respect to ye ministry, which is a rare virtue

---

* This is the book whence these and all the preceding extracts are taken. Goldsmith, 1672.

in these days. So I take my farewell of my friend and neighbour in his bed of earth, in which I, myself, must shortly lie, and you that heare me must follow me ; wherefore let us pray to GOD and labor for faith and repentance and new obedience, and then, 'Come Lord JESUS, come quickly."

"The notes of ye sermon, preached at ye buriall of *Mr. Richard Shortland*, by Mr. Jessop, December the 13th, 1667 :—

"Now for the occasion. I was in a great dispute in my thoughts, whether to speak or to hold my peace, of this my worthy friend, considering the teachyness and cencoriousness of ye place we live in. I thought at first to omitit, but considering death hath placed my friend above your censures I shall offer somewhat to it. My worthy friend, his parentage you all know, his parents were persons of substance and repute among yee. His father intended him for learning and sent him to ye University of Cambridge, where he was brought up at the feet of Gamaliell, and his tutor was Mr. Joseph Mede. But for want of health he was incapacitated for a further progress in study, wherefore he was sent for home to succeed his father in ye sometime beneficiall trade of clothing. This 5 year I have had ye happiness to be acquainted with him. He would often complain that his soul was hindered by ye clog of ye body. I am confident there be sundry here that can protest his abilities in ye publick busyness of ye towne ; he was courteous to his neighbours and to my knowledge he was a forgetter of injuries ; he was a loving husband, and as you know he was not negligent in ye bringing up of his children ; and he was firme for government both in church and state ; as for religion, to my knowledge he was well versed in Scripture, and what was ingraven on his memory was ingraven on his heart too ; he was orthodox in his opinions and he was a constant attender on GOD's publick worship, which I know he did out of conscience. Many people enter into publick worship as ye high priest into ye Holy of Holies but once a year, if they do that. But (above all, to return to my worthy friend), this I looked upon as ye flower of all his vertues, that he had a great esteeme of our Lord and Master, JESUS CHRIST, he never spake of Him without great submission and affection and resignation of soul. The last words I heard him speak were—'Oh what are we ! we have nothing without JESUS CHRIST ;' I shall speak no

more of him but to you my loving neighbours. I would exhort
you to step in and supply his place, that by your interposing he
may be ye less missed. Some of you have abilities sufficient for
publick busynesses. Let it not be said that GOD gave you not a
heart to make use of them. My loving neighbours, if now that
our serviceable member is 'cut off, if whatever was imitable in
him may be redoubled in you that are alive, it will be a good
thing."

"Notes of ye sermon preached at ye buriall of young *Mr.
Thomas Guyon*, at Coxall, by Mr. Brooks, of Yeldham, June 17,
1673. :—

"Concerning ye person brought hither to be buried, he lived
but a little time in all; but yet something I shall say of him.
He was a gentleman very likely to have been usefull in his place
if GOD had continued him here; he loved to be in imployment
and followed it diligently which is very commendable, and though
his calling carried him into places of great temptation, yet I never
heard him charged with any miscarriages. He owed much to
GOD for restraining grace, and as I hope for renewing grace. It
pleased GOD to visit him with a lingering consumption; and he
often complained of ye vanity and folly and hardness of his heart,
and that he had not made returns to GOD as he should have done
for his many and signall deliverances; and he has told me many
times with tears in his eyes, that though he was kept from grosse
sins yet he could never be sufficiently humbled for these and other
sins. He was often in private devotion and fervent in it. He
gave much good counsel to his surviving brothers and often
begged of his sorrqwfull mother that she would not be troubled
for his death. . . . . He lay a considerable time in a very
submissive frame of sperit and willing to be at GOD's disposing.
Tis true, for a long time he desired life and hoped to recover, and
used meanes and who can blame him for it. But when he saw
meanes proved ineffectual he seemed to me not to be troubled,
but rather rejoiced that the time of his dissolution was so neare.
And though he had enough to defend ye world withall and many
dear relations loth to part with him, yet he was not solicitous to
live but willing to die. A little befor his death when he was told
some parts of the body were cold, he seemed not troubled at all,
but wished his body were all over so if GOD saw it good. The
Lord grant that we may all be so instructed by his death, that we

may lay to heart and labor to prepare for our owne death, that so we may die ye death of ye righteous as I hope he did."

"The notes of the sermon preached by Mr. Lithermore, at ye ffunerall of the old *Lady Honeywood*,* at Marks Hall, October 26, 1681 :—

"The occasion of this present assembly is plaine before you, being to performe the last piece of service that we can doe to ye body of ye pious and renouned Lady Honeywood. . . . .
I know, now, you expect I should say something of ye pious lady here deceased. Her light was too great to be put under a bushell. Her works were such as now praise her in ye gate. I shall say no more than what may be truly said and to which you will say amen. I shall begin with her birth and descent. She came of pious and religious parents such as were tried and growne up under persecution. She was ye daughter and coheire of John Lamot, Esq., marchant, in London, whose parents came from Flanders, thence driven by persecution. She was piously educated and so she continued all her dayes, making good that saying, 'Traine up a child in ye way he should go and when he is old he will not depart from it.' She was twice married, her last husband was Sr. Thomas Honeywood by whom she had 7 children, of which but two survive her. She stood in severall relations. As a wife she was one of the best of wives, so kind and loving in all respects; I have often heard her say, 'I love a Honeywood,' which she made good by making much of her husband's friends Take her as a mother and a grandmother, she was a loving, care full and indulgent one. As to her servants, she was one of ye best of ladyes, more like a mother than a mistress. She was a lady of admirable parts of quickness of understanding, &c. . . This noble and never to be forgotten lady is gone from us, never to come again. Let us live, so that we may meet her in heaven and live with her in everlasting happyness."

---

* A history of the family of Honywood and of the parish of Marks Hall is obviously outside the province of this work. It would of itself fill a fair sized volume.

ANCIENT HOUSES, FIELD NAMES,
ROADS, BRIDGES, &c.

THE most interesting part of the town will be found centred round the Market Hill, and an endeavour will here be made to call attention to the principal buildings which still remain, as well as to record a few notes relating to those which have fallen into decay and are now no more. There are doubtless many choice little pieces of carved woodwork in the old houses here, which are now covered with plaister, but which will be brought to light in years to come. Other carved work of two to four centuries back may be seen in many of the existing houses, but eighteenth and nineteenth century vandalism· has removed much that should have been treasured with reverence. Fortunately the circulation of archæological literature among all classes of society is doing much to make people understand that the value of these relics of byegone days is utterly destroyed when the handiworks of their forefathers are removed from their original situations.

In the centre of Market Hill, there formerly stood a little chapel which in later years, as has been shown on a previous page *(ante* p. 174*)*, was a Corn and Butter Market; later still, we find the upper part converted into a Wool Hall. Here, too, was the Turret with its Clock and Bell, for the better ordering of apprentices. This building, also known as the Market Cross, was

doubtless of a similar character to many such buildings as are to
be seen at the present day, the lower part being open and the
upper part, consisting of a spacious apartment adapted for meetings. The Market Cross was pulled down in 1787.

Close by on the west side was, and still is, the CHAPEL INN, a
sign almost if not quite unique. It is also known as AYWORTH'S,
or Edgeworth's and Seals or SEWELLS, and it is probable that here
stood the house of John Sewell, who was Sheriff of Essex in the
4th year of King Richard II. (A.D. 1381,) an allusion to whose
residence is contained in the Assize Rolls of Divers Counties, 5th
Rich. II., No. 7, in these words, "They all (*i.e.* the insurgents of
the days of Wat Tyler) "rode about armed in a land of peace
with the company aforesaid, who rose up against the King and
his lieges to the Temple of the Prior of St. John of Jerusalem, to
Cressyng, and to the house of John Sewall, of Coggeshall, and
overthrew the houses and buildings of the same Prior and John,
and feloniously took and carried away their goods and chattels
there found." And elsewhere we read that the insurgents took
away one thousand four hundred marks in money belonging to the
same John Sewall (*Essex Arch. Soc. Trans. N. S.*, Vol. I., p. 217).

Below this house at the southern end of Stoneham Street, is
the LION Inn.

On the south side of the Market Houses is the large block of
buildings known as CONSTANTINES, or LADY VENTRISS'S, comprising the shops occupied by Messrs. Lawrence, Barton, Frith and
Goodchild, and a building used as a Temperance Hotel. The
property takes its name from Richard Constantine, who was the
owner of it in the reign of King James I., in which year he
granted a lease of these houses to Robert Cooke for 5000 years.

Passing to the south side of East Street, we find ourselves in
Market End, and here in the days long passed away could have
been seen an interesting display of trade signs, not all taverns or
public houses as some might imagine but the pictorial sign boards
of traders in all kinds of goods, wares and merchandise. Mr.
Miller Christy points out, in his interesting work on the *Trade
Signs of Essex*, that in the days when only an infinitessimally
small proportion of the population could read it would have been
absurd for a tradesman to have inscribed above his door his name
and occupation, or the number of the house, as is now done, but
if each dealer displayed conspicuously before his place of business

a painted representation of the wares he sold, the arms of the
trade-guild to which he belonged, or those of his landlord or
patron, or some other device by which his house might be known,
there would be little probability of mistake.

The principal of these houses appears to have been the
CROWN, which was, as we have seen (p. 66), an ale-house. It is
now the Post Office and the printing and publishing establishment
of Mr. Edwin Potter. It is this house that Bufton was referring
to when he recorded that, on February 15th, 1692, "There was a
bonfire made at the Crown for joy that Squire Honeywood got
the day of Sir Eliab Harvey and was not cast out of Parliament;
and when he came home from Chelmsford, the night after he was
chosen, abundance of candles were lighted up for joy." But the
sign of the Crown in this town dates back to a much earlier
period, as will be seen from the extracts from the Court Rolls of
Great Coggeshall Manor *(ante,* p. 112) ; from this document it
appears that in the days of Queen Elizabeth (in the year 1567)
the owners of the Crown were required to take up the gate in the
water lane, and to widen the lane. Where the particular lane was
is not now apparent, but as it is known that formerly the water
from St. Peter's well used to flow in an open channel down Church
Street, it is probable that the Crown, of Queen Elizabeth's time,
was on the same site as the present Post Office, if so the water
lane referred to was on or near this property. In connection with
the open water-course in Church Street, it may be mentioned that,
in 1792, Mr. Fisher Unwin, brewer, laid down pipes under the
highway from the well belonging to his malt house in Church
Street, for the purpose of conveying water from that well to his
brewhouse, called the cellar, at Market End, such pipes being laid
with the consent of the Lord and tenants of the Manor of Great
Coggeshall and the inhabitants of the town. This well adjoins
the public well, known as St. Peter's Well, in Wain Lane. The
sign of the Crown is one of the oldest of English trade signs, and
if time had not altered the manners and customs of the people
the title page of this book would have announced that it was
"Printed and sold by Edwin Potter, at ye sign of ye Crowne, at
ye Market End, Coggeshall."

Next to the Crown, proceeding westward, was a house, called
MAVESONS or MABSONS, a name probably derived from the person
who possessed it upwards of 300 years ago (p. 129); the east

part now belongs to Mr. William Mount, but the western part is the more ancient and is of interest, the construction of the uppermost chamber in the roof being somewhat singular.

Proceeding further in the same direction, the adjoining house is the WHITE HART HOTEL. It appears to have been called MAYKYNES in the reign of King Henry VIII., and then belonged to the Paycocke family (*ante p. 129*), being held of the manor of Coggeshall Hall, but the sign post belonging to it was built on the waste of the Manor of Great Coggeshall. Bufton records the death, in 1675, of Ambrose Armond, of the White Hart. The sign is generally considered to have had an heraldic origin.

Opposite the White Hart was the BLUE BOAR. Adjoining the White Hart on the west is a house which was called the TRUE-BLUE *(ante*, p. 131*)*, a sign which does not appear to exist elsewhere in Essex, at any rate it has not come under the notice of the author of *The Trade Signs in Essex.* The property possessed this name in 1758, when the Coggeshall Hall Manor Map was prepared.

The block of property between the White Hart and Bridge Street, or Cellar Lane, was, in 1758 and 1789, known as the GREEN DRAGON, a sign, it may be imagined, which did not harmonise very well with its neighbour, the True-Blue. The True-Blue and the Green Dragon may together represent the property which, in the 17th year of King Henry VIII. was an inn called the DRAGON. The Dragon is a very ancient trade sign in England, and would seem to have been taken from the flag of the cohorts of a Roman legion. As a national ensign this winged serpent was long continued in this land; it was borne by Harold's standard-bearer, and in later years was carried before the kings of England in their wars.

There was a house in this locality known as the MAVICE.

Passing Bridge Street, and proceeding towards the Gravel, we find from the Great Coggeshall Manorial Survey that the SHAMBLES, or the stalls where the butchers exposed their meat for sale, stood in the triangular piece of ground here. These business premises, called the OLD HALL, in 1775 *(ante* p. 120*)*, were on or near the site of the Cricketer's Inn, and belonged to the Manor of Great Coggeshall. The roof of the back part of the Shambles, Bufton tells us, fell in on the 25th February, 1686. Here also was probably the CASTELL OF GYNES, which in the reign of Edward IV.

was nothing more than a cottage *(ante,* p. 122*)*. Its name imports that in byegone days it was a residence of some note, but, unfortunately the only traces of its history lie in the mention of the property in the manorial records.

The FISHMARKET (p. 119) was near the Shambles, and in this locality was a house called the BELLS AND BREWERS, abutting upon Hares Bridge towards the north. A house called the FOXES adjoined the last-mentioned property.

Opposite the Castell of Gynes was the lord's tenement called the COCKE, now part of the brewery premises of Mr. John Kemp King, the field at the back being still known as Cock Orchard. The Cock is a good old English sign, and was in use in Coggeshall in the times of Edwd. IV. and James I. (pp. 86 and 123), and from the fact that this house was one of the monastic properties at the time of the dissolution of the Abbey, it would seem that the name may have been assigned to it by the monks whose seal, as has been noticed (p. 94), bore three cocks; one is, however, more inclined to believe that the sign owes its origin to the days of cock-fighting—a pastime which was indulged in generally on Sunday, in reference to which practice Stubbs, in his *Anatomie of Abuses,* written in 1585 (see *Brand Pop. Antiq.,* Vol. II. p. 57), says, " They flock thicke and threefolde to the cock-fightes, where nothing is used but swearing, forswearing, deceipt, fraud, collusion, cosenage, skoldyng, railyng, convitious talkyng, fightyng, brawlyng, quarrellyng, drinkyng, and robbing one another of their goods, and that not by direct, but by indirect means and attempts. And yet to blaunch and set these mischiefs withall (as though they were virtues) they have their appointed days and set houses where these devilries must be exercised. *They have houses erected to the purpose,* flags and ensigns hanged out to give notice of it to others, and proclamation goes out to proclaim the same, to the end that many may come to the dedication of this solemn feast of mischiefe." To Bufton we are indebted for the record that on " 29 March, 1697, there were a great many fighting-cocks carried through Coxall on horseback in linen bags or clothes."

The CORRECTION HOUSE was located between the Gravel and the stream running from Hares Bridge to Short Bridge, and in the 17th century belonged to Matthew Guyon.

SHORT BRIDGE spans the ancient course of the River Blackwater, and from the presentments in the Court Rolls of the Manor of Little Coggeshall, it appears that it was maintained by the Surveyors of the Highway.

The bridge over the artificial channel between the old river and Grange Hill is known as LONG BRIDGE, the HORSE RIVER BRIDGE and STEPHEN'S BRIDGE. It was doubtless originally built under the direction of the monks as lords of the manors and owners of the land in this locality, shortly after they settled here,

STEPHEN'S BRIDGE.

but it is improbable that any part of the original structure, except it be the foundations, is now extant, though it would seem that many of the bricks used in the first erection have been worked into the present bridge. Some years ago iron rails were substituted for the protecting wall of the bridge, and on this wall over the middle arch there was a stone with the arms or badge of King Stephen, a *saggitarius*, a creature half man and half horse, carved on it, and there was formerly also this inscription in free-stone inlaid in the upper part of the bridge—"This bridge was repaired in the year 1705, at the cost and charge of Nehemiah Lyde, Esq., Lord of the Manors of Great and Little Coggeshall, and of the severall fee farmers and proprietors of the Lands and tenements late parcell of Coggeshall Abbey."

Adjoining Long Bridge on the north east is a house called the ROOD HOUSE. Foxe tells us that in the year 1532, "The image of the crucifix was cast down and destroyed in the highway by Coxhall;" but whether this crucifix stood here or not there is nothing to show. This property, as the writer has shown more fully elsewhere *(East Anglian Notes and Queries, N.S.*, Vol. II., p. 67), was on the 1st May in the 3rd year of King James 1st, conveyed by Cyprian Warner, Thomas Shortland, Thomas Aylet and Nicholas Richold to Michael Hills. In 1664 it is described as the Roode House, adjoining the north side of the Common River near the Great Bridge there. It is probably on the site of Roode's land (as to which see *ante*, p. 80), a surmise which is confirmed by the fact that Randolph Wolley, of London, merchant tailor and Thomas Dodd, citizen and grocer, of London, were the grantees from King James I. of, among other properties, one house upon the north side of Long Bridge, as fully as the same came or ought to have come to the hands of Kings Henry VIII. and Edward VI. or Queen Mary or Queen Elizabeth, by reason of the dissolution or surrender of the monastery, &c. The Rev. E. L. Cutts *(Essex Arch. Soc. Trans.)* gives a sketch of Long Bridge, and says this house very likely took its name from the erection in the small space before it of a Rood to mark the en-trance to the Abbey demesnes ; and in a note he calls attention to an illumination in the 14th century MS. in the British Museum, No. 10,293, fol. 186, in which is a representation of a bridge with a tall cross beside it just as suggested above.

GRANGE HILL derives its name from the Home Grange of the Abbey at the top of the hill, a grange being another name for a farm house or granary belonging to any of the monastic orders.

In Church Street, commencing from the upper end, the first house of note is that known as the WOOLPACK, a most appro-priate name for a hostelry in a town whose growth was due in a considerable degree to the wool-merchants of the fifteenth and sixteenth centuries. This house, which is situate on Church Green, has received some notice already *(ante* p. 140), having been the residence of the Rev. Thomas Lowrey, an ejected minister of the Church of England. It has a double-gabled front with projecting upper floors, and carved oak-work within and without. As early as 1708, it is in the title deeds called the Woolpack, but in documents, dated 1769 and 1803, the Inn is called the WOOLPACK AND PUNCHBOWL. It was probably this house that Bufton was referring to, when he noted that on 1st May, 1693, 'ye soldiers set up a maypole at ye Woolpacke door,' and here it was, too, that Abram Emming roasted a small bullock whole, on the 12th February, 1678, being Shrove-Tuesday, for

Bufton says, that this culinary achievement took place on Church Green. Another house, situated half-way between the Church and Market Hill, bore the name of the Woolpack, as appears from the Great Coggeshall Manorial Survey.

On the south side of Church Street and now forming part of the CEDARS, formerly stood the GREEN DRAGON, a name which was attached to the property as early at least as 1693, as is evidenced by the Court Rolls of Great Coggeshall Manor. It was pulled down about 1809 and the site laid into the garden or yard of the Cedars, sometime the property of Thomas Andrews, a solicitor of this town, who died in 1826.

Lower down the street, on the opposite side of the road and east of Wain Lane, is a treble-gabled fronted house with some carved woodwork. Over the doors are texts, *e.g.*, 'Except the Lord build the house,' &c., and on the wall plate in Wain Lane, 'Richard White, 1736,' is inscribed. It was at the back of this house, as has been shown (p. 215), Dr. Jegon, Bishop of Norwich, was probably born.

WAIN or VAIN LANE is doubtless a survival of the Anglo-Saxon *Wægen*, which means ways, perhaps because the lane connects Church Street with Church Lane. It will be seen from a presentment in 1720 (*ante* p. 119), that this place was then called the Wayne Yard of Mary Cox adjoining PETER'S Well, as to which see *ante* p. 15.

HORN LANE, opposite Wain Lane, may have some connection with the May-day custom of blowing with and drinking out of horns, which prevailed till comparatively recent times.

The BULL INN, on the north side of Church Street, was so called in 1731, previously to which time it was known as the COCKE-ATTE-HILLES.

Almost opposite this Inn, is a house (Ordnance Bench Mark, 113.8) with an oak frieze carved in relief, bearing date 1565 and initials T.C. or T.G., probably the initials of a member of the Cox, Guyon, or Gray family. The upper floor projected until the wall of the ground floor was built up flush with the dormitories. This frieze is one of the relics of old Coggeshall which should be jealously preserved for all time.

The THREE-STORIED HOUSE, belonging to Mr. John Beard, opposite the Baptist Chapel, attracts attention as one of interest. The first floor projects about a foot into the street, and the second is built still farther outward. In 1689 the house belonged to William Armond and Elizabeth his wife, and was about that time occupied by John Buxton, a member of the wealthy family of that name, which for considerably more than three centuries has been connected with this town.

The cottages on the west are called SPOONERS, from the name of a former owner. Farther on is the GREYHOUND INN.

On the west of Swan Yard is HERRINGS, so called as early as 1394 (p. 121). It belongs to Mrs. Appleford and is occupied by Mr. David Mount.

The house adjoining Herrings, towards the west, is known as PLUMMERS, and was so called in 1576 (p. 81). In 1740 it belonged to and was occupied by Mark Grime, doubtless of the same family as Colonel Grime, who, for his bravery in the wars in Flanders and the Spanish Netherlands, was awarded a pension by Wm. IV. (see *Memorial Inscription*, p. 45.)

Opposite Plummers is the Parochial Reading Room, which, with the garden in front of the two red brick villas standing some way back from the street, was formerly called WYBORS, probably a corruption of the name of a family called Wilbore, which resided in this town. In 1789, the property was known as the GREEN MAN. William Mayhew, who was member for Colchester, resided here for some time; his opponent, Spottiswood, was first returned to Parliament, but on petition was unseated, and it is related that Mayhew arrived at the House of Commons just in time to record his vote in favour of the Reform Bill, of 1832, which was carried by a majority of only one vote.

On the same side of the road, but nearer the Market Hill, is the BLACK BOY, so called since, if not before, 1803. This, and the house between it and the Market Hill, was, in 1708, known as the CORNER HOUSE.

In Church Lane is a fair sized house opposite Wain Lane, on a mantle piece in which are the following lines with appropriate symbols (compare Gladwin's *Memorial Inscription*, p. 51) :—

The hour runneth	An hour glass
And time flieth	The sun
As flowre fadeth	A withering flower
So man dieth	A skull

Sic transit gloria mundi.

Beyond the Town Clock, which was restored in 1888 as a memorial of Queen Victoria's Jubilee, is a house, in Stoneham Street, which, in 1731, was called the WOOLPACK AND CROWN.

Where the Friends' Meeting House now stands one is disposed to locate the CROUCH HOUSE, which, in 1426, was nothing more than a decayed cottage (*ante*, p. 122). The field at the back is still called CROUCHES, as to which reference has already been made (*ante*, p. 16.)

On the north of Crouch's Alley the WORKHOUSE stood until the establishment of. the union house at Witham.

Near the upper end of Stoneham Street, and on the west side is a row of cottages called MOSES, or Moises, by which name it was known as early as 1462, when it belonged to Richard Bullock (*ante* p. 122).

At the junction of Robins Bridge Road and Tilkey Road is the YORKSHIRE GREY built in the south-eastern corner of Hart Field. There does not appear to have been any house here in 1758, and the sign in this town is probably not more than 50 years old. Mr. Miller Christy suggests that the Yorkshire Greys are named after some famous racer.

Nearer the Market Hill, on the east side of the street is the ROYAL OAK, a sign which is intended to perpetuate the memory of King Charles II.

Below Church Lane is CUCUMBER HALL, but why so called is unknown. Nearer the Market Hill was the BLACK HORSE, now the LOCOMOTIVE, a name given to it about 35 years ago by a ganger on the railway, who occupied the house after the completion of the line.

The new residence called MOUNT PARK, at the east end of East Street, was built by Mr. T. C. Swinborne and now belongs to Mr. Robert Curzon, J.P. It belonged to John Stacey in 1731, and afterwards to the Skingley family. About 40 years ago the old house was ransacked by a gang of burglars, who, when they had possessed themselves of the valuable contents set fire to it and levelled it to the ground.

The STAR Inn, in East Street, was opposite the eastern entrance to Starling Leeze, and was freehold of the Manor of Coggeshall Hall, but the porch of it was built on the waste of the Manor of Great Coggeshall, and at the time of the survey of that Manor, in 1731, the inn had the double sign of the SWAN AND STAR. As a star is the crest of the Innholders' Company it is not surprising that it should so frequently have been adopted by publicans as a distinguishing mark for their houses. The combination of the Swan and Star appears to be inexplicable but there was doubtless some reason in its origin.

On the north side of East Street, a house or two west of Starling Leeze, was called the BLUE BOAR, a sign which very naturally occurs in this district as it was one of the cognizances of the De Veres, Earls of Oxford, who held large estates in Earls Colne and the neighbourhood. It may be that the first holder of this Inn was one of the Earl's retainers who, out of respect to his late master and to show his former connection with so noble a family, had the signboard fresh painted, and henceforth the boar, not in its natural colour but of blue, was suspended from above the door of the hostelry. This was the sign of the house one hundred and sixty years ago, but how much earlier is a question the answer to which has yet to be supplied.

The SWAN, on the north side of this street, was possessed of the same sign in 1731. Francis Lay issued a token in the 17th century payable at the Swan ; the word is not written but the bird appears in the centre of the coin (p. 195). Next to this inn on the west was the SUGAR LOAF, which leads one to suppose that the house belonged to Edmond Spicer, whose trade token bore on one side a sugar loaf (p. 195). It was at one time called the KING'S ARMS.

Between the Sugar Loaf and the Bird-in-Hand was a house called BUCKS, probably the name of a former owner.

The BIRD-IN-HAND was formerly called the *Through Inn*, possibly from the fact that there was a right of passage *through* the house from East Street to Church Street. As a curious coincidence it may be mentioned that a few years back the name of the tenant of the *Bird-in-Hand* was Joseph *Bird*, and that of the owner Richard *Bird* Holmes. This ornithological sign in this town dates back at least 160 years. A reference to p. 193 will show that it was from this house that one of the last processions of weavers set out in the year 1791, just a century ago. The signboard formerly had on it a hand holding a bird recalling the proverb—

"A bird in the hand is worth two in the bush."
The premises belonged at the time of the dissolution to the Abbot and Convent of Coggeshall.

The house, now four cottages, immediately opposite the Bird-in-Hand, has been known at different times as the Blue House and the George. The upper floor formerly projected, but a brick front was a few years ago introduced to the lower floor, on the top of which can still be seen the carved wooden beam or frieze with the date 1585.

About ten yards west of Blue House Lane, is an ancient house which until recently had some good carved wood-work in it. The cellar of this house is of interest.

Next to the Bird-in-Hand is a house which, in 1731, was called Rices, but about a century later converted into an Inn called the New Bird-in-Hand. On the opposite side of the road were houses called Staffords, Durdens and the Dyehouse.

Near the western extremity of West Street stands, as it stood 160 years ago, the White Horse..

Opposite the Vicarage Field were houses and land called Windloves, or Neals and Ladywoods, now called Sunnedon.

The Fleece is situate opposite Sir Robert Hitcham's School, and still retains the name it had in 1731. This sign is associated with the wool trade.

Paycocke's House, as it is called, is on the east side of the Fleece. It has already been referred to, and an illustration of the gateway figures on page 161. The house 160 years ago belonged to Isaac Buxton, senior, and was occupied by John Buxton. It is much to be regretted that this interesting relic of the domestic architecture of several centuries back ever left the possession of this family as in their hands it would doubtless have been preserved from decay. Behind the house and extending westward is Vincent's Close, which, in the 16th century, belonged to John Paycocke or Peacock (*ante* p. 80).

The Roman Road from Saint Albans, through Bishop Stortford and Braintree to Colchester, although it has already been slightly noticed in an early part of this work (pp. 1 and 6) has not yet received the attention which it deserves. Close to Black-water Bridge is an enclosure of land which, until 1889, formed a detached portion of the Parish of Great Coggeshall; it was formerly in four fields and was freehold of the Manor of Coggeshall Hall, being held of the Lord by the annual free rent of 2s. 6d. The Bridge has been noticed on p. 9, and it will be remembered that when it was rebuilt, 30 or 40 years ago, planks of board were

found at some depth below the bed of the river. From the in-
quests, published by the Record Commission (London, 1811, fo.
p. 303), it appears that an enquiry was instituted in the first year
of King Edward II. (A.D. 1307) concerning the refusal of the
Abbot of Coggeshall to repair this bridge, and it was held by the
jury that he was not liable to repair the bridge of Stratford (the
Street Ford) between Braintree and Coggeshall, as within the
memory of man there had been no other bridge over the river
than a certain plank of board *(planchea de borde)* which, as the
jury found, had at all times been considered sufficient for horsemen and pedestrians. The Abbot was again troubled on account
of non-repair of this bridge in the reign of Edward III (Pat. 15
Edw. III., p. 2, m. 5 & 39, see also 51 Edw. III. *Calendar of In-
quisitions, post mortem*). Among the Westminster Abbey manu-
scripts there is a rough sketch of Blackwater 'Brigge,' with notes
of the holders of land in the vicinity in the time of Henry IV.,
also copy proceedings (*temp.* Henry VIII.) against various persons
in reference to the repair of the bridge ; among these persons was
the Abbot of Westminster, on account of his fishery there and
his tenements adjoining the bridge.

The road has to be traversed about a mile eastward before we
are again in this parish, at which point Braintree is 4 miles and
Colchester 11 miles distant. On entering Coggeshall parish here
the road is called STOCK STREET, names which, when found in con-
junction, have great significance as the work *Stock* or *Stoc* is the
Anglo-Saxon for a stockaded place or an enclosure protected by
stakes or piles, and the word *Street* indicates that at one time that
part of the road which is so called was a well-constructed, if not
actually paved, way with houses on either side. The Romans
called it *Stratum*, but their successors transformed the word to
Stræte or Street, hence the two words when thus found associated
can lead to no other conclusion than that in Saxon times this was
a stockaded place on the old Roman road. These villages of the
barbarians were formed in most instances by the *felling* of the
trees of a wooded district—they sometimes called the open space
a field, *e.g.* Old-*field*—and on the ground which had been cleared
they built their rude huts for their own habitations and still ruder
buildings for the folding of their cattle, using the fallen trees for
the construction of their houses and for the staking of the enclosure. Without some explanation it would strike the general

reader as strange that a farm-house with six or eight cottages some distance apart should be called a Street.

A mile further eastward is Crow or Crop Field, or Crop Barn Field, where so many Roman remains have been found from time to time (pp. 6-8). From this point to Hares Bridge the road is called West Street, the condition of which was such that Thomas Paycocke, three hundred and seventy years ago, gave £40 for its repair, referring to the road as "foulways."

HARES BRIDGE is at the south-east corner of the Vicarage Grounds, and was so called when the before mentioned Thomas Paycocke made his will. The name is derived from the family of Hares, one of whom was a grantee from the lord of the manor of Great Coggeshall of a piece of land lying next to Sir William Coggeshall's meadow, (*ante* p. 122) As Sir William Coggeshall's meadow was close to Hares Bridge it follows the piece of land granted to Walter Hares was also in this locality. The bridge crosses the stream which conveys the waters of the Marks Hall drainage area to the river, discharging them at a point where the TYE MILL formerly stood; the word *Tye* here doubtless indicating the junction of the *two* streams, unless it derives its name from the British word Ty, a house. Passing through the old market place EAST STREET is reached, and by this name the road is known as far as Dead Lane. In ancient documents this part of the highway is frequently referred to as GALLOWS STREET. Where the Gallows stood is now a question which must probably remain unsolved; Joseph Foster, aged 70, had it, by relation, that this instrument of execution stood near the present Gas Works, but it is worthy of note that there is a field, copyhold of the manor of Feering with Pattiswick, which is called Gallow Croft. It is No. 143 on the Ordnance Map of Feering parish, and lies to the east of Lees Farm on the south side of the road from Coggeshall to Colchester. That there was a Gallows here, as in nearly every parish, there can be no doubt, for it is referred to in the Hundred Rolls (*temp.* Edw. I.), and at that time it belonged to the Abbot of Coggeshall, whose right to possess it was not disputed by the Crown when the writs of *Quo Warranto* were issued. From Dead Lane, for some distance along the Colchester Road, the highway is known as ROTTEN ROW, a name which it may have acquired through lack of proper attention on the part of the Surveyors of the highways.

R 2

DEAD LANE may in some manner be associated with Gallows
Street, but one rather inclines to the opinion that its name origi-
nated at the time of the Black Death, those awful days in the
middle of the fourteenth century when nearly three-fourths of the
population of certain districts succumbed to that pestilential
disease, or perhaps it is traceable to the pestilence which the registers of the parish show, destroyed so many of the inhabitants of
this place between 1578 and 1604, (*ante* pp. 37 and 38), or it may
be that it is to the Great Plague of 1665, when in London, and
many towns beside, the mortuary cart went round at night, preceded by the bellman crying in solemn tones "Bring out your
dead," that we must look for the origin of this ghastly name, but,
as to the last mentioned plague, there is no evidence from the registers that its ravages extended in any marked degree to this town.

In connection with Dead Lane it may be well to record here
that a field on the east side of Colne Road, (No. 190*) is called
DEADMANS HILL in the Court Rolls of the Manor of Great
Coggeshall, and on the other side of the same road is an enclosure
(No. 160) which, in the Coggeshall Manor, &c., Survey, is known
as DEADWOMAN'S HILL.† To the west of this field is LEECH POND
LEYS, or LEES POND FIELD (No. 153 and 161).   Though the
word, leech, may here have reference to the medicinal blood-
sucker it must be borne in mind that it is not improbable that the
field is another burial ground or field of corpses (*leich*, a corpse),
and if such should be the case it is doubtless the resting place of
our Saxon predecessors.   In the north-west corner of No. 153 is
a cottage which still retains the name of the PEST HOUSE. Lying
on the north of Deadman's Hill, immediately opposite to Deadwoman's Hill, is an enclosure called CHURCH PASTURE, and the
field north of Leech Pond Field is called CHURCH FIELD. North-
east of Church Pasture is the FOLLY (Nos. 186, 188), a word
which *Edmunds* says is derived from folc-ley, meaning the people's
or public land, held by all persons in common.   There is in this
remarkable association of names—pointing, as they seem to do,

---

* The numbers refer to the Ordnance Map of Great Coggeshall except
when followed by L.C. when they refer to the map of Little Coggeshall.

† Called STAR-WALLS in Tithe Survey, as to which see Edmunds (p. 104),
who says the word *Wall* marks the site of Roman works, and as an instance
he gives Cox-wall.   This note should be considered in reference to the Ety-
mology of our town's name, as to which see *ante* p. 6-13.

to the holy acres where "the rude forefathers of the hamlet sleep,"
—involved a history the pages of which are for the present locked
by the clasp of obscurity, but, as time rolls on, the husbandman,
the potter and the builder may bring to the light of day once
more the urns, the bones, the swords, the spear-heads and the
beads which our Saxon predecessors in deep reverence laid to
rest in the distant past. Such a discovery was made near the
river bridge, at Kelvedon, and the following note with reference to
it appeared in the *Essex Naturalist*, for July, 1888: "Mr. G. F.
Beaumont exhibited an adult human skull, a cinerary urn, four
beads of red earth ornamented with green and yellow (the ornamentation of two of them consisting of an encircled snake), a
large amber bead, a cross-shaped bronze fibula, an iron buckle,
and an iron knife-blade or spear-head, all of which he believed to
be of Saxon date. These remains were exhumed by Mr.
Beaumont in the south corner of a field situate near the river
bridge at Kelvedon, and No. 7 in the Ordnance Survey map of
Inworth parish. Mr. Beaumont remarked that although the
ground had been levelled, and there were *no external signs of
barrows*, he had ascertained from an old survey (A.D. 1758) that
the field was called 'Barrow Field,' and the lane running along
its south-west side bore the significant name of 'World's End
Lane.' The fields numbered 436A and 437 (Ordnance Survey
Map, Feering Parish) which adjoin No. 7 (Inworth Parish) towards the north, are known as 'Barrow Hills.' A great many
antiquarian articles, similar to those exhibited, were found in this
locality some years ago, notably in the disused gravel pit, No. 9,
Inworth Parish Map, but, unfortunately, they have for the most
part either been destroyed or lost. Mr. Beaumont announced
that he had decided to hand his exhibits to the Essex Archæological Society for the Colchester Museum." The lands (called
Longlonds, *ante* p. 128) adjoining the field where these interesting
remains were found were formerly freehold of the manor of
Coggeshall Hall, although more than half a mile distant from any
land in Coggeshall Parish; and from the abuttal description it
appears that in immediate proximity to the Barrows was a field
which, till the reign of Henry VIII., was known as Shadwell,
perhaps indicating that here was a well or font dedicated to St.
Chad, one of the earliest Bishops of London, who is said to have
been sainted for bringing the inhabitants of these parts again to

Christianity after their apostacy, and it is reputed that he erected several churches in this county. The latest discovery in the Barrow Field was made in November, 1889, when a stone coffin hewn out of a solid block of oolitic limestone was brought to light. It was six feet seven inches long and two feet four inches wide. The body was encased in lime, and, had it not been for the ignorance of the workmen, it is probable an almost perfect cast of the corpse could have been obtained. The skull and other bones were in an excellent state of preservation.

It will be convenient here to call attention to a similar aggregation of weird field names, which, though in Kelvedon Parish, are just on the south border of Little Coggeshall Parish, and appear on the map of Ltttle Coggeshall Hall Manor. These are Callows, or GALLOWS END LANE (Pantling Lane in Ordnance Survey), leading from Bradwell into the road from Coggeshall to Kelvedon. DEADMAN'S HILL forms the south-western portion of No. 68, Kelvedon Parish (Ordnance Survey). LEACH POND FIELD is No. 50, and LEACHPOND LEYS SLOP the western half of No. 49. Of one or more of these fields it may be said—

> " Perhaps in this neglected spot is laid
> Some heart once pregnant with celestial fire,
> Hands that the rod of empire might have swayed,
> Or wak'd to ecstacy the living lyre."

The western half of No. 51 (K.P.) is called PLUMLEYS, which seems to denote that here was formerly a plum orchard, afterwards *laid* down to pasture. The south-eastern part of the same field is called ROMLEY, which apparently points to Roman associations, literally the Roman meadow. PANTER LANDS are Nos. 20, 21, and 22 (Ordnance Survey, Kelvedon Parish). Nos. 18 and 19 are called BURNT HOUSE. Such names as TOM, or TOWN'S ACRE, and GROGGERY (No. 93, L. C.) remind us of the Saxon Tun or Town and its Christian missioner, St. Gregory.

There are also, in Little Coggeshall, fields called GULL HOLE (No. 127, L. C.), GULL CROFTS (No. 149, L. C.), GULL FIELD (No. 152, L. C.), GULL MOOR (No. 153, L. C.), and GULL FIELD MEADOW (No. 155, L. C.), RAIN CROFT, or RFND'S CROFT, and SHRIVES (No. 129. L. C.), CHURCH FIELD (No. 125, L.C.) KITCHEN FIELD (No. 126, L. C.) [See Seebohm's *Vill. Com.*, 262 and 432.] PIT FIELD (No. 116, L. C.), SHIRLEYS (No. 114, L. C.), BOON SHOTS (No. 103, L. C.), CUTHEDGE FIELD (Nos. 98 and

110, L. C.), CUTLER'S CROFTS (Nos. 104, 106, and 107 L. C.),
PORTER'S CROFTS (Nos. 96 and 97, L. C.), COURT FIELD (No.
87, L. C.), HARE FIELD (Nor 134, L. C.), Ditto (No. 135, L. C.),
HOP GROUND (No. 136, L. C.), TENTER FIELD (No. 134, L. C),
Ditto (No. 50, L. C.), WINCHGATE FIELD (No. 148, L. C.),
KEYSES FIELD (No. 92 L. C.), CURD HALL FARM, on the Tithe
Survey is called BLEST END FARM, but Blest End itself appears
to be further west, between CAPON'S FARM and HERRING'S FARM,
STOCK FIELD (No. 71, L. C.)

To return to Great Coggeshall Parish. We have fields bearing
the following names, BABB'S FARM YARD, &c. (Nos. 243 and
247) at Stock Street. Coote *(Romans of Britain)* considers that
the surname Babb is the radical portion of the Roman name
Babbius, a fact which is not without importance in connection
with the Roman remains which have been found near this locality.
BUNN FIELD is No. 254, COKER'S is No. 234, ADAM FIELD is No.
265. The VINEYARD, near Holfield Grange, is shown on the
map. BARREN DANSON'S is No. 117, BROCKMAN'S is the north-
western part of No. 249, HUNGERTON'S is No. 94, CROSSPATH
BRADLEY is No. 87; PENNY LANE leads from Hovell's to Potash
Farm, and the field on the west of it (No. 51) is called PENNY
LANE MEADOW, names which lead to the surmise that Roman
denarii, of which our English pennies are the representatives, have
been found here in some quantities (see *ante*, p. 10.) Here, too,
are HIGH HALL FIELD (No. 50), WHALEY or VALEY CROFT (No.
67), GREAT GATE FIELD (No. 65), LITTLE GATE FIELD (No. 85),
COGGESHALL GROVE (80, 81, 82, and 83), QUARTER MILE FIELD
(No. 113), BROOM FIELD (No. 52), MOAT FIELD (No. 21),
FINCH FIELD SPRING (No. 48), LITTLE BUNGATE (No. 46), to
the north of which is BUNGATE WOOD. BAKER'S LAND (No. 73),
NEW ENGLAND (the eastern parts of Nos. 43 and 44.) The
western half of No. 2 is called MOUNT FIELD, and it will be observed from the map that it is at the north-western extremity of
the parish. There are no traces of barrows in this field. Round
Gate House Farm are GATE FIELD (No. 126), HIGH FIELD (No.
76), HOD'S CROFT (No. 124), GOLDEN FIELD (north part of No.
133), CHURCH PASTURE, the southern portion below which is
TOWN FIELD (No. 134), and TOWN LEY (No. 269), to the west
of which two last-mentioned fields are COLEMAN'S CROFTS (No.
129), GREAT LOWS, or THE LOWS (eastern half of No. 121),

HIGH LOWS (the part of No. 137 which lies north of No. 143 and the adjoining plantation, which is numbered 138 on the map). Wide Wide Croft, otherwise JOHN'S CROFT (No. 141) adjoins it towards the east, ROOKLANDS, or RUCKNEY (Nos. 169 and 170), WISDOMS (No. 162), DAMOKE FIELD (No. 177), JOHN'S CROFT, or DAMOCKS No. 179), JOHN'S CROFT (No. 180), WINTERFLOODS (No. 187), POPLARS (Nos. 181 and 182), FRENCH LANDS (No. 185), PEASELANDS (No. 190), FABIAN'S FIELD (No. 381), TOWN FIELD (No. 390), LITTLE TOWN FIELD (No. 389), ROW FIELD (No. 388), WINDMILL FIELDS (Nos. 388 and 395), HACKLEY FIELD (No. 396), RAIN CROFTS (Nos. 401, 402, and 403) which seems in this instance to be derived from the old English word *Raine.* a boundary, for the boundary line of the Parish runs along the south-eastern side of these fields. MOUNT FIELD is No. 393 ; THE MOUNT, Nos. 344, 345, 346, 347, and 348 ; COOK FIELD, No. 343 ; SHEFPCOATS, No. 354 ; BRAZIERS, No. 355 ; CHURCH FIELD, Nos. 360, 361, and 362 ; BUTT FIELD, No. 364 ; GREAT AND LITTLE DOLE, or DOOL, FIELD, No. 372 ; BASIN POND FIELD, or BENT FIELD, Nos. 373 and 375 ; INGORY DOWNS, Nos. 280, 292, and 276 ; JAGGARD'S, Nos. 365 and 367 ; STARLING LEES, Nos. 350, 351, and 352 ; POPES LEES, Nos. 333 and 334 ; COCK FIELD, the upper part of No. 300 ; COCK MEADOW, No. 327 ; VINCENT'S CLOSE, No. 329 ; CROPS, No. 321 ; BISSING GUTTER FIELD AND MEADOW, No. 322 ; KING'S CROFT, No. 323 ; EARSWELL, or Earl's Well and Low-field,* lie between Highfields Lane and the Gelatine Works. TENTER FIELD is No. 310 ; CROW BARN FIELD, No. 315 and south part of No. 314 ; CROUCHES, Nos. 294 and 295 ; TYEMILL PIGHTLE, No. 45 ; BLACK HALL, No. 316, at south-west corner of No. 315.

---

* Low is the Saxon word for a barrow.　Read this note in connection with the note on page 83.

FAIRS, CUSTOMS, FOLK-LORE AND
MISCELLANEOUS.

IT is probable that fairs are the survival of the ancient pagan festivals, as may be gathered from the letter addressed by Gregory the Great to Mellitus (A.D. 601), wherein he says that some solemnity must be provided for the English people in exchange for their former celebrations, and they were consequently to be allowed "to build themselves booths from the boughs of trees about those churches that have been turned to that use from temples." The fair in many places is held on the same day as the feast of dedication, and, as we have seen on a previous page (*ante* 19), the fair at Coggeshall was to continue for eight days, namely, from the eve and on the day of St. Peter ad Vincula, and for six days following. On page 16 attention has been called to the site of an earlier church, near a property which about two centuries ago was called "Old Ales," in reference to which it may here be remarked that Dr. Pettingal derives the word *Gule*, which is synonymous with *Ale*, from the Celtic or British word *Gwyl*, signifying a festival or holiday, and explains "Gule of August" to mean the holiday of *St. Peter ad Vincula* in August when the people of England under Papal rule paid their Peter's Pence (Brand's *Pop. Antiq.*, *Vol.* i., p. 347.) This association of the fair with the dedication of the church, and the survival of the name *Old Ales*, are facts of no mean significance.

The grant which was made to the monks of Coggeshall of the right to hold a fair was probably more in the nature of a confirmation of an existing custom than in itself an original grant. At these festivals the gathering was not only of a religious nature, but was used for pleasurable pursuits, and for purposes of trade and business generally. The fair was in ancient times held in the churchyard, but an Act passed in the 13th year of Edward I. provided that henceforth fairs and markets should not be kept in churchyards.

Adjoining the present churchyard is an enclosure known as "Butts Field," indicating that the shooting at *butts* was one of the sports which in days of yore was here indulged in, and although the field has not been used as a playground within the memory of the oldest inhabitants, yet some of them have heard their parents say that it was formerly so used.

The following notes from Hall's *Precedents* may have reference to the feast of dedication :—

"1543, 22nd May. Coggleshall. — Thomas Clarke and Richard Trewe had not maide 11 mo torches, nor yet kepede the drynkinge in the Parish of Coxsall, accordyne to the laudable use and custome of the same parish."—*f* 111 *b*.

"1543.—Coggleshall. . . . We present Thomas Paykoke, yt he hath broken an old awncient and laudable custome of or Church, in makynge of torches, that haith bene usid every oute of mynd of man. And that the same Thomas is elected to be one of the torchwardyns, and doth refuse to take upon him the same office, accordynge to the laudable custome of the same parishe."—*f.* 28 *b*.

𝕭urial 𝕮ustoms.

OF the ceremonies which were observed at the funerals of some of the principal inhabitants of this parish at the end of the 17th century, Bufton has left us a few notes, in addition to the notes of the sermons (*ante*, p. 226) which were preached on these occasions.

"'The Lady Guyon (Sir Mark's second wife, and Sir Thomas Abdy's daughter) dyed June 24th, 1679, and was buried ye 26th late in the evening, by torches without a sermon."

"1685, Nov. 18.—The first wife of Mr. Boys was buried. Six gentlewomen carried up the pall, with white hoods and night gowns ; and Mr. Livermore preached at her funeral, and I was gone to London."

"1690, Nov. 1.—Sr. M. Guyon was buried about 10 o'clock

in ye evening, by torches, without a sermon ; there was about half a score coaches, and about 30 or 40 men had black gowns and caps ; they carried the torches to light the coaches. There was one breadth of black cloth hung round the chancill, and ye · pulpit was covered with black, and the great Bible."

" 1691, Aug. 21.—Wm. Guyon, Esq. Sr. Mark's son, died at London, being 21 years old, and was brought down to Coxall with great pomp, nigh 200 horsemen riding before, about 40 or them with black cloaks, and about 10 coaches following, about 9 o'clock at night, by torches, and abundance of people."

It was formerly a very common custom when a virgin died that one nearest to her in size and resemblance should carry before the corpse, or the funeral procession, a garland, which was afterwards hung up in the church.

> " To her sweet mem'ry flow'ry garlands strung,
> On her now empty seat aloft were hung."

So we read in Bufton that on " 5th July, 1686, a daughter of John Church, singlewoman, was buried, and a garland hung up ;" and on " June 5, 1691, A maid, daughter of the widow Chilton, was buried, and a garland carried before her."

Witches.

IN every place and parish every old woman ·with a wrinkled face, a furrowed brow, a hairy lip, a gobber tooth. a squint eye, a squeaking voice, a scolding tongue, having a ragged coat on her back, a skull cap on her head, a spindle in her hand, a dog or cat by her side, was, says Gaule, in his *Select Cases touching Witches*, 1646, not only suspected, but pronounced for a witch.

Such an unfortunate creature there was at Coggeshall about two centuries ago, and Bufton tells us about her thus :—

" 1699, July 13.—The widow Comon was put into the River to see if she would sink, because she was suspected to be a witch, and she did not sink but swim. And she was tryed again July 19, and then she swam again and did not sink. July 24. The widow Comon was tryed a third time by putting her into the river, and she swam and did not sink. Dec. 27. The widow Comon that was counted a witch was buried." The manner of her death is left untold.

The Coggeshall Volunteers.

IN 1779 the Volunteer system of national defence was brought into prominence, by reason of the threatened invasion of Ireland by France and Spain, but it was not until about 20 years later that the organization became complete. Several Acts of Parliament were passed between 1794 and 1804 to provide for the administration and discipline of the force which in 1805, when the invasion of Napoleon the First was imminent, amounted to 429,165 men.

The loyal little town of Coggeshall raised a small band of warriors as its quota to the general muster for the defence of the kingdom, and what they did, and how they did it, is told in the form of " A farce in two acts, by an Inhabitant of Great Coggeshall," entitled " The C*******ll Volunteer Corps." So popular was the skit that it reached at least four editions. The writer was one Thomas Harris, a schoolmaster, who in his preface says that, " notwithstanding the deficiency of the corps in respect to privates—there were only three, the rest of the members were officers—and its abrupt breaking up, the plan for raising the corps was perfectly judicious; nor, indeed, could it be otherwise, as it was a work of profound deliberation, the wisdom of the parish being thrice concentrated for that very purpose; but as the best concerted schemes, from some trifling accident, have failed, so in this instance, from a too hasty zeal in its execution, the whole fell to pieces, the cause of defect being that the business was begun at the wrong end." The preface proceeds : " As some individuals have applied certain of the characters to themselves, it may be necessary to say that nothing personal is intended; but if gentlemen will, in defiance of this assertion, obstinately persist in the contrary, and will, against all truth and reason, say, ' I am meant for Sergeant Scroggins or for Corporal Drill'em,' or 'I am the old woman,' &c., the only reply will be—Sir, upon my honor you are mistaken; the cap was not intended for you; I neither took the dimensions of your head. Have you tried it? Does it fit? If so, and you have a particular fancy to it, why, Sir, in that case you are welcome to wear it."

The caps fitted the heads of many of the Coggeshall folk, for it is reported that although Thomas Harris had his joke, he paid dearly for it, for he lost his pupils, and got into much trouble.

Here are a few extracts from the farce.

Scene—A Market Place. Enter Cryer ringing his bell, and followed by a mob of boys, &c., huzzaing.

Cryer—O yes ! O yes ! O yes ! This is to give notice that the committee for conducting the business of the Volunteer Corps is now sitting—all persons who are desirous of entering as privates, and will find their own clothes, guns, and gunpowder, are desired to attend. Wanted, two drummers and a fifer, also a few men for pioneers—the more grim and ill-favoured the better. As the Corps at present consists mostly of officers, no more will be admitted ; but should any neighbouring Corps be in want of a few, it may be accommodated at the rate of one officer for one private, and in every dozen so exchanged an officer will be thrown in extra. GOD save the King.

Scene—A Street. A bell tolls. Enter old woman meeting Dobbins.

Old Woman—Pray neighbour Dobbins, who does the bell toll for ?

Dobbins—For the Volunteer Corps.

Old Woman—Whose Corps ?

Dobbins—The Volunteer Corps.

Old Woman—You don't say so ! And so poor Mr. Volunteer is dead at last ? I have heard great talk of the gentleman. They say he was very harmless and inoffensive ; it seems he has left a numerous family. And pray, neighbour Dobbins, when did he die?

Dobbins—You are under a mistake, old lady, the bell tolls for the inhabitants of the parish to meet at the Church vestry in order to form themselves into a military society to kill Master Buonaparte if he should happen to come this way.

Later on we learn from Scroggins, the Sergeant (No. 15 in the illustration), that in case of invasion, and if the enemy were advancing from Colchester, the corps was to take route for Braintree, or which, as Scroggins explains, is just the same thing, suppose the enemy came north the orders would be to march south, keeping as near as they could at least a distance of 10 miles.

Scene—The Vicarage Field. Enter Corporal Drill'em (16) with a muster-roll followed by a group of mechanics dressed according to their several occupations.

THE COGGESHALL VOLUNTEERS.

Corporal—Gentlemen soldiers, halt! Now fall back, and let each man come forward as his name is called over. Attention! Jeremiah Clodpole (1) [here!]. Thomas Appletree (2) [here!]. Roger Pebbleback (3) [here!]. Fall into the rank, Master Pebbleback, take your hand out of your breeches and hold up your head. Obadiah Slendershanks (4),. Obadiah Slendershanks, answer to your name. [*He is pushed forward.*]

Slendershanks—An please your Corporalship, I'm deaf.

Corporal—How long have you been deaf?

Slendershanks—Yes, three children. My wife died of a quinsey.

Corporal—I ask how long have you been deaf?

Slendershanks—The youngest is 3 years come Whitsuntide.

Corporal—Daniel Thickset (5) [here!] Abraham Chub (6) [here!] Peregrine Paunch (7) [here!] Timothy Splayfoot (8) [here!] Lazarus Feeble [here! *faintly,*] come forward, Lazarus! How old be you, Mr. Feeble?

Lazarus—Threescore and five, come the time.

Corporal—Are you a marksman?

Lazarus—Yes, but I must rest my gun upon my forked stick. I've killed many a sparrow so!

Corporal—Well, Lazarus, for the present I must set you with Mr. Slendershanks. Attention! David Cowleech, (10) [here!] Humphrey Sharpshins (11), [here!] Timothy Fillpot (12), [here!] Anthony Hamstring (13), [here] Simkin Stradem (14) [here]!

Other Soldiers at Coggeshall.

A MONG the MS.S. of G. A. Lowndes, Esq., is a letter dated 1643, July 3rd, Coxhall, from Thomas Honywood to Sir Thomas Barrington, in which the writer says, "there are some soldiers willing to go their colors if they had money to bear their charges. If Sir Thomas will let Mr. Crane, of Coxhall, lay out some money for them, they will march, otherwise they will not move."

On 4 Feb., 1679, a Watch house was set up in Mr. Hubbard's corn fields (Bufton).

On 1st March, 1688. There was a guard house set up for the soldiers at the Market House. On 13th of the same month the soldiers went away *(ibid)*.

On the 27th July, 1690. Two companies of the Trainbands which lay here were marched up to the church in the forenoon, being Sunday, with their arms, and drums beating and flags flying *(ibid)*.

Bufton has a reference to the Rye House Plot, "1693, Sept. 9, being Sunday, it was kept as a day of thanksgiving for the discovery of a plott about 3 months before against the King's life, and there was much ringing of bells and shooting off musketts and ye drakes and making of bon-fires" *(ibid)*.

1694, June 19. Our two great guns were fetched away from the church *(ibid)*.

Coggeshall Jobs.

F OR some strange reason Coggeshall is remarkable for its 'Jobs,' and there are several extraordinary stories told about this place and its people, thus we read, that when the Coggeshall folk wanted to divert the current of the river, they fixed hurdles in the bed of it for the purpose.

Another tale says, that a mad dog bit a wheelbarrow and the people fearing that the injured object would go mad, chained it up in a shed *(Brewer's Dic. of Phrase and Fable)*.

There were two windmills here, in close proximity, but as there was not sufficient wind to turn both of them, one was levelled to the ground.

If an epidemic prevailed in a neighbouring parish, it is said the people were wont to hang up blankets in the roads to prevent the pestilence being borne hither by the wind.

An enthusiastic fisherman, seeing, as he supposed, the moon in the river, and being somewhat curious as to its structure, did his best to draw it out with a rod and line.

The following lines have an allusion to Coggeshall :—

" Braintree for the pure,
Bocking for the poor,
Cogshall for the *jeering town*, and
Kelvedon for the boor."

Fuller, in his 'Worthies,' mentions the expression, 'Jeering Coxhall,' and adds, " How much truth herein I am as unable to tell as loth to believe ; sure I am that no town in England of its bigness afforded more martyrs in the reign of Queen Mary, who did not *jeer* or jest with the fire, but seriously suffered themselves to be sacrificed for the testimony of a good conscience. If since then they have acquired a jeering quality it is time to leave it off, seeing it is better to stand in pain till our legs be weary than sit with ease in the chair of the scorners."

Earthquakes at Coggeshall.

BUFTON tells us that on the 8th Sept., 1692, "being Thursday, and the same day that Jacob Cox dyed, about two o'clock, there was an earthquake at Coxall and many towns beside hereabouts, and at London and severall other countries we heard, and the news-letter said it was at the same time in Holland and ye rest of ye provinces in ye Netherlands. I was in our garret at that time and heard the house crack and perceived it shake, and was afraid it would fall, and therefore ran down stairs."

Nearly two centuries afterwards, namely on the 22nd April, 1884, about twenty minutes past nine in the morning, another earthquake occurred here, and throughout the greater part of Essex and in the neighbouring counties, the shock being most intense near the east coast of this county where very considerable damage was done. At Coggeshall some of the chimneys in houses in Church Street and Bridge Street were thrown down ; a looking glass was thrown off a table and broken, a panic was caused among the girls in the National School, clocks were stopped, bells rang violently and an oscillation was generally experienced by the inhabitants similar to the passing of an express train through a station, or of a heavy traction engine along the road ; wells which had before been almost useless now yielded a plentiful supply, while in other cases some became almost barren. An old crack in the Church tower was intensified and the parapet so loosened that a sum of £170 had to be expended in the work of reparation.

Extracts from Bufton.

" APRIL 23rd, 1680, a *new pillory* was set up in Coxall."
This was a pillar, usually of wood, with a hole made in it through which the head of the miscreant was projected ; there were sometimes other holes for the arms or legs. The punishment of the pillory was inflicted for various offences among others upon bakers for selling short measure, and was in vogue from Saxon times down to the year 1837.

"1682, July 6th, a *Ducking Stole* was set up in Coxall.' Another name for this instrument was the Cucking-Stool. It was first invented for taming female shrews, and is said to have been an ecclesiastical engine of popish extraction for the punishment of fornication and other immoralities.

"1681, Feb. 1. There was a man, a stranger, whipt up Church Street at the cart's tail.

"1682, Dec. Ye widow Mootone paid £15 because she had had a bastard. £10 of it was given to the poore.

"1684, Dec. It was said that 7 butchers were robbed by 4 thieves of above 500 pounds ; above 100 of it of Nicholas Fosters, and above 40 of Roger Mullings.

"1697, June 15. Old Mr. Buxton was robbed on the London Road.

"1686. About March the meal men first began to come to Coxall Market, and had their meal cryed 15 pounds for a shilling, and the bran was taken out and 14 pounds for 14 pence.

"1693, May 18. The poor did rise because the bakers would not bake because some of their bread was cut out the day before for being too light.

"1695, Oct. 8. The poor did rise at Coxall in ye evening to hinder ye carrying away of corne. And Jonathan Cable beat a drum to gather them together, for which he was carried before a

s

Justice but not sent to Jaile. The poor did rise at Colchester and
other places about ye same time and it is said burnt several wag-
gons. The combers broke up their purse. It was occasioned by
Jonathan Cable being so unreasonable. It was thought if he
might he would have had all the money belonging to the purse."

ⴲersonaƚ ⴼlames.

HERE is a collection of personal names derived from animals,
trees, trades, places, &c., borne by persons who have been
connected with this town in times past. The list might be con-
siderably extended :—Sparrow, Larke, Raven, Martin, Starling,
Jay, Bird, Duck, Mavis, Sparhawke, Teale, Cocke, Cockerell,
Mutton, Lamb, Ram, Roe, Hart, Wilboare, Bull, Calfe, Colt,
Coney, Hare, Seal, Sammon, Whitinge, Beeke, Maggot, Olive,
Armond, Peartree, Crab, Plum, Cherry, Berry, Beane, Pease, Rice,
Pollard, Bush, Hedge, Root, Parsley, Garland, Lilly, Butcher,
Baker, Tanner, Turner, Skinner, Cooper, Fuller, Weaver, Tailor,
Tiler, Draper, Glover, Dyer, Carter, Wheeler, Fisher, Chandler,
Gunner, Potter, Slater, Mason, Sawyer, Miller, Cartwright, Gard-
ener, Shepheard, Ringer, Groom, Clerk, Chamberlain, Smith,
Grocer, Cooke, Nurse, Page, Swain, Man, Huntsman, Squier,
Savage. Stafford, York, Norfolk, Sudbury, London, Hedingham,
Flanders, Tunbridge, Cornwell. Pope, Monk, Abbot, Vicars,
Righteous, Church, Death, Marriage. Frost, Summers, Summer-
son, Christmas. Black, White, Greene, Gray, Scarlet, Fairhead,
Whitehead, Head. Broome, Cask, Cape, Sling, Bell, Club, Hunt,
Blud, Proud, Joy, Write, Streight, Weight, Miles. Waters, Rivers,
Wells, Pool, Pond, Shed, Towers, Castle, Bridges, Cliff, Clay, Sand,
Stone, Diamond, Farrow, Webb, Cotton, Keyes, Marsh, Field,
Hills, Streete, Lee, Creek. Wood, Boughtwood, Drywood, Dog-
wood, Eastwood, Westwood, Hazlewood, Underwood, Woodward,
Hayward, Appleford, Walford, Fishpole, Whiteacre, Holmstead,
Overhill, Holditch, Stanbridge, Highgate, Springate, Shortland,
Cowland, Headland, Park, Archpool, Litherland. Pitchforke,
Gimlet, Picknut, Glasscock, Cockshief, Slowman, Wiseman, Bear-
man, Deadman, Love, Loveday, Goodday, Goodwine, Crackbone,
Spiltimber, Pinchback, Shakeshaft, Cutlipp, Wildblood, Jelle-
browne, Goldwire, Leapingwell, Maydwell, Lesswell, Thorough-
good, Hopper, Skipwith.

𝔍n 𝔐emoriam.

JOSEPH BEAUMONT.

THE high esteem in which the late Mr. Joseph Beaumont*
was held in Coggeshall and throughout the County of Essex,
as evidenced by the remarkable assembly at his funeral and by the
lengthened obituary articles which appeared in the columns of
the press, leads the author to believe that extracts from the literary
testimonies to the sterling worth of his deceased father will not be
considered out of place in the " History of Coggeshall."

The East Anglian Daily Times gave an account of the professional and social career and sudden demise of Mr. Beaumont in
a long article which appeared on the day following his death.
From this article the following short notes are extracted :—

"One of the leading professional men of East Anglia has
been suddenly called over to the majority. A cheery face, beam-
ing upon all smiles that were contagious, will henceforth be only
a memory. On Thursday morning, when the good people of Coggeshall rose to begin the labours of another day, the saddening
and unexpected news fell upon their ears that in the still hours of
the night one of their most highly respected fellow-townsmen, Mr.
Joseph Beaumont, had been summoned from the affairs of life,
in which for many years he had played so active a part. A man
more generally esteemed by those who knew him best, it would,
indeed, be hard to find, and it is no exaggeration to say that there
is universal mourning in Coggeshall and the neighbourhood at his
death. . . . . . His delight was to serve them in whatever
way possible, and what is more, his manner of doing it was devoid
of the least appearance of having conferred a favour. For over a
score of years he had been a member of the Coggeshall Church
Restoration Committee, and as President of the Coggeshall Cricket
Club and in other matters of local amusement, the intense geni-
ality of the man constantly asserted itself."

The *County Chronicle* and *Essex Herald,* after devoting considerably more than a column of their space to an account of
Mr. Beaumont's life, death and burial, again referred to him in
these eulogistic terms :—

"The sudden death of Mr. Joseph Beaumont will be heard

---

* Died, 18th July, 1889.

of everywhere in Essex, and in many other parts of the country, with feelings of the sincerest regret. Mr. Beaumont possessed— and that in goodly measure—qualities which will always command respect so long as Englishmen remain what they are. He was a man of far more than common ability, of rare industry, and of the friendliest disposition. His practice as a solicitor was large and varied. He was equally at home in conveyancing work and as an advocate in the courts, his sagacity, penetration, and clearness of view and utterance never failing him. He knew how to buy and how to sell property; he knew how to manage it; he knew how to give wise advice to a multiplicity of clients; he knew how to deliver an effective speech, and he knew how to make himself in- teresting and agreeable in company. It has been said, very truly, if somewhat severely, that no man is entitled to public esteem unless he does something beyond the bounds of his well-known duties and obligations. Tried even by that test, Mr. Beaumont comes out satisfactorily, for he was of constant and valued assist- ance to institutions and movements intended for the general good both in the neighbourhood of his own home at Coggeshall and in the county at large. From time to time he discharged with true zeal and fidelity various unpaid offices; he did all he could to elucidate and settle the more difficult questions of agricultural politics by taking a leading part in the discussions at the Essex Chamber of Agriculture, at the Farmers' Club, and elsewhere, and, in fact, there was nothing, from a county meeting to a village concert or a cricket match at Coggeshall, in which he did not exhibit the kindliest and the liveliest interest.

"Such a citizen will be really missed. Men may be no worse than they ever were, but, whether that be so or not, there are not too many of Mr. Beaumont's sort among us. How seldom it is that you meet with a man whose industry scarcely knows a pause, and yet with as much capacity for play as a boy, and yet as amiable a nature as a woman. Those were the characteristics of Mr. Beaumont in a marked degree. In his time he went through trouble, but he bore it well—not defiantly, but in a becoming spirit at once of manliness and resignation. He seemed to be helpful, in some way or other, to most people who came across him, and so was deservedly popular. To us and our predecessors he was frequently of good service. As a youth he was a corres- pondent of the *Chronicle*, and his interest in the paper never flagged to the end, for there were several valuable and interesting paragraphs in our last number which were founded upon information furnished to us by him. Like many in all parts of Essex, we shall long remember Mr. Beaumont with gratitude both for the sake of his public work and his personal kindness. It was due to him that we should lay this little tribute upon his bier."

The Essex Weekly News, after a feelingly written memoir of the deceased gentleman, summed up his character in these well-chosen lines:—

"The death of Mr. Joseph Beaumont is an event which will cause wide-spread regret wherever it becomes known. Mr. Beau-mont was not an ordinary man, his admirers were not confined within the narrow limits of the ancient town of Coggeshall, nor even of the County of Essex, in the remotest corners of which he had become familiar by more than a mere name. As a power-ful advocate and a trusted legal adviser he had few compeers ; his wide experience of human nature and of public business made him a valuable ally and a formidable opponent, while his genial disposition and extreme kindness of heart rendered him one of the most agreeable of companions. In all the relations of life during the last quarter of a century we have ever found him a genuine Englishman, as full of fire as of affection."

The Essex Standard, supplementing its obituary article, alluded to Mr. Beaumont in its Country Notes in these words :—

"The death of Mr. Joseph Beaumont removes from Essex a man who has played a prominent public part for more than a quar-ter of a century. Mr. Beaumont, as one of the leading Solicitors of the County, was naturally a public man in virtue of his profes-sion, but beyond this, he was by the sheer vigour of his character and opinions, constantly to the fore in many other public matters. Politics, agriculture, and philanthropic objects aroused his interest and enlisted his services, and he was a remarkable illustration of the well-known fact that the busiest men always have most time to spare. He was the author of several useful legal works, and he had indeed a right to be considered a legal authority after the long and large and very varied experience which he had enjoyed in the course of his practice. As a public man Mr. Beaumont will be greatly missed in Essex. His private worth was known to hosts of attached friends, by whom he will be remembered as one of the most amiable, and most genial of men. His sound common sense, and his earnest and generous help to those in whom he was interested made him, as many could testify, a valuable friend in need."

 Mr. Beaumont was descended from John Beaumont, who was born about 1470, and who, when he made his will, in 1543, resided at Bildeston, in Suffolk. On the death of John Beaumont, his property at Hitcham passed under his will to his son, Robert, who also became possessed of other lands in the adjoining parishes of Bildeston and Kettlebaston; Robert died in 1554, leaving a son, Michael, who was buried in Bildeston Church, in 1614, beneath a black marble stone inscribed to his memory. Michael's son, John, died in 1641, as appears from another stone, which, in the recent restoration of Bildeston Church, was built into one of the walls; it bears the arms of the family impaling those of Alabaster. The former arms, duly recorded at the Herald's College, are azure, semée of fleurs-de-lis and a lion rampant or; Crest, a lion passant or. John had twelve children, of whom was John, baptised at Bildeston, 13 Oct., 1623, and buried there in 1703; his eldest son, John, took the family estates which appear to have been of considerable extent; another son, Jonathan, baptized at Bildeston, in 1660, settled at Nayland, and died in 1743, leaving his house in that village to his sons, Jonathan and Thomas; the latter had a son, John, who also lived at Nayland, where he owned a house called the Guildhall. John had eleven children, of whom was Joseph, born 12th November, 1787, whose youngest son, the subject of this memoir, was born at Colchester, 4th March, 1827, came to Coggeshall about 1856, and died there, 18th July, 1889. These genealogical notes are taken from a pedigree of the family containing the names of nearly 200 of the descendants of John Beaumont of Bildeston.

THE END.

General Index.

Index of Places.

Index of Personal Names.

www.ingramcontent.com/pod-product-compliance
Lightning Source LLC
Chambersburg PA
CBHW020856020726
47497CB00005B/1432